While quarrels between man and woman are nothing new, and could be dull, they take on a freshness and merriment extraordinaire in the hands of Philip Rapp. My best wishes and fond admiration for The Bickersons, and may they live unhappily ever after.

—Goodman Ace

Somebody said that trying to analyze wit was like dissecting a frog. You can see what he's made of, but when you get through, the subject was expired.

—Philip Rapp

For access to archives, please go to: **www.bickersons.com**.

THE GRIPES OF RAPP
THE AUTO/BIOGRAPHY OF THE BICKERSONS' CREATOR, PHILIP RAPP
©2011 BEN OHMART

ALL RIGHTS RESERVED.

No part of this book may be reproduced or distributed, in print, recorded, live or digital form, without express written permission of the copyright holder. However, excerpts of up to 500 words may be reproduced online if they include the following information, "This is an excerpt from *The Gripes of Rapp*, by Ben Ohmart"

All photos from the Paul Rapp collection unless otherwise noted.
The Bickersons and Philip Rapp's writings copyright © 2011 Paul Rapp.

Published in the USA by:
BEARMANOR MEDIA
P.O. BOX 71426
ALBANY, GEORGIA 31708
www.BearManorMedia.com

ISBN-10: 1-59393-656-7 (alk. paper)
ISBN-13: 978-1-59393-656-3 (alk. paper)

DESIGN AND LAYOUT: VALERIE THOMPSON

TABLE OF CONTENTS

INTRODUCTION . . . 1
FOREWORD . . . 5
CHAPTER 1: ENGLISHMAN . . . 6
CHAPTER 2: BANJO EYES . . . 34
CHAPTER 3: FANNY LADY . . . 61
CHAPTER 4: WAR & PEACE OF HEAVEN . . . 75
PHOTO GALLERY: SECTION ONE . . . 86
CHAPTER 5: SNORING THROUGH IMMORTALITY . . . 113
CHAPTER 6: WINTER IN BRAZIL . . . 127
CHAPTER 7: DANNY KAYE, MGM AND *THE BISHOP'S WIFE* . . . 142
CHAPTER 8: THE BICKERSONS VS. THE HONEYMOONERS . . . 153
CHAPTER 9: *TOPPER*, JOAN DAVIS AND THE GANG . . . 182
PHOTO GALLERY: SECTION TWO . . . 193
CHAPTER 10: HIRAM HOLLIDAY . . . 202
CHAPTER 11: JOAN DAVIS AND THE MARX BROTHERS . . . 214
CHAPTER 12: THE 1960S CHANGES EVERYTHING . . . 229
CHAPTER 13: AT THE END OF THE DAY . . . 267
PHOTO GALLERY: SECTION THREE . . . 281
APPENDIX 1 . . . 294
APPENDIX 2: RAPP'S OUTLINE FOR HIS AUTOBIOGRAPHY, JUST AS HE WROTE IT . . . 353
APPENDIX 3: SOLD SKETCHES FROM PHILIP RAPP'S 3X5 JOKE FILE CARDS . . . 359
APPENDIX 4: MISC. OUTLINES AND FILM TREATMENTS . . . 371
APPENDIX 5: NOVEMBER 27, 1984 LETTER FROM MARIAM RAPP TO COLUMNIST JIM MURRAY . . . 381
APPENDIX 6: LETTER FROM PHIL WHILE IN LONDON TO PAUL RAPP . . . 385
APPENDIX 7: BRIAN RAPP'S THOUGHTS ON HIS GRANDFATHER, JUNE 9, 2009 . . . 387
CREDITS . . . 390
INDEX . . . 394

To

Martin Grams, Jr.

Prolific writer, friend, and just like Rapp, a master of his craft

Introduction

It's truly unfortunate that one of the byproducts of living in a strictly commercial world is that the lack of dollars will stop some people from writing their story. Philip Rapp started an autobiography in the early 1970s called *The Gripes of Rapp* ("with apologies to John Steinbeck"), but when he failed to click with a publisher, he set it aside and never completed it. I have tried to put in every word of *Gripes* (and other tidbits) that he wrote, highlighting them in **bold** for your viewing pleasure, but I'm not sure that I'll follow his own prefaced instructions:

> **(A note to the typesetter, proofreader, editor and publisher)**
>
> **Gentlemen:**
>
> **If the piece regarding my self-serving typewriter ever sees the light of print I ask that it be printed in its original form, typos and all. As you will see, that is the heart of the matter and will make no sense in any other form. Maybe it makes no sense anyway but I felt I had to record it just to prove that Man has still not conquered the Machine.**
>
> **—P. R.**

He had even constructed a five-page outline, which promised to be an engaging read, and I have tried to quote from it as much as possible, when decipherable. What cannot be decoded from Rapp's own mind has been set into the Appendix, for all you theatre/film puzzle lovers out there.

At some point, he called his memoirs "With Love and Curses," which initially caught the interest of publisher J.P. Tarcher (an imprint of Penguin Group). But J.P. was more interested in Fanny Brice than Phil Rapp, requesting a sample chapter of four to six thousand words on his old Snooks star. Though Phil had sent him the Bickersons albums as a sample, the publisher didn't think such humor would make a very saleable book; he was looking for all the items that Phil did *not* want to write, as they were too personal.

"Well, I publish books not the things that are kept out of them," wrote Mr. Tarcher, "and I am terribly concerned that the things you can't tell are what might make these pieces truly come alive."

About *Gripes*, Rapp wrote, "This is not a funny book. It is a philippic. It is all true to the best of my recollection and like the cook who adds bran to his hamburger to make it go further, I shall employ the use of a few stretchers."

I beg to differ with a Master that this is not a funny book. As you'll see, his autobiography would've been as hot as anything by the Jack Benny writers or Irving Brecher, and dotted with samples of Rapp's many scripts throughout his career, the laughs tend to pile up.

Phil Rapp will forever be a part of history—not as Eddie Cantor's writer, Danny Kaye's writer, Fanny Brice's writer, or the man who brought the Marx Brothers back for a final (though aborted) encore—but as the creator of one of radio's most durable episodic fantasies: *The Bickersons*. The influential Don Ameche/Frances Langford satire on domestic bliss is still revered in the annals of radio. It ranks with *The Jack Benny Program* and *Fibber McGee & Molly*, though for some, the acidic comedy proves too strong.

This book began because of my strong love for The Bickersons. Indeed, it was easier to write the complete history of that series (see *The Bickersons, A Biography of Radio's Wittiest Program*), plus editing two books of Bix scripts, than laying to rest the story of their creator and eternal champion, Phil Rapp. For there is *much* more to Mr. Rapp than meets the pun. Having lived and actively participated in five decades of Hollywood, Rapp touched upon many projects, both finished and unfinished, filmed and unfilmed, and it is Phil's son Paul that should share a good fifty percent of the blame for it taking me seven long years finally to assemble into book form the incredible load of material that Paul lent me: over thirty—maybe forty—boxes of scripts, contracts, letters, photos, scripts, personal papers and scripts. From this came the aforementioned three books, plus two Baby Snooks script books (with about five more in the planning stages), *Phil Rapp's Joke File* (which had me going through thousands of dusty index cards upon which Rapp placed one joke each), *The Television Scripts of Philip Rapp* (for the first time publishing the last pilots of the Marx Brothers, Joan Davis, and Ben Blue) plus it gave me the courage to write a book on Don Ameche, and start one on Frances Langford, all with the help of their respective estates.

But I have never, ever been privy to *this* much information or generosity, and will probably never be sent my own private warehouse of material to wade through *again*, and because of this, with SO much to quote, etc., it's taken a while to finish the story of this intelligent, sometimes difficult, and much beloved comedy writer.

Because this is a biography of a writer, I've tried to let Phil's work speak for itself as much as possible, without repeating too much of the material in the previous books. So, if you want the *whole* story on The Bickersons, and the infamous court case in which Phil sued Jackie Gleason about his stealing Bix to make *The Honeymooners*, you will have to get the Bix bio book. Ditto: to appreciate Phil's joke file to the fullest; Baby Snooks scripts; etc. But contained within these pages is a smattering of that, and *all* the rest. You'll be amazed at this man's prolific output.

Thanks go to the following people for helping make this book as complete as possible. Of course, there would be NO book without Paul Rapp. He has accomplished the seemingly impossible—he preserved his father's entire legacy, and loaned said massive output to this author. More scripts and papers than you could believe, which have since been donated to the Thousand Oaks Library (which he let me choose) once I scanned *every* piece of paper in the 30+ boxes.

Thank you also: Randy Bonneville, Janet (daughter of Eddie Cantor) & Brian Gari, Frances Langford, Laura Wagner, the Don Ameche family, John Franceschina, Martin Grams, Jr., Frank G. Peppiatt, Sandra Grabman, Joel Rapp for unlimited permission to quote from his autobiography (*Radio, TV, Mother Earth & Me*), and the very generous Yutaka and Yoshie Fukushima, for all you do.

And thank you, Mayumi Ohmart, my lovely wife, for always listening and for always being there.

—**BEN OHMART**
KYOTO, 2010

FOREWORD

I have, I must frankly confess, only the vaguest idea of how to write a book. I have never read any instructions on the subject, nor had any conversation with an author of books regarding his craft. Naturally, this will become evident to the reader but I offer no apologies. This is not an ordinary book, a biography of the characters depicted, although I believe I have the credentials to construct such a work. To some readers it will appear a diatribe, to others a labor of love. Both of these emotions are valid. Close to forty years of writing comedy for this wild breed of man and woman, under the most intimate conditions, gives me the right to put into print the quirks and foibles and virtues of nearly every major comedy star who ruled the airwaves and cinema screens since the early thirties. The list of names is virtually endless, and to those I have left out I can only say, aren't you lucky!

I had looked forward to making this a collaborative affair with my young brother, Johnny, whom I always believed had a far nimbler wit and would have been a restraining influence—but it was not to be. John, whom I raised and tutored in the business, a great comedy writer in his own right, and probably the mainstay of Bob Hope's staff for better than fifteen years, was suddenly taken from us in April 1968. He left this vale of comedy without notice, but not before he had made his mark. It is to dear Johnny I dedicate this work, such as it is.

—PHIL RAPP,
BEVERLY HILLS, 1974

(Original foreword written for Phil's incomplete autobiography)

CHAPTER ONE
ENGLISHMAN

The stand-up comics. Most of them should sit down.
—Phil Rapp

Maurice Rapp, Philip Rapp's father, was a silversmith in Austria (though "book publisher" was given as his occupation on Phil's birth certificate) who soon became a tailor when he and his wife, Anna Waldman, were driven out of their country in 1901 by a fascist regime who were stripping Jews of their wealth. Moving to Hull, England, on March 26, 1907, Philip Neville Rapp was born.

Soon came siblings Ben, Louis, Johnny, and a baby sister, Roslyn.

Phil's eldest son Joel relates, "My dad tells the story that while he and his family were ensconced in an underground bomb shelter during a blimp raid in World War I, my grandmother went into labor with Uncle Johnny and my ten- or eleven-year-old dad had to run for the doctor in another shelter, zipping around the streets with the blimps dropping bombs from overhead."

Paul, Phil's youngest son, takes up the story: "Grandfather Rapp [Maurice] was born in Vienna, and so was Grandmother Rapp. It seems their parents were there at the time. After they grew up and married, they moved to Hull, England. Grandfather Rapp went into the book publishing business. After their second son, who is my father, was born, they moved to London. It was in London that my grandfather decided to go into the antique silver business. At the outbreak of the First World War, my grandfather was interned to the Tower of London, as were all aliens, since England could not take any chances.

"Grandmother Rapp had her hands full trying to raise four children, so that at the end of two years, when Grandfather was allowed to return home, he found that his business had failed. My father went to school in London. His education, like that of his brothers, was complete. Grandfather Rapp was a slight, bespectacled man who believed in education. His own education was a good one. In 1923, the Rapps came to America with their four sons and one daughter. They settled in New York in the Bronx. At first they found life very strange. They spoke English, but it was different from the English they heard in New York. The vowels were pronounced like R's and the R's were pronounced like *oi*. The children on the street mocked them, and at the same time stood in awe of them. Their manners so bewildered the other children, that they were called sissies. The Rapps—Father and two eldest sons—soon found employment and life settled down to the usual routine, as is lived in America almost everywhere."

By 1926 Philip Rapp was feeding his urge to perform by hoofing it up on the vaudeville stage with Bobby Morris, and sharing the New York stage with some of the top comics of the day. Not to mention a certain Mariam Fishbein, who was also part of a dance act, a "sister act," though not with her sister. He would marry this hoofer and stay married to her for sixty+ years.

Born November 11, 1911 in Chicago, the brown-haired, brown-eyed, five-foot-two Mariam (Mary) was the last of twelve children born to Frank Fishbein and Anna Meltzer. She actually didn't know her real birthday was November 11—later known as Armistice Day—until she sent for her birth certificate to start collecting social security at age sixty-five. It seems that with so many kids in the house, her parents simply forgot to write it down. They knew it was near *some* winter holiday (so they picked December 28), but that's it. Upon learning her true birth date all those years later, she said, "No wonder my life has been such a mess. I've been reading the wrong horoscope for sixty-five years!"

Paul Rapp, again: "My mother's mother and father were born in Poland, and while they had been educated, it was mostly in the teachings of their forefathers, Hebrew. They were people of the Torah or the Books of Law, as had been handed down through the thousands of years of Jewish history. Dad didn't do a lot of Jewish things, but when I was young, we went to Temple. But it was for the reformed type of Jew, the one who went once a year.

"While both sets of grandparents had been taught Hebraic Law, and both were religious, my maternal grandparents were more of the peasant stock, physically strong, with a deep and passionate zest for life and its full meaning. After their first child was born in Poland, they migrated to America, and settled in New York City. After nine children were born, they decided to join relatives in Chicago, where my maternal grandmother gave birth to two more children. Grandfather Fishbein was a tailor who opened and successfully managed a cleaning and dying and tailoring establishment in Chicago, where my mother grew up. Theirs was a happy home, where eight girls loved to sing and dance and play instruments. At an early age, my mother (having experience in amateur theatricals) decided to become a professional entertainer, and started her career as a dancer at the Metropolitan Opera House in Chicago, only to forsake it for vaudeville, because it paid better and seemed like a more exciting kind of life. When she met Dad she was working as the private secretary to the manager of the Waldorf Astoria and dancing in various chorus lines on Broadway. (When we would go to Sun Valley she would ice skate beautifully.)

Joel Rapp admits, "It's strange, but at one time I knew the entire history of both sides of my family—today, I can't remember my maternal grandfather's name (I never met him—he died before I was born) or the full set of facts about my dad's parents. They, and all my father's siblings except Johnny, lived in New York, so my only contact with my grandparents and my uncles and aunts was when I was under ten and when we made yearly train trips back east (they lived in the Bronx, 1546 Jerome Ave., I think). I have no clear memories of anything to do with my grandparents, sad to say.

"I don't recall anything really about my grandparents' financial circumstances but I do remember that Dad sent them a substantial check every month [when he became an established radio writer]."

Phil and Mary plunged into wedded bliss in 1931, at the beginning of the Great Depression, sharing tough times eking out a living on the vaudeville stage. Phil often told the tale of how he and his wife made a solitary potato last for three days by nightly cooking the poor thing in hot water. The thin tomato soup made from ketchup and boiling water made a welcome change. But better times lay ahead.

Making the rounds of New York's stages put Phil in touch with a lot of comedians whom he charmed with a similar quick wit. It wasn't long before he was writing a few jokes for them for pocket money. "I wrote vaudeville acts for long-forgotten teams," he later told the press, "then wrote an act for my wife and myself—disaster. My agent said, 'Give it up and stick to writing for other people.'

"I started in radio in 1931, writing a series for Georgie Price, for Chase & Sanborn Tea. It was a fifteen-minute program, twice weekly, over Columbia/CBS, called *The Chase & Sanborn Tea Program*, for a year. Then I wrote *The Chase & Sanborn Coffee Program* with Georgie Price on NBC, from the New Amsterdam Theatre, for about ten weeks. Both series went on at same time. The *Tea Program* had Paul Douglas as the announcer. I subtitled it 'The Prince of Parody,' since Price was a singer and a mimic. Georgie sang an original song, and then sang a parody on it, which I had written for him, and as a tour de force somewhere before the program was over he would do an impersonation of a famous star. There was very little dialogue employed. I remember writing less than three minutes of monologue. The *Coffee Program* ran for an hour, with more dialogue, skits and other people. Elastic, but not variety, more like Milton Berle's TV show. All my professional life, I have directed whatever dialogue I have written.

"I then went on the air myself as an actor-writer," Phil continues. "I worked for U.S. Industrial Alcohol Company for an anti-freeze producer called Pyro. I was master of ceremonies and general factotum on this program."

Called *The U.S. Industrial Alcohol Program*, the fifteen-minute Pyro program was Phil's first outing (as announcer, touting Pyro anti-freeze) with a company that would be quite important to his radio writing career: the J. Walter Thompson ad agency.

IN THE BEGINNING

In the beginning there was Georgie Price, a small man with large talents. I was already thru with my career as a vaudevillian, determined to become a comedy writer for the new medium of radio, and was the youngest member of the old and original Friars Club in New York. Out of work, penniless and married, Mariam and I lived in a basement room on the west side of New York. It doesn't seem possible now, but we survived solely on potato soup, thinned out daily, for weeks at a time. If my darling wife ever reads this book she will discover how I managed to scrape up the rent money for our goat's nest. She always believed that I had sold a few jokes here and there to actor-members of the Friars, but the truth was I took a job as a professional eyewitness for/an unscrupulous insurance company that specialized in taxicab-accident policies. The agreement I had with their representative was as follows.

I was given the barest description of some accident that had occurred months or years ago that was just coming to trial, an accident that I was supposed to have witnessed, and told to give testimony favorable to the company. I was also told that the chances were remote that I would ever have to take the stand, but if I did I would receive twenty-five dollars. If I was at the trial and not called I would receive ten dollars. I held that disgraceful job for two weeks, spent every/morning outside one courtroom or another, and thank the dear God in Heaven, I was never called upon to testify. At the end of the second week, wrestling with my conscience all the time, I quit, finally deciding that poverty was far better than perjury.

The fact that Mariam had taken a job as secretary to an assistant manager at the Sherry Netherland Hotel, which paid a pittance, had nothing to do with my decision. But my experience, curiously enough, paid off. I wrote an article called "Professional Byewitness" for a blackmail type of magazine for which I was paid the munificent sum of thirty dollars. The piece was anonymous, of course, and exposed the entire criminal methods of the now-defunct insurance company. I was launched on my career as a writer, but there was no comedy involved.

Now, what has all this got to do with Georgie Price, you may well ask? First, a little about Georgie's background. He was a superb performer, blessed with a powerful singing voice, and easily the most gifted mimic in big-time vaudeville. He was one of the original kids in Gus Edwards' Schooldays, a flash act that boasted, among others, such future great names as Eddie Cantor, Walter Winchell, Lila Lee, Eddie Buzzell and Georgie Jessel. Lou Holtz, then a star in his own right, and some years older than the Edwards troupe, recalls meeting young Jessel in San Francisco when they played on the same bill. As Lou describes it, "That kid was wearing a cashmere coat with an astrakhan collar, white spats, a derby hat, carried a cane, and smoked a cigar you could row a boat with!" And Jessel was only 15! Georgie Price was not that precocious, very much on the conservative side, and unlike my dear friend Jessel, saved his pennies. When Price finally retired from show business he already owned a seat on the New York Stock Exchange, had his own brokerage house, a Rolls complete with chauffeur and footman, and died a multi-millionaire.

Georgie Price was still very active in show business when I first met him at the Friars Club. Vaudeville having slacked off a bit, or possibly Georgie was a little tired of traveling, he signed to do a radio program for the Regal Shoe Company. The program was called *Regal Reproduction*, which was the slogan of the company, and tied in with Georgie's talent as an impersonator. It was only a fifteen-minute show, three times a week, and Georgie needed some gingerbread, or small bits of humor, to go between his musical numbers. I offered my services as a comedy writer and we made a deal.

The salary was meager, but it was sufficient to pay the rent and get us off the potato soup. The program lasted thirteen weeks and I even saved a few dollars. While I worked on Georgie's programs, I used the typewriter in the press room of the Friars club, and had the opportunity of meeting/another George—George Burns of Burns and Allen, more familiarly known as Nat. That wonderful comedy team had just come into prominence, and Burns, unlike most performers who never changed their act, had the good sense to freshen his routines from time to time, a fact which I believe resulted in his long-lived success in all three media: radio, pictures and TV.

He was always searching for new material, and whenever Burns and Allen were in town I was able to provide them with one page of "he and she" jokes, guaranteed original. Without even glancing at the page, generous George would always give me twenty-five dollars. I was learning and earning.

Now ten days after the Regal Shoe program folded, Georgie Price got a call from the J. Walter Thompson Company, then the largest advertising agency in the business. They wanted him for a show being sponsored by Chase and Sanborn Tea. Together we prepared the audition, billed as Georgie Price, the Prince of Parody, and the sale was made—the deal was still a fifteen-minute show, three times a week, but the money was, for those early days of radio, stupendous! I was provided with a desk at the agency, the only freelance worker in the establishment, and shared an office with Sam Moore, then a copywriter. Sam subsequently graduated to comedy writing, and we worked together on many scripts, all for clients of Thompson.

The boys at the agency were a magnificent bunch, headed and master-minded by the tall, handsome John U. Reber, a legendary name in radio. Because of my vaudeville background, I played small parts on nearly all the Thompson programs and I was making money hand over fist. Mariam and I were now secure financially and we moved into a luxurious apartment in Jackson Heights.

It was at JWT that I met David Freedman who was writing *The Eddie Cantor Show* for Chase and Sanborn Coffee, besides writing novels and plays. He needed help, and he offered me a full partnership on all his projects. I was enthralled by the man, his personality, and his remarkable knowledge; I was enchanted by his family, which consisted of his three small sons, Benedict, Noel and Toby and his wife, Beatrice, and we embarked on a relationship that lasted for many years and ended in tragedy for David [he died of a heart attack on December 7, 1936]. I will go into this in my later chapters, but 15 years after our first meeting I was already a millionaire with a stable of racehorses, a huge home in Beverly Hills, a 50-foot yacht, a ranch in Encino, and

I was the father of two beautiful and talented sons. David, was the only man I ever knew who ran a million dollars into a shoe-string three times! I ran him a close second.

David Freedman, born in Romania in 1898, was a towering hulk of a man (six-feet-five inches tall and 300 pounds) who penned several books and many plays for Broadway, including 1929's *Mendel, Inc.*, which became the basis for the 1932 Smith and Dale film, *The Heart of New York*. He also collaborated with Eddie Cantor on the comic's autobiography, *My Life Is In Your Hands* (1928), which became a Pulitzer-nominated best seller.

At their meeting, Phil was twenty-five years old and David was already a great gag salesman from his Upper East Side apartment, where the two of them built up a veritable joke factory, pitching "exclusive material" to anyone who could afford it, including some of the top comics of the day.

Phil learned a lot more about the selling of comedy from David. In his autobiography, *Radio, TV, Mother Earth & Me* (BearManor Media, 2006), Joel Rapp wrote that David "was my father's mentor (this was in the early 1930s) and they wrote sketches and jokes for all the top comics. I remember my father telling me that the apartment had a back entrance, and if, say, Comic #1 was there buying jokes, and Comic #2 was on his way up, they'd shuffle #1 out the back door . . . all day long they were coming and going.

"Dad told me an anecdote that illustrates David's 'chutzpah.' There was a big heavyweight fight at Madison Square Garden that they wanted to see but they had no tickets. David's plan was he would go up to a ticket-taker and with his enormous bulk and enormous bravado he said, 'When Mr. Rapp gets here, tell him I'll meet him (wherever)' and in he'd go . . . . Dad showed up, told the guy he was Mr. Rapp, and was let in by the guard who didn't want to risk upsetting the big guy, whom he assumed was some sort of big shot."

As of 1935 Freedman and Rapp were writing for Eddie Cantor's radio program. (Phil had been hired via a July 11, 1933 telegram from Cantor, in which he asked him to come to California to work on his show "for a couple weeks.") Phil also worked on sketch material for the Broadway musical *Life Begins at 8:40*, with music by Harold Arlen and lyrics by Ira Gershwin, although only David Freedman's (and other writers) name appears on the credit list. It was to be the first of many ghostwriting instances Rapp enjoyed for the good money involved.

The team also contributed sketches to *Ziegfeld Follies of 1934*, which ran for 182 performances (from January 4, 1934 to June 9, 1934) and introduced Rapp's second-most enduring creation: Baby Snooks. The great Eve Arden played Snooks' mother, Victor Moore was the father, and 43-year-old Fanny Brice began her long career as that precocious brat Snooks. (See Chapter 3 for the whole story.) Snooks returned two years later in *Ziegfeld Follies of 1936* (January 30–May 9, 1936) in a skit called "Baby Snooks Goes Hollywood."

Phil didn't stick solely with David. He was doing a lot of writing on his own, and had at least a few separate collaborations. One of these was with George Beck on a play called *Open House* in 1939, which opened and promptly died after a three-day run at the Lobero Theatre in Santa Barbara. The cast included Judith Allen, Lillian Bond and William Brisbane.

Phil wrote a lot of sketches for radio comics, including Tommy Riggs, George Burns & Gracie Allen, Harry Richman, Block & Sully, Jack Oakie, and many others. One such bit, written for Beatrice Lillie, is reprinted below (complete with commercials), and is typical of Rapp's zany 1930s comedy style.

ROYAL GELATIN PROGRAM
(Audition)

SIGNATURE: **(MARCH WITH ME)**

WILSON: (over theme) **This is Ward Wilson, setting off the Royal Gelatin Program under the musical direction of William Artzt, featuring Arthur Anderson, bass baritone of the Metropolitan Opera Company and starring Miss Beatrice Lillie, her Own Repertory Company and her personal guest star. Miss Lillie!**

(Applause)

(Music concludes as Miss Lillie reaches the microphone)

LILLIE: (Elegantly) Thank you! Helllllooooooooooo everybody! How do you DO?

WILSON: (Politely) Pardon me, Miss Lillie.

LILLIE: Pardon *me*, Mr. Wilson! Am I protruding?

WILSON: I have just one more special announcement to make. Do you mind if I stand here while I make it?

LILLIE: Not at all! But please get off my foot!

WILSON: Confidentially, ladies and gentlemen, I watched Miss Lillie at rehearsal this afternoon and I just want to say she was . . . er . . . just a little off! However, I feel safe in saying that this evening she will surely be much, much . . . worse!

LILLIE: How FORtunate, Mr. Wilson! (A sour chord from the orchestra) This is The Royal Gelatin Program, under the musical direction of . . . Where have I HEARD that beFORE?

WILSON: I said it all, Miss Lillie. I'm the announcer!

LILLIE: Oh I see! Announcer prevention. (Ho-Ho) And now a word about my little repertory company. Wait till you HEAR them. They are waiting impatiently in the wings, champing at the bit, pawing at the ground . . . at least I *hope* that's all they're pawing at. They will give their all to Art.
And my good people, they give until it *hurts*.

| | And my guest singer for this evening . . . the renowned Eye-talian opera singer . . . Mme. Hicienda. Her voice is really . . . different—so big . . . so full . . . so round . . . so—so—frightening. It frightens even ME. Wait till YOU hear her. I first ran into Mme. Hicienda in the steam room of a Turkish Bath, and the goings on there my dear—and the goings *off*. |

WILSON: I can imagine!

LILLIE: (Shocked) My DEAR Mr. Wilson! Tonight my repertory company . . .
(Orchestra starts tuning up)
(Louder) Tonight my repertory company and guest star offer . . .
(Orchestra tuning swells)
(Still louder) Tonight my repertory company . . . Oh very well then have it your way . . . play, vagabonds . . . puh-lay!

1. MEDLEY FROM MISS LILLIE'S SHOWS
ANDERSON ORCHESTRA

You Know That I Know (Oh Please!)
You Forgot Your Glove (Third Little Show)
Dance, Little Lady (This Year of Grace)

WILSON: (Over introduction to number) A medley of tunes honoring Miss Beatrice Lillie . . . tunes from the many shows in which she has starred. And introducing, Arthur Anderson of the Metropolitan Opera Company who was NOT brought here tonight by Miss Lillie.

LILLIE:	(Music fades after vocal) Mr. Wilson. May I ask whose voice that really was?
WILSON:	His own, Miss Lillie.
LILLIE:	How fortunate, Mr. Wilson!
	(Music up to full finish)
WILSON:	(In own voice) Women know a lot more about fruit gelatin desserts than they used to. For instance, most women realize that if they serve a gelatin dessert that is flat and weak-flavored it's not *all* the gelatin's fault . . . it's largely the way the package was handled. You see, *weak* gelatin is just *old*, "shelf-stale" gelatin. But now you needn't risk getting *old* packages because you can order *Royal* Gelatin, the *one* kind you can *count on* for full-strength fruit flavor. Royal Gelatin is handled as *all* gelatin *should* be! It's delivered to grocers as often as twice a week, and only a few packages at a time. This rapid distribution is handled by that same famous system that delivers Chase and Sanborn's Dated Coffee and Fleischmann's Fresh Yeast. It's your *insurance* against flat, disappointing gelatin desserts. So why not follow the lead of smart women everywhere. Ask for *Royal* . . . the *fresh* Fruit Gelatin!

2. SOMETHING IN THE NIGHT
TRIO AND ORCHESTRA

LILLIE:	(At conclusion of number) The show must go on! I want you to meet my repertory company. Come, my brave band! Give them

music—music of the stars—something historical . . . courage my little puppets—face the music . . .

3. FUNERAL MARCH OF THE MARIONETTES ORCHESTRA

WILSON: (Over music) What's this—a masquerade?

LILLIE: These good people are—I might say—unique; in fact I *will* say it—UNIQUE . . . they play for nothing . . . nothing whatsoever. They are imatures—a—amateurs right down to the ground! They stand for Art. For Poetry. Music. Science. Agriculture. Physical Culture. They stand for everything! Wait till you *see*! First—I present Joe Hennessy . . . cab driver, gentleman, and leading man. It was he who brung me. Ah—it was not *I* who hailed his taxi this evening but FATE!

JOE: (Tough) Oh Ye-ah!

LILLIE: The moment I entered his taxicab and saw the back of Joe's neck, I said to myself, "There sits my hero!" Come you 'ere—'ero! Take a bow, Joe.

JOE: I don't want no bow. All I want's my two dollars and fifteen cents. That's what the meter read when we come upstairs. See.

LILLIE: My good man, forget your sordid trade. Tonight you are no longer Joe Hennessy . . . public hack driver number 24-0-58-X. Tonight you are a fiery French lover.

JOE:	Tonight I'm stuck for two dollars and fifteen cents. My cab's downstairs with the meter tickin'!
LILLIE:	Let it tick! The show must go on! Next . . . our leading lady . . . Mrs. Bertram Eiderdown . . . my next-door neighbor.
EIDERDOWN:	I have a bone to pick with you, Miss Lillie! You're telling all the neighbors that I'm just as foolish as I look.
LILLIE:	No—no, my dear! I said you *couldn't* be as foolish as you look!
EIDERDOWN:	They say my talent hasn't reached its full flower!
LILLIE:	I just know it will—a cauliflower!
EIDERDOWN:	I'll go to any length for my art!
LILLIE:	Indeed! The moment Mrs. Eiderdown moved in next door she came to borrow my washing machine. What technique—my dear!
EIDERDOWN:	I'll return it tomorrow, Miss Lillie.
LILLIE:	Keep it, my dear. Your husband is bound to look much handsomer in a clean shirt.
EIDERDOWN:	I won't stand for any more of this.
LILLIE:	Quite right, my dear—sit down!
EIDERDOWN:	Humph!

LILLIE: Tonight I have chosen a part for Mrs. Eiderdown that fits her like a mitten. She will play a frail but spiritual woman of the streets . . . dying . . . dying . . . dying!

EIDERDOWN: How should I know how a woman of the streets dies?

LILLIE: Ah-ah! Now don't be modest!

EIDERDOWN: Do you mean to insinuate that I'm a loose woman?

LILLIE: You're not tight, are you? (Laugh)

EIDERDOWN: Miss Lillie . . . I want you to understand I have a position to maintain in this community. My husband is an outstanding figure in the fur industry. He handles more undressed pelts than . . .

LILLIE: (Shocked) My DEAR Mrs. Eiderdown! Let's not get personal! And now—the third member of my little repertory group: Dr. Murgatroyd Jerkowitz . . . my dentist! Have you a word for my public, my dear Doctor?

JERKOWITZ: (Heavy Russian Jewish accent) So you should see your dentist at least twice a week.

LILLIE: Exquisite! Please! My dear doctor, tonight you are to play the heroine's father. Of course, you are familiar with Mrs. Eiderdown's work.

JERKOWITZ: Sure . . . I did it myself. And a very neat little job, too!

LILLIE:	Yes—yes, I know! But tonight, Doctor, you play the heroine's papa. He died eleven months before the play opens. If he had lived one more month he would have been dead a year.
JERKOWITZ:	Sure, I was even lucky to be here tonight. My wife is very sick!
LILLIE:	Not dangerously?
JERKOWITZ:	No! She's too sick to be dangerous!
LILLIE:	How fortunate!
JERKOWITZ:	Did I come here to be insulted by you!
LILLIE:	Yes! I do EVERYTHING. Now—here are your parts. Joe, Joe—Hey taxi—
JOE:	Where to?
LILLIE:	Joe, you are a fiery French lover like Francois Villon, D'Artagnan—the Three Musketeers—and so on!
JOE:	What! Fifty million Frenchmen for two dollars and fifteen cents?
LILLIE:	Now—now, Joe, this is art!
JOE:	Yeah—well this is Joe! An' if any of you guys at the garage is listening in, this ain't the Joe Hennessy you know. This is another guy. There's two of us Joe Hennessies and I don't know how I got mixed up in this. All I know's I want my two dollars and fifteen cents and I'm going to get it, see! Art or no art!

LILLIE: (Applauding) What fire, Joe. But when you play the lover use just a LEETLE more of a French accent. I will show you how.

JOE: You can't show me nothin'!

LILLIE: Oh yes I can! George Bernard Shaw said nobody acts quite like I do. And when I get to heaven I will ask Shakespeare what *he* thinks of my work!

JOE: Oh, yeah? Well supposin' he ain't in heaven?

LILLIE: Then *YOU* ask him! (Laugh)

3. (a) FUNERAL MARCH OF THE MARIONETTES
ORCHESTRA

WILSON: (As previous number fades) Arthur Anderson sings—"Drums in My Heart."

(Music immediately)

4. DRUMS IN MY HEART
ORCHESTRA

LILLIE: (At conclusion of number) What a voice! Do you think I could get him for my repertory company Mr. Wilson? I would have him sing "Far—Far Away!"

WILSON: How I wish you could sing like that, Miss Lillie.

LILLIE: My dear boy—I ought to receive a hundred thousand dollars a year for my singing.

WILSON: A hundred thousand dollars? Why, that's more that the President gets.

LILLIE: Then—get Hoover to sing for you! (Laugh)

(Sound of Whistle)

WILSON: What's the idea of blowing that whistle, Miss Lillie?

LILLIE: Isn't it lovely. I got it from a man on the curb.

WILSON: Your broker?

LILLIE: No. My doorman. He calls taxis with it. I rather fancy its birdlike note.

WILSON: If that's a birdlike note then my canary's a little brontosaurus.

LILLIE: A what?

WILSON: A Brontosaurus!

LILLIE: Then your canary should gargle! (Whistle again)

4. ~~(a) FUNERAL MARCH OF THE MARIONETTES ORCHESTRA~~ (Scratched out on script)

(Music fades)

WILSON: Wait a minute, Miss Lillie, what's this play about?

LILLIE: It's a mystery!

WILSON: It certainly is!

LILLIE: It's been said I should put more fire into my plays!

WILSON: You should put more of your plays into the fire.

LILLIE: Oh flatterer! Now if you'll just be patient, I'll explain the action of this play. It's a sort of a tragedy—comedy—the whole thing takes place on a rainy Thursday—

WILSON: Frankly, Miss Lillie, I don't think it matters.

LILLIE: Well—we've buttered our bed—we must lie in it! Now company, are you all quite sure of the parts you play?

ALL: No!

LILLIE: Perfect! Joe Hennessy, you are a very rich man, found dead in your Tudor library! It's a lovely place. Early American in the living room . . . Renaissance Italian in the drawing room . . . and Queen Anne in the bedroom.

JOE: Now you're talkin'.

LILLIE: Mrs. Eiderdown . . . you are a French coquette. Of course you must understand the nature of a coquette.

EIDERDOWN: Oh, my husband loves them . . . he makes them himself. Chicken croquettes.

LILLIE: How fortunate. And now you, Doctor. You are Inspector MacGregor of Scotland Yard.

While I . . . I am the dead man's faithful wife. Lie down, Joe . . . you're dead . . . I have discovered my dead husband when his mistress enters. That's you—Mrs. Eiderdown. Here we go now.

Come on—enter!

EIDERDOWN: (Acting) I have come to see your husband.

LILLIE: (Acting) My husband will not speak to you.

EIDERDOWN: I just spoke to him on the telephone. Oh how I wish I knew where he was when he called me ten minutes ago.

LILLIE: Ah so do I. He has been dead for two hours.

EIDERDOWN: Joe—Joe! Speak to me! Are you dead or alive!

JOE: I'm just laying here!

EIDERDOWN: You killed him!

LILLIE: Trollop! Do you dare accuse *me*, his faithful wife?

EIDERDOWN: The pistol you hold in your hand is smoking!

LILLIE: Do you mind if I smoke?

JOE: I don't care if you burn!

EIDERDOWN: I loved your husband. You cannot get away with this. What is being done about his murder?

LILLIE: I have phoned Scotland Yard. A man from the Yard will be here any moment to see about him!

EIDERDOWN: I won't have him buried in the yard. You won't dig up my nasturtiums. You'll bury him in the yard over my dead body.

LILLIE: Splendid! Over your dead body! Now just fling yourself on your dead lover and sob!

JOE: What's that?

LILLIE: Be still, Joe, you're dead!

JOE: She ain't going to fling no hundred and sixty pounds on me.

LILLIE: Oh dear! He won't play!

JOE: **I'VE HAD ENOUGH OF THIS ART STUFF!** Get him to go to it.

(Joe gets up)

LILLIE: Joe—you failed me. Mr. Wilson, would you be good enough to lie down and be a dead lover. No, wait a minute. You're lighter than Mrs. Eiderdown. YOU be the dead lover, Mrs. Eiderdown . . . and Mr. Wilson you be the French cocotte.

WILSON: I be the French coquette. Don't be ridiculous, Miss Lillie!

LILLIE: Now, Mr. Wilson, you know you give lovely imitations.

WILSON:	Well . . . I don't know—I can imitate Floyd Gibbons . . . but . . .
LILLIE:	There! Certainly if you can be Floyd Gibbons you can be a French coquette. Come now . . . try.
WILSON:	All right. But I'm warning you. It'll sound just like Floyd Gibbons.
LILLIE:	Well, never mind! Go ahead and sob, Mr. Wilson . . . sob.
WILSON:	(In the Gibbons manner) Oh my poor dead lover . . . what a poor dead lover, folks . . . this old headline hunter has seen many a dead lover . . . whenever there's news there's your little Floyd—i.e., folks, and I want to tell you, boys and girls, that when it comes to dead lovers . . .
LILLIE:	Please Mr. Wilson . . . just sob softly from now on. (Acting) Ah—here is the man from Scotland Yard. My husband had many enemies, Inspector MacGregor.
JERKOWITZ:	Uh-huh!
LILLIE:	Three knife wounds and a dagger were found in his back. A man's fingerprints were on his neck. There were two glasses on the table—one smelled of poison. And the walls are full of machine gun bullets—so is my husband. How did he meet his death, Inspector MacGregor?
JERKOWITZ:	Well—I'll tell you . . . tzuizide!

(EIDERDOWN GROANS)

LILLIE: Mrs. Eiderdown, please keep quiet. You're not dying, you're *dead*.

WILSON: I beg your pardon, Miss Lillie. I think there's really something wrong with Mrs. Eiderdown.

(MRS. EIDERDOWN GROANS LOUDER)

I think she has acute indigestion.

LILLIE: This is no time for compliments. What shall I do!

JOE: Give me my two dollars and fifteen cents.

LILLIE: You brute! You beast! How can you think of money when a woman is suffering—I'll settle for seventy-five cents.

5. MEDLEY FROM "TAKE A CHANCE"
ORCHESTRA

WILSON: Miss Lillie has prevailed upon me to present her personal guest star for this evening . . . it is with profound apologies and the deepest regret that I introduce Mme. Hicienda!

LILLIE: Thank *you*, Mr. Wilson.

This way, Madame. Oh, my dear, dear radio friends . . . I just wish you could see Mme. Hicienda. She is tremendous! In fact, she is one of the biggest singers in the world.

HICIENDA: (Gushing) Thank you, Miss Lillie!

LILLIE: She is so big she hasn't even *tried* to get into the Metropolitan Opera House.

HICIENDA: OH—you're too kind, Miss Lillie.

LILLIE: The doors are too small!!! Her last concert was a huge success. I wish the people had at least stayed to hear the second number! Now Madame, this little thing is a microphone. Don't be afraid of it! You can go right up and touch it!

HICIENDA: I'm not afraid.

LILLIE: Come closer to it! Oh! I see you can't get any closer to it!

HICIENDA: Like this?

LILLIE: No—No—try standing sideways.

HICIENDA: Is this better?

LILLIE: No . . . that won't do either, maybe you'd just better lie down!

HICIENDA: Mi-mi-mi-mi-ahhah.

LILLIE: No—no—not yet, my dear. Pardon me, if it's not an inquisition—but isn't that the gown you wore when you sang for the Longshoremen's Benefit last year?

HICIENDA: Why yes! I think it is!

LILLIE: Don't you think it's just a little too young for you!

HICIENDA: (An expletive going into vocalization) Bahh-ahhhh-ahhh.

LILLIE: Madame Hicienda comes from one of the leading musical centers of Italy . . . Bologney!

HICIENDA: Mi-mi-mi—ahhhahhh.

LILLIE: She offers as her first number . . . one of the finest things in all music . . . "Lo, Hear the Gentle Lark."

HICIENDA: I am going to sing "The Mad Scene" from *Lucia*.

LILLIE: "Lo, Hear the Gentle Lark."

HICIENDA: "The Mad Scene."

LILLIE: My dear, where *did* you get that gown?

HICIENDA: I had it made specially for me—in Paris!

LILLIE: Really—and where were *you* at the time! (Vocalizes) Oh pardon me. And now, "Lo, Hear the Gentle Lark" . . . (Sings) As it has never been sung before . . . or since!

HICIENDA: (Sings) Are you trying to ridicule me!

LILLIE: (Sings) My dear Madame—that's impossible. Come now, "Lo, Hear The Gentle Lark."

HICIENDA: (Sings) "The Mad Scene."

LILLIE: (Sings) "Lo, Hear the Gentle Lark."

HICIENDA: (Sings) For the last time, "The Mad Scene."

LILLIE: Thank you (Sings) Madame. Now if the leader's ready we will hear Mme. Hicienda sing "Lo, Hear the Gentle Lark."

HICIENDA: "The Mad Scene. The Mad Scene." For the love of mike . . . "The Mad Scene." Mi-mi-ah-ah-ah . . .

LILLIE: MAR-VEL-OUS! Madame . . . I have never heard "The Mad Scene" done better . . . that was simply superb. And now Madame Hicienda will sing . . .

HICIENDA: "The Mad Scene" or nothing!

LILLIE: "Lo, Hear . . ."

HICIENDA: (She goes hoarse) No. No. No. No. No.

LILLIE: Lovely! Don't let a little cold bother you. Sing *over* it! Under it—around it—through it!

HICIENDA: Cold. Cold! I've lost my voice! I'll sue you for this. I'll scratch your eyes out . . . I'll I'll . . .

LILLIE: "Lo, Hear the Gentle Lark."

HICIENDA: (Hoarsely) I feel my throat contracting.

LILLIE: There you are! I knew you'd get a contract if you sang for me!

HICIENDA: I'm ruined.

LILLIE: How fortunate!

HICIENDA: I'll see my lawyer. You haven't heard the last of this.

LILLIE: But you can't go, Madame. You must sing, "Lo, Hear the Gentle Lark!"

HICIENDA: Bah! You are a—you are a—a—a witch!

LILLIE: Temper—temper—Wait, Madame, wait a minute. Don't go . . . Madame . . .

(DOOR SLAM)

Oh, dear. What did she call me, Mr. Wilson.

WILSON: A . . . witch, Miss Lillie!

LILLIE: How fortunate!

WILSON: Shall the orchestra play "Lo, Hear the Gentle Lark" . . . anyway?

LILLIE: Indeed, Mr. Wilson. The show must go on. I will jump into the breech.

WILSON: The . . . *what*?

LILLIE: My dear Mr. Wilson. I shall sing "Lo, Hear the Gentle Lark." This will kill you—I hope!

8. LILLIE SPECIALTY
LILLIE

9. REPRISE FINALE: "DANCE, LITTLE LADY"
LILLIE AND ENSEMBLE

WILSON: (In own voice) Fruit gelatin desserts have never been more popular. Because more and more women have discovered that a *Royal* Fruit Gelatin Dessert is a success ten times out of ten. It's easy to see why! Royal is delivered to stores so frequently that it does not get weak and flat. Whether you get Cherry flavor, Raspberry, Strawberry, Lemon, Orange or Lime . . . you get fruit gelatin that tastes *like the real fruit*! Then, Royal *sets* quickly . . . in about *half* the usual time. Any woman knows what a convenience that is in arranging her afternoon's activities. Royal is inexpensive, too, which is a help to any budget. And Royal gelatin makes a big hit with the children who love the color and consistency as well as that delicious Royal flavor. So if you haven't tried this tempting dessert lately . . . do so very soon! Just ask your grocer for Royal . . . the fresh gelatin that tastes like *real fruit*!

CHAPTER 2
BANJO EYES

Our favorite doctor story is about the time Sidney Skolsky, Eddie Cantor and Phil Rapp, the champ Hollywood hypochondriacs, were sitting around discussing their ailments, with each trying to top the others. Finally, Skolsky, who couldn't stand the bragging any longer, challenged, "I'll tell you what—let's all go a doctor for a physical examination. Man with low blood pressure pays!"
—**Walter Winchell's column,
March 12, 1936**

Israel Iskowitz, A.K.A. Eddie Cantor, was one of vaudeville's biggest names, being a star as early as 1917 when he made it big on Broadway with *Ziegfeld Follies of 1917*. His appearance on Rudy Vallee's radio show in 1931 soon snowballed into Cantor's own starring vehicle, heading *The Chase and Sanborn Hour* (scripted by Freedman and Rapp) that same year.

Below is an undated example of the lunacy that was still going on a good ten years later:

HUSING: Oh, this is terrible! Here comes Eddie Cantor in a full dress suit with no sleeves!

(CANTOR ENTERS IN FULL DRESS SUIT WITH NO SLEEVES)

CANTOR: Listen, I've got a right to bare arms for my country.

HUSING: Why are the sleeves off?

CANTOR: It's that crazy tailor of mine in California. I wrote and told him to send me my full dress suitso this is what I got. And listen to the note he sent me—"Dear Eddie, I'm sending your fulldress suit by airmail, and in order to save postage I'm cutting off the sleeves and puttingthem in the pockets!"

HUSING: Well, why did you put it on?

CANTOR: I've got nothing else to wear. And tonight I'm giving a party to the man who makes the New Pebeco.

HUSING: Say, you certainly are a hundred percent loyal to this toothpaste.

CANTOR: Loyal? You know that Jersey cow I bought for my farm?

HUSING: Yes.

CANTOR: Well, I named her Pebeco.

HUSING: Really?

CANTOR: Sure, I taught her to brush her teeth twice a day and now she gives dental cream!

HUSING: Wait a minute, what are you doing with that book under your arm?

CANTOR: Oh, this is a book of etiquette, Ted. I don't wanna make any social errors at the party tonight.

HUSING: A man who's traveled as much as you should know all about etiquette.

CANTOR: Say, there's lots of things I don't know. Look what happened to me in Italy when I went to visit Mussolini. I didn't know you have to bring your invitation.

HUSING: Common sense should have told you that! The guard didn't let you in, did he?

CANTOR: Didn't let me in? He threw me right out of the side entrance.

HUSING: Well, why didn't you tell him who you were?

CANTOR: I did—I said, "Look here, I'm Eddie Cantor, you can't throw me out of the side entrance like that."

HUSING: What did he do then?

CANTOR: He apologized, took me in again—and threw me out the front entrance!

HUSING: At least he was polite enough to apologize.

CANTOR: Oh, yes. But those French people, they're really polite. One Sunday on the river Seine, a Frenchman and two French ladies were in a canoe, when it capsized, and they all fell in the water.

HUSING: Really?

CANTOR: Yes—and just as the Frenchman was going down for the third time, he tipped his hat, and said, "Pardon me, ladies—I can't stay up any longer!"

HUSING: Well, in France they're all polite.

CANTOR:	Not only the people—even the animals. I went out to the race track, and I bet on a horse. He was the politest horse I ever saw.
HUSING:	A polite horse?
CANTOR:	Yes—he let all the other horses go first!
HUSING:	Well, if a horse could be so polite, *you* certainly don't need a book of etiquette.
CANTOR:	I'll tell you the truth, Ted. I'm taking lessons from that social authority, Madame Blintz, and she'll be here any minute.
HUSING:	Is she very high class?
CANTOR:	High class? She's so ritzy, she won't eat lady fingers unless they're manicured!
HUSING:	Is that her getting out of a cab?
CANTOR:	Yes—I'll tell you what you do, Ted. Take this book of etiquette—go behind the screen, and when I'm stuck, read me the answers.
HUSING:	Well, how will I know when you're stuck?
CANTOR:	I'll sing something—uh—(SINGS) "My Bonny Lies Over the Ocean"—then you'll know.
HUSING:	Here she is—I better hide. (DOOR SLAM)
WOMAN:	Why, how do you do, Mr. Cantwah?
CANTOR:	Cantwah? –A Park Avenue Parkyakarkus!

WOMAN: I can see you still don't know etiquette. There's a lady in the room—and where is your hat?

CANTOR: *Where is my hat?* You're *looking* at it, here—right on my head!

WOMAN: No, no, when a lady enters the room, what do you do with your hat?

CANTOR: Oh, er, don't tell me—what do you do—(SINGS) My Bonny lies over the ocean . . .

HUSING: (SOTTO) Remove it.

CANTOR: Remove it!

WOMAN: That's correct. By the way, I've arranged for you to take some dahncing lessons from my assistant, Miss Hefty.

CANTOR: Who—that fat dame?

WOMAN: Don't say fat. They say plump—in the best places.

CANTOR: Yeah? Well, in the best places she's fat!

WOMAN: You must remember always to be very grammatical. For instance, when your butler brings in the cake, which is correct, "Place it there," or "Put it there?"

CANTOR: Ah—er—

WOMAN: While you're thinking, I'll sit down.

CANTOR: Put it there!

WOMAN: (AGHAST) What?

CANTOR: (SINGS) My Bonny lies over the ocean . . .

HUSING: (SOTTO) Place it there.

CANTOR: (QUICKLY) Place it there!

WOMAN: Of course, at your dinner, you will have a lady sitting on your right hand.

CANTOR: Sitting on my right hand? What'll I eat with?

WOMAN: Oh, silly! Now you remember what I told you about the servants at the dinner table.

CANTOR: Oh, yeah, I know. One ring means we're ready for the next course. Two rings means to clear away the dishes.

WOMAN: That's right—and what is three rings?

CANTOR: A circus!

WOMAN: No, no—three rings means you're ready for dessert. What are you having for dessert?

CANTOR: I think bananas.

WOMAN: Not bananas—You mean bahnahnahs.

CANTOR: Bahnahnahs?

WOMAN: Certainly. If you want a bahnahnah, you simply ask for a bahnahnah, and immediately you get—

CANTOR: The rahspberry!

WOMAN: Oh, you don't know your etiquette!

CANTOR: You don't know my house!

WOMAN: No, no—didn't you ever eat bahnahnahs with crahm?

CANTOR: With crahm? No—but I've had sardoons with let*toce*.

WOMAN: Sardoons?

CANTOR: Yes—fish's pups!

WOMAN: Preposterous!

CANTOR: No, pups.

WOMAN: Will you stop that?

CANTOR: Pups.

WOMAN: What do you mean—pups?

CANTOR: Pups I will and pups I won't!

WOMAN: Oh, instead of all that banter, you'd be better off if you'd study your etiquette book.

CANTOR: (RITZY) I shall be delighted to ahnswer anything you ahsk. Go ahead, Toots.

WOMAN: Now let me see if you remember last week's lesson. Do you serve the cigars and cigarettes before or after coffee?

CANTOR: Why, er—you—er—(SINGS) My Bonny lies over the ocean . . . Ted . . . (SINGS) The answer's on page forty-three.

HUSING: (SINGS) I'm sorry but that page is missing...

CANTOR: (SINGS) Oh, Ted, you're a great help to me!

WOMAN: Did I hear another voice?

CANTOR: No, Madame Blintz, I'm a ventriloquist. Look...

(DOES VENTRILOQUIST BIT)

WOMAN: I can readily see that you've learned nothing in the way of etiquette since your last lesson. I'm going to phone home that I'll be here for three hours, and see that you learn every word in your book.

CANTOR: Three hours?

WOMAN: I shall return presently.

CANTOR: Hey, Ted!

HUSING: Yes, Eddie?

CANTOR: If she stays here three hours I'll be a wreck.

HUSING: Do you want to get rid of her? I'll scare her to death. Here she comes—I'll get my gun!

WOMAN: Now, Mr. Cantwah, I'm going to ask you—

HUSING: Stick 'em up—both of you!

CANTOR: A hold-up man!

WOMAN: (SCREAMS) Good heavens!

HUSING: (TOUGH) Young feller, I want all your money—and you, lady—I'm gonna kiss you, and kiss you good!

CANTOR: Now, just a minute—you can take all my money, but I'll never stand for you kissing Madame Blintz!

WOMAN: You mind your business—a hold-up is a hold up!

Anybody over the age of twenty-five will recognize the sobriquet as the sole possession of Izzy Ishkowitz. Of course, everybody knows that early in life Izzy changed his name to Eddie Cantor. The descriptive nickname, which he bestowed upon himself, fitted him like the proverbial glove. He was as wiry and vibrant as the strings on the almost obsolete instrument, and taut as the skin of its sounding board. He needed no pick to duplicate the twang, his high-pitched voice sufficed. Nobody ever strummed a banjo in slow tempo (as they do with the now popular guitar), the fingering and the business hand flew, at lighting speed. That was Eddie.

Onstage he was a dynamo—running up and down the stage, clapping his hands and bringing songs to life with a mediocre voice. I once asked him why he covered so much ground while singing and he told me that a moving target had less chance of being struck. This unique method of delivering a song evolved during his days as a youngster scrounging for a dollar in amateur nights, later in saloons with the fabulous Jimmy Durante at the piano, in order to avoid the debris and beer bottles thrown by the entirely uninhibited audiences of the day. Nowadays, this vicious habit of savage viewers occurs only at ball games. While Eddie raced up and down, poor Jimmy was nailed to the piano, but he swears he was never the victim of attack.

His enormous, hypnotic eyes were the direct result of chronic hyperthyroidism. My Dorland Medical dictionary defines this condition as due to excessive functional activity of the thyroid gland. Symptoms include exophthalmoses (bulging eyes), weight loss usually with increased appetite, overactive behavior, and other bizarre manifestations such as driving hard bargains and performing practical jokes that bordered on cruelty. The last two symptoms are not to be found in any medical book, but are brought to light as Rapp's Findings, thoroughly demonstrated by Cantor during our many years together. I will return to this matter but I feel that our stormy relationship should be recorded in some chronological form.

Eddie Cantor was a star long before I met him, therefore I can claim no credit for his rise to success. With all due modesty, and Eddie would have been the first to admit it, he frequently did so with full-page ads in weekly *Variety*. This, I feel, was partly responsible for his RE-rise to success via radio. The other party partly responsible (that almost sounds like double-talk) was the late great David Freedman, with whom I collaborated during the early years of grinding out the hour-long Sunday night *Chase and Sanborn* radio programs.

It was the year of the Demise of Vaudeville, to which I contributed with my dancing partner and comic half of the act, Bobby Morris. We were good hoofers, most of our comedy routines were borrowed, we had our fair share of bookings, but the real culprits that deprived us of our livelihood were the "Talkies" and the advent of radio. Of secondary interest to me at the time was the economical holocaust labeled "The Wall Street Crash."

It was the end of '29, I was already married (still am) to a young Chicago beauty who had to lie to the registrar about her age. For almost a year we lived in a room over an undertaker's establishment, nursing our last few dollars, and to this day I cannot stand the smell of formaldehyde. While still in vaudeville, Bobby Morris and I got a three-day stand at the Stratford Theater, a small-time movie and vaudeville house.

We had cut out nearly all the hoofing and had embarked on a comedy act that got plenty of laughs. I've forgotten whose act it was, but the original owners of it would never have played that joint in the first place. There was a band onstage and a young, brash M.C. who sang and introduced the acts. His name was Bob Hope, his jokes were exorable and he said, "Constantinople." We were such a hit that Hope asked me if we had any surplus material that he might use. No money was mentioned, but he had a steady job, and larceny crept into my mind. "You need rapid fire, special material—stand-up topical stuff," I said. "I'll write something for you."

My partner stared at me in amazement. He was about to open his mouth but I impaled him on a stiletto look.

"Did you write your own act?" asked Hope.

"What do you think?" was my curt answer. At least I didn't lie.

"But, hil—" Morris started to blurt. I cut him off.

"I know, Bobby—we still have a few dates to play in Chicago, and it'll take me no time at all." Turning to Hope I said, "I'll have some stuff ready for you next Friday. We'll talk about the fee after you read it."

When we reached our dressing room, there was silence as we removed our makeup, then Bobby turned to me.

"What's that about you writing stuff for that guy? You're not a writer."

"Who wrote our act?"

"We stole it!"

"Borrowed it. From Norwood and Hall. And they lifted it from Lloyd and Brill, who did it after Joe Penner."

"How does that make you a writer?"

"Didn't I put in the nectar gag?"

"Sure, but—"

"Then I'm a writer." Bobby was unimpressed.

"Balls," he said. "You couldn't even write home for money."

"That's unoriginal and also not true. I'm always writing home for money. Last week I wrote home for fifty dollars, the week before I wrote home for twenty dollars—"

"So what did you do with the money?"

"They never sent it."

That got a smile out of Bobby. Unless you live in a monastery you must have heard that joke a thousand times. I cherish the belief, possibly mistaken, that I made it up. We used it in the act and it always got a big laugh. I was convinced that I could write comedy. I never sent any material to Bob Hope who apparently made it on his own.

But why do I keep getting away from Cantor?

To illustrate Eddie's idea of a practical joke I submit the following incidents. I was now Cantor's only writer, having split with David some time earlier. It was the summer hiatus of his radio show and Eddie was making personal appearances all over the country. Since I was being paid fifty-two weeks a year I was forced to accompany him and make preparations for the new season to begin. At the same time Jack Crandall, a somewhat mysterious associate of Cantor's (I never did find out what his function was) was with us at every appearance.

Crandall seemed a pleasant enough person, but he had one trait that always seemed to drive Cantor up the wall. Jack could sleep anywhere, anytime, and at a moment's notice. Eddie suffered from grave insomnia. I always played a small bit in Eddie's act and when we returned to his dressing room, Crandall was invariably fast asleep on a lounge, snoring lustily. The noises he made were practically indescribable.

"That son of a bitch!" Eddie's exclamation dripped with venom. "Listen to him! He sounds like a Hotchkiss reciprocating force pump draining a peat bag in Clonakilty!" I don't know where he got the phrase but the comparison sounded accurate.

"Listen, Eddie," I ventured tentatively, "if he bothers you so much, why do you carry him along?"

"You mind your own business!" Eddie explained. Then he proceeded to apply makeup to Crandall's face—the stuff he used for his blackface number. Crandall never stirred. Having washed up and dressed into street clothes, Eddie covered the mirror with a towel.

"What are you doing?" I asked.

"Shake the bastard out of it," he commanded. "We're going out to get a bite."

I needn't go into the rest of it. The only thing I must mention is the fact that really put the icing on the cake. Crandall, in blackface, ordered watermelon for dessert.

This particular scene took place in Detroit, and could easily have been the tinder that lit the fuse for the dreadful race riots that occurred many years later. But Cantor was not yet satisfied. That night we boarded the midnight train bound for New York. We entered the drawing room, bags were stowed, Crandall climbed into the upper berth and fell asleep while shedding his clothes. I was undressing, preparing to lie down on the sidewall berth and Cantor sat on the edge of the lower berth getting madder by the minute as Crandall began his night music. The train had not yet left the station. I could see Eddie's jaw muscles beginning to work and I sensed some sadistic plan was beginning to germinate in his head. The train began to move. As soon as it gathered speed, Eddie spoke up.

"Okay, Phil—put your clothes on."

By this time I had learned enough not to ask questions. I obeyed and watched as he lathered half his face in the small bathroom, still fully dressed except for his jacket. He then emerged and began to shake Crandall vigorously.

"Get up, you big idiot!" Cantor yelled in Jack's ear. "We'll be in Grand Central in 15 minutes!" Crandall sat up, half unconscious. "Get dressed and we'll meet you in the dining car." He wiped the lather off his face and donned his jacket.

"Jesus Christ," mumbled Crandall. "Feels like I only slept five minutes!" And he began to scramble into his clothes.

Eddie and I left the drawing room and went straight down the corridor to the main washroom. The Pullman porter was already busy shining shoes. At the sound of Crandall lumbering drunkenly down the corridor, the porter stuck his head thru the drawn drapes.

"Sir?"

"Which way to the dining car?" was Crandall's sleep-filled growl.

"Back the other way, sir. But it's closed now."

Cantor held back his laughter, almost choking with glee as Crandall retreated in the other direction. After a few moments Eddie and I made our way back to the drawing room. Do I have to tell you? There lay Crandall in the upper berth, fully clothed, snoring lustily.

I will return to the saga of Eddie Cantor in a later chapter describing, to the best of my recollection, the radio years, motion pictures to which Eddie introduced me, his great talent for finding and grooming new stars like Deanna Durbin, Eddie Fisher, Bobby Breen, Dinah Shore, Parkyakarkus, and a host of others. Right now I am assailed by so many vagrant thoughts about the other personalities who shaped my long and checkered career that I must beg the reader's forgiveness if I seem to record the ensuing chapters in unorthodox style or chronology. This may be considered heresy by accredited book writers—but as I stipulated earlier, I don't really know the rules.

Unfortunately, Rapp did not find the spirit to complete his autobiography, but he did make significant notes to himself on most sections. While it's difficult to decipher and date some of it, they are quoted below in their entirety for clues as to what might have been chronicled.

CANTOR

Freedom was writing for Cantor in 1932. I was writing for Brice. Both programs JWT [advertising agency]. John Raber thought David needed help. I had meeting and we both agreed to go to Washington where Cantor was playing his revue with [George] Jessel in order to write his next Sunday program. Cantor charmed by Freedman's attitude on train. Worked out whole program, met Cantor briefly, returned on train that night and roughed out Canada Dry audition for Jack Benny. Back in NY. Cantor got his leave to go to coast to make picture. I went with Freedman. Brought Brice and lost Cantor. Salary cut. Quote telegrams to Coldwell from Cantor. Holzman. Jack Crandall story of train from Detroit.

He had now engaged Frank Gill to help me. Eddie Davis remained in B.G. This must have been on return trip, office in apartment on Vine St. I think the Ravenswood. We broadcast from theatre in downtown L.A. Parky, Sid Fields, Louis Gress.

First meeting, Cantor's apartment. Frenchy rubbing him down, Crandall with cigar, Holzman, and steam coming from bathroom. Eddie Davis, limp and wet emerging. 1933 wire from Cantor to Colwell. Turned it down. Doing Follies. Went to California. Lived at Knickerbocker Hotel. Wrote in Eddie's dressing room at Goldwyn studio. Palatial. Took *Virginian* thru canal to work on *Strike Me Pink* and Pebeco programs. Never saw upper deck except fancy dress ball. Locked in stateroom grinding away on articles, program and picture.

Lived on Norton Ave. First night typing in dining room. Buzzer on floor. Last time in Calif—1927. Death trail. Starving. Continental Hotel—Shanley and Furness. Room and bath, grifters sleeping on floor.

The days of Rubinoff at the New Amsterdam theatre in N.Y. How I acted on program. Then followed him as MC of PYRO program. Story of Norman Brokenshire—This is the pyorrhea program!

Story of Bea Lillie and audition piped into Standard Brands. Rebar thought script written by Doc McGonigle was atrocious but Bea loved it—John insisted I work on it—no dice from McGonigle. Bea compromised by having me play a large part on program. Result: Standard Brands didn't want her but wanted me.

My decision to quit Cantor. Johnny [Phil's brother] was now with me. Living on Weyburn Ave in Westwood. Famous line: Rapps deserting a sinking ship. Johnny goes back with Eddie. Subsequent wires from Cantor pleading with me to reconsider. Quote telegrams. Dinner he gave for me at Hillcrest. Five hundred dollar check for my faithful years of service.

The large Arden Milk house on Sunset Blvd. Krasna in Rolls, Merman, even, star in Hollywood. Theatre downstairs, complete stage. I once shot a movie there using the entire Cantor family.

Cantor was the first performer in radio to do a dress rehearsal with an audience. Some flunky sat with a pencil and recorded the laughs on the script. Then came the "judicious cutting" (refer to cutting line in notes) whereby all the lines that didn't get laughs were cut out and (the script was naturally overwritten for this very purpose) by airtime was completely emasculated. I fought bitterly against this procedure but was overruled. This was the beginning of the end.

Jimmy Wallington. With us for years. Cantor was first man to wear costumes for a radio audience (in studio). Laughs were mystifying to the home listener. Laughs were provoked by gestures and other means, entirely baffling to the radio audience. No wonder when the script lines that didn't get laughs were cut we wound up with nothing but trash. I could never convince him of folly. Still, and possibly because there was very little to listen to in those days, the Cantor program remained on top of the rating services (Crossley) and his personal appearances produced huge audiences. It is ironic that his decline in the ratings stemmed from opposition by Major Bowes on the other network. The world's greatest professional toppled by amateurs. He then decided he needed still more writers—refusing to recognize the fact that if he had left the original writing alone he would have fared better.

The serious spot. Safe driving. Brotherhood. Many others. In the hour Chase and Sanborn show it was necessary to use one serious spot. Like most comedians, when success comes, the bishop complex sets in. See Danny Thomas. Red Skelton and his Pledge of Allegiance taken right out of Roget's Thesaurus.

Tell the story of the "Two Dogs" written on the train to Pittsburgh after David's father's death. Stolen from *Life* or *Judge*, I don't remember which. The lawsuit and the discovery by Freedman. Cantor and Wallington liked to play a "let us suppose" spot. Two dogs. Two women. Two children. Out of this grew the March of Dimes. Happily endorsed by FDR.

Cantor sadistic in many ways. Used to stand at the foot of Ida's bed and hold a horrifying pose until she woke up and screamed in terror. Insomniac. Called many times in the small hours with improbable ideas for programs. Waking up Jack Crandall five minutes out of Detroit. Stories of Jessel on tour with him. Joke at the Palace. Chase and Sanborn dated coffee. Next day was labeled and sold as Maxwell House. Lawsuit, hushed up. Memory is vague but I believe he smoked small cigars.

After my release from hospital Cantor insisted I take a short rest in Florida. Left him with a program but it was never broadcast. I never got paid, either. He was not a generous man.

Cantor was always on a diet. Thin, nervous, dynamic—a way of talking and not looking at you—looking out into the far distance as though addressing a vast audience a half a mile away. He would never take a drink, except once in a great while a drop of sherry—but loved to make his table companion drunk, and forced pickles, spicy foods, any stuff he himself could not eat upon me. Vicarious. He took great care of himself physically, was rubbed down every day by his valet, Frenchy—remember Bunky Arthur too—great story here—Bedini and Arthur, Cantor the stooge—did pushups, played badminton and swam.

We used to go roller skating—all of us. Eddie, Ida, Margie, Madam, Parky and Benny Rubin. And play bingo at Venice. Insert photo on phony train. Penthouse in N.Y. Insert story of Polly Adler renting place. Cantor now came up once a week to talk. I'd place my hand on stack of blank papers and reassure him.

The Rapp/Cantor relationship was obviously a love-hate one for Phil. Indeed, when jotting down the first notes ("Rapp's Law") to his autobiography, in a wirebound notebook, the first thing he wrote was: "Comedians are paid in direct inverse proportion to their (lack of?) comedic talent. Thus, Cantor in his radio heyday outsalaried all others." Yet Phil found it hard to walk away from the steady money that writing for a major comic produced.

"Dad lived in the luxury of Beverly Hills from 1934 until his death in my home in Beverly Hills," says Paul Rapp. "He was never without luxury. I wish I had the custom Packard Station Wagon today; it would be worth over a million dollars."

According to Joel Rapp, when Cantor got picture offers out West, he brought Phil with him, thus opening up a world of opportunities.

Eddie's daughter Janet Cantor Gari recalled, "I remember Phil very well from my childhood. My sisters and I would go to school here in New York and spend the summer in rented houses in California, while my father made a movie. There were so many of us traveling that we took up an entire railroad car—no plane travel in those days! What fun it was for me to be able to bounce in and out of every compartment and be greeted by friendly, funny people like Phil Rapp. I realize now how young he must have been, but to a little kid, all adults are in a different space entirely."

"One summer in particular is very vivid to me," Janet continues. "We were living in what was called the 'Birch' house, because they were the owners. It was a huge place right on Sunset Boulevard, and it had lots of rooms we didn't need, like a sun room, a ball room, a formal dining room, etc. Mother had rented it only because it was the one place she could find that summer with enough bedrooms. In the back was an enormous swimming pool, and we had lots and lots of company. I even have a home movie of that summer where Phil and Mariam Rapp are helping their darling little boy walk across the gravel in the driveway without stumbling. I guess that must be Joel [Rapp, Phil's son], eh? He was so cute."

In 1935, Eddie and Ida went to Florida to rest in the sun and talk radio scripts with Phil (in New York) on the phone. Rapp was now head writer since David Freedman did not want to change coasts, staying in his beloved New York. With the new West coast sponsor, Phil found his weekly radio salary increased to $10,000 a week. Freedman was to receive 10% for previous material, via a verbal contract.

The Cantor "vacation" was the perfect opportunity to brainstorm over some new film ideas. As Rapp explained, "The plot of *Shoot the Chutes* concerned Eddie Pink (Cantor), a meek man who gathers courage from a book on assertiveness and is hired to manage an amusement park. Gangsters, who had murdered the park's previous

November 29, 1936.

six managers, try, with the aid of [Ethel] Merman, a singer with whom Pink is hopelessly smitten, to force Pink to install their slot machines. Pink finally realizes she's in league with gangsters, and the crooks are apprehended following a long chase on the Ferris wheel. Eddie winds up in the arms of his supportive secretary, played by the attractive Sally Eilers." This became *Strike Me Pink*, which finished filming in mid-December.

The final screenplay of *Strike Me Pink* (1936) was adapted by Walter DeLeon, Francis Martin, Frank Butler, with additional dialogue by Philip Rapp. The film's songs were by Lew Brown and Harold Arlen. Reviews were ecstatic for the film, and especially for Cantor. *Screenland* claimed that "every Eddie Cantor picture seems to me his best," while *The New Yorker* raved, "*Strike Me Pink* is big and fast. It seems to me that it's about as big and fast as the Marx Brothers' *A Night at the Opera*, and as there is only one Cantor and there are three Marxes, the Cantor piece may be regarded as even more of an achievement."

Based on the novel *Dreamland* by Clarence Budington Kelland, *Strike Me Pink* premiered at Radio City Music Hall in New York on January 17, 1936. The novel had first appeared in serial form from May 25 to June 29, 1935 in *The Saturday Evening Post*. While Rapp received Additional Dialogue credit, some news items reported at the time that Goldwyn had also hired the successful Broadway team of Howard Lindsay and Russell Crouse to adapt Kelland's book. If so, they, along with writers William Conselman, Arthur Sheekman, Nat Perrin, Bayard Veiller, Edward Chodorov and Lawrence Riley, received no screen credit, however, for their possible work.

First called *Dreamland*, then *Shoot the Chutes*, the name *Strike Me Pink* was adopted almost at the last minute, most certainly to cash in on Ethel Merman's 1933 hit Broadway musical of the same name. The film cost around $1.5 million, an incredible sum in those Depression years. The famous Cyclone Race rollercoaster in Long Beach, California, was rented by Goldwyn and repaired for the final chase sequence. It was to be Cantor's last film for Goldwyn.

The story involves Eddie Pink (Cantor) as Super Service handy man ("Shoes and pipes broken in") on the Millwood University campus, where he is continually picked on by "fun-loving" students. Dumb Butch Carson (Gordon Jones), a three-year senior, looks after the poor timid fellow who has been taking a correspondence course that promises "to make a man" of him. The instructions and record also come with a coin: "On one side of this coin is a man; on the other, a mouse. Whenever you find yourself in a situation that demands courage, dominance and magnetism, toss the coin. If it comes up a man, you are to plunge through fearlessly. If it comes up a mouse, continue to toss the coin until it comes up a man."

Butch's mother runs the Dreamland Amusement Park, where Eddie and Butch are made co-managers; she needs help, as she's being pressured by Vance (Brian Donlevy) to install crooked slot machines (which Vance will control) in her park. But when the imbecilic Butch finds himself enlisted in the Navy, Eddie—and his coin—is all alone to face the continually threatening presence of the gangsters. Eddie is a great bluffer, however, and uses a trick of blanks in a gun to make himself seem invincible to one hoodlum and successfully puts the evil eye on another (Edward Brophy), making him dance out of the office spreading flowers everywhere, in possibly the funniest moment in the picture. He's also aided by the rather helpless Harry Parker (Harry Einstein, the English-mangling Parkyakarkus from Cantor's radio show) who comes at Pink's request of a bodyguard. To prove his strength, Harry takes a phonebook and begins tearing it apart.

"You're tearing one page at a time," says Eddie.

"I ain't in a hurry," explains the dope.

Of course, Harry takes his job too seriously; at one point he even hijacks Eddie's girl in the tunnel of love. "Don't worry," says the bodyguard at the wrong moment, "I watch you like a stork."

Eddie is infatuated with nightclub singer Joyce Lennox (Ethel Merman), who turns out to be Vance's girl. After a hilarious chase at the climax, the gangsters are ensnared by the police and all turns out well for the heroes.

Invitation telegrams were sent out to attend a 9:15 performance of *Strike Me Pink* on January 16, 1936, and to an after-show party "in the Music Hall Studio Apartment in honor of Eddie and also Ethel Merman whose birthday it is. Kindly telephone acceptance to publicity department as soon as possible."

It wasn't long before Eddie was knocking on Phil's hotel door with another film idea.

May 4, 1936

Mr. Phil Rapp
Knickerbocker Hotel,
Hollywood, California

Dear Phil:
Following up my telegram, I am signing a contract for you to write the next Bobby Breen picture.

I thought of the story two days ago, told it to [producer Sol M.] Lesser as coming from you—he was crazy about it even though I ad-libbed it in the roughest form. The outline follows:

We open in a courtroom where we hear a Judge talking, I've had before me some of the most hardened criminals in this city, individuals who are a menace to the community, but you're different—you're a puzzle—I can't make you out at all." And we pan with our camera and disclose Bobby Breen to whom the Judge has been referring.

The Judge continues, "You say you don't know these crooks and yet the officer swears you're a part of the gang."

Bobby answers, "The officer is nuts—I didn't know the guys until they came around my block and asked for me. I was playing with the boys."

And as he continues we dissolve into an East side street and show Bobby with a group of boys playing a game when three smug looking boys in their early twenties approach and the leader addresses the kids, "Which one of you fellows does the singing around here?"

The kids point to Bobby, who delighted with the prospect of maybe getting a job, responds gratefully, "Gee mister, you ain't going to put me on the stage, are you? Why I could sing better than all those actors."

The leader stops him with, "How would you like to make a dollar?"

The kids yell, "Bobby is going to get a dollar!" and Bobby, eyes popping, gulps, "And here's a little sample." He starts to sing a few notes, but the leader puts his arm around his shoulder and answers, "Not here—come with me."

The three crooks take Bobby by the hand and, followed by the other kids, walk up a few blocks, where they find a soap-box, place Bobby on it and command him to sing. This he does and to such great effect that in a little while a crowd gathers and as the crowd increases, our three suave well-dressed pickpockets start working. When they have tapped the mob of their wallets, watches, etc., we go back to the Courtroom and pick up Bobby who is telling the Judge, "I didn't know they were pickpockets—I don't like to sing for crooks—I like to sing to make people happy—that's what I've been doing all my life."

The Judge questions Bobby further and we find that Bobby's mother has run away because of his father who is a nice fellow when he is sober, but he is never sober. Bobby lives for a week at Mrs. Murphy's home—the next week shifts to Mrs. Cohen's three-room flat then to Mrs. Battalio, one of the Italian neighbors. In fact he is called Everybody's Boy, because no one really owns him.

As the Judge is about to sentence Bobby to the reformatory, he is interrupted by a Court visitor, a Mr. John Hudson, a well-to-do citizen and a member of the Big Brother Association. He makes arrangements with the Court to take Bobby in his custody and be responsible for him. Bobby becomes a part, and a large part, of the Hudson household. He prevents a divorce and he stops the elopement between Hudson's daughter and a cad—a money-hunter.

At one stage of our story, Bobby is virtually kidnapped by

his drunken father. When Bobby finds out that his father took him to the country not to spend the day, but to keep him for good, he is enraged and tells his father, who is a little "stewed" at the time, that he must go back to his Daddy Hudson. This inflames the drunken father who slaps Bobby, knocking him down. (We can get a good scene out of this.) The father later is killed in a drunken brawl. Bobby is returned to Mr. and Mrs. Hudson, who are brought closer together because of their great love for their newly adopted child, who by now is an outstanding radio star.

Phil, I have written no story in this letter, but I have given you several characters, a good opening and a chance for you to invent some action in the Hudson home.

You have full sway—go ahead and write from scratch, keeping in mind the things I have given you above. Forget radio for the while, although I know I can't stop you from thinking of Texaco sub-consciously. Take a couple of weeks and knock out a rough draft, without dialogue and send it to me to Cleveland. I will make some notes and suggestions and return it to you, so that when I arrive on the Coast, about a month from now, you should have the story in good enough shape to submit to Sol Lesser.

As you know, the broadcast went quite smoothly last night and am hoping the one next week does as well, but I don't see how it can miss, with the Mother's Daddy spot, Parkyakarkus as an intern and whatever we can get out of part one.

Let me hear from you on receipt of this letter and I hope that you found a house by now.
Affectionately,
Eddie Cantor

P.S. In the story—the more you can play the Big Brother movement—the better.

Phil must have liked the idea, because a May 12, 1936 letter from Eddie relayed the following: "Keep working on the Breen story. Am leaving tonight for Cleveland where I will play for a week; then to Chicago for another week, and after a few days in St. Louis, I will be on my way to the Coast."

Nine days later *Variety* reported that the title of the Breen picture as *Happy Go Lucky*; and also that Rapp's new play, *The Hard Way*, had been scheduled to open on Broadway at the Cort Theatre in the fall.

On May 25, 1936 Eddie wrote from Chicago:

Dear Phil:-
Am glad to know that you are working out the rough edges of "EVERYBODY'S BOY."

I am looking forward to the second draft. There is no question in my mind but that it will be a good vehicle for Bobby in a few short weeks. After that we can discuss my problem, but right now I would like a little rest.

We are doing five performances daily here, having broken all records of this theatre the first three days.

Harry and Bobby send out love to you and yours.
Affectionately,
Eddie

Eddie Cantor was determined to make Bobby Breen a star. The June 12, 1936 edition of *RKO Newsette* announced "CANTOR'S BOY STAR MAKING 3 MORE," stating that the eight-year-old singing sensation of Cantor's radio show had just been signed for a three-picture deal, the first to be *Everybody's Boy*, which was written by Rapp. It's unclear whether the project fell flat or became one of Bobby's immediate pictures (*Rainbow on the River*, released December 18, 1936; *Make a Wish*, released August 27, 1937). Rapp certainly went uncredited if *Everybody's Boy* was made under a different title.

Thanks to Cantor, Rapp was now living in California, and trying his hand at as much writing as he could—even for the movies. The

April 28, 1937 edition of *The Hollywood Reporter* announced, "Maurice Conn has purchased an original, 'He Had to Fight,' by Phil Rapp, as a Frank Darro and Ken Richmond feature."

But it was *radio* that was taking up most of his time.

On December 5, 1936 Cantor wrote again to Rapp:

> My dear Phil,
> Well, we go to court with that "momzer" [arrow pointing to handwritten "Freedman" in a penciled circle] on Monday. From the way the testimony shapes up, I feel 100% sure you will not have to come on. In the examination before trial, he has perjured himself one-half dozen times. That must have a telling effect when he gets on the stand.
>
> I hope you all liked last week's broadcast, although we were surprised not to have heard from you. Johnny has been doing a swell job for us, and while I am not sure, there is a possibility of bringing him out to the Coast when I return the week after next.
>
> I certainly was elated to see the way you looked and the way you felt when you left. If it keeps up, I am sure that you and Frenchy can open up a health school in Hollywood. Frenchy could do the massaging while you do the blackouts on the side.
>
> And speaking of blackouts, I want you to write and tell me if you are as interested now, as you were when I spoke to you a short while ago, about working two weeks a month on the script. If you are serious about it, I shall make you a definite proposition. Write or wire me so I can arrange my plans accordingly.
>
> I have engaged Jack Murray for eight weeks, and he is coming with us to the Coast. He is doing nice work, although Davis has "wacked" him up too.

My very best to Mariam and the baby.
Affectionately,
Eddie

P.S. John Reber, Jesse Block, Bill Murray, Jack Larson are all going to be expert witnesses for me.

CHAPTER 3
FANNY LADY

It's unclear whether George McManus's 1904 comic strip *The Newlyweds*, in which a couple and their child Baby Snookums appears, was an influence on Fanny Brice's first performing the role of the eternally youthful, innocently vengeful, Baby Snooks, in 1912 on the vaudeville stage. One scholar claims that Snooks was introduced on *Ziegfeld Follies of the Air*, with Jack Arthur as Daddy, and acknowledges David Freedman and Phil Rapp as the creators of the character.

Phil himself asserted the following, included in his autobiography, in a short chapter entitled:

THE BIRTH OF BABY SNOOKS

To begin with, Fanny never called her Snooks. It was always Schnooks. You can imagine the trouble she had signing autographs in the old radio days. Fortunately, she never had to say the name on the air in any of the scripts I wrote for her. She had done the child character at parties and for friends but never professionally until I prepared the first five-minute sketch which was aired in the late 1930s on a long-forgotten radio program. It came about this way.

David Freedman and I were collaborating on a number of radio programs at the time. We had Block and Sully, Eddie Cantor, George Givot, Lou Holtz, Lulu McConnell—even a dramatic series starring Mady Christians. The money was rolling in, the amount of work was staggering, but we had a card file and a larcenous system. The joke file provided us with basic material which I must confess was slapped together in the most haphazard fashion, but in those days radio comedy was so new that the people would listen to anything.

To prove that they hardly knew what they were listening to, David and I would merely switch the names of the performers we were writing for, so that Holtz's script on Monday night was a thinly disguised version of what Eddie Cantor fractured the studio audience with on Sunday. The same applied to the rest of them.

But Fanny Brice was a problem. She was a Jewish dialect performer, doing a weekly sketch concerning a husband and family, and she played a character known as Mrs. Cohen. The sketches were just that, and labeled "Mrs. Cohen at the Beach," "Mrs. Cohen at the Movies," etc. The other half of the program was a historical satire, also done in dialect, with Fanny playing the part of some famous or infamous female figure of the past. Obviously, none of the material we supplied the rest of the performers fitted these two categories. So we had to actually *write* them.

Fanny always had trouble with her teeth and David had sent her to a dentist on the East side, a man he recommended very highly. A professor! A genius dentist. A man who had worked on the crowned heads of Europe. Fanny went to him. His knowledge of dentistry was so scant that she showed up on rehearsal night with her dentures gone. Cracked. He almost ruined poor Fanny for life. Freedman was beside himself. "You idiot," he roared at the woebegone and toothless Fanny, "why did you go to that butcher!" forgetting that he had sent her. She whimpered like a child. We both stared at her, I with compassion, but Freedman's brilliant mind was already churning. "That baby character," he said. "What do you call her?"

"Schnooks," lisped Fanny, in tears.

Freedman was already at his bookcase searching frantically. Fanny was weeping hysterically, vowing that she couldn't go on the next night or ever again until her teeth were fixed. I agreed with her, knowing that she could never play a satire as Mme. Pompadour, even in dialect, in her present condition.

"Here it is," said David, and he pitched a small book at me.

It was *Chimes from a Jester's Bells* by Robert James Burdette, an out-of-print collection written way back when. Public domain, of course. "Look up a sketch about a kid and his uncle and switch to a girl. Fanny'll get her chance to play Schnooks."

The sketch by Burdette was a simple but humorous piece called "The simple story of George Washington." The only switch I made was to change "Schnooks" to "Baby Snooks."

It was most probably in 1912 that Brice began performing a baby routine in vaudeville, but it was miles away from the Snooks character known today. In 1921, the same year she introduced her famous song "My Man" to Ziegfeld audiences, Schnooks emerged again at a party, when she was asked to entertain. The lisp, wide eyes and innocence flashed that night, but wasn't cultivated until February 29, 1936, when *The Ziegfeld Follies of the Air*, written by Rapp, began. The series ended quickly, but was moved to NBC's epic (in length and prestige) *Good News of 1938*, in which Snooks and her great straight man of a Daddy (Hanley Stafford, the perfect foil) became a regular feature of the sixty-minute show.

Snooks kept her poor Daddy pulling at the leash for a long, long time, though it's clear that the man just did *not* know how to handle or ignore difficult (or *any* kind of) children, as the following hell from the *Good News* episode of July 18, 1940 easily demonstrates.

ANNOUNCER:	And now, ladies and gentlemen, here is Fanny Brice as Baby Snooks!
	(MUSIC . . . APPLAUSE)
POWELL:	Well, Daddy, played by Hanley Stafford, is putting on a minstrel show for his lodge. In order to make a thorough job of it, Daddy has decided to visit the public library for technical research and to browse through a few joke books. Naturally, he couldn't escape the clutches of his dynamic offspring, so we find them both on the steps of the library. Listen…

FATHER: Now, Snooks, before we go in you must understand one thing.

BRICE: No noise.

FATHER: Exactly. You must be as quiet as a mouse—don't raise your voice above a whisper and walk on your tip-toes.

BRICE: Is anybody dead in there?

FATHER: Nobody's dead in there! But a lot of people come to the library to cogitate.

BRICE: Don't they feel good, Daddy?

FATHER: They feel fine. But people who go to the library don't wish to be disturbed while they're meditating. That's why you'll behave better than you ever have before!

BRICE: Will I?

FATHER: You will if you want to go in with me.

BRICE: I will.

FATHER: All right. Then let's go—but remember—conduct yourself like a little lady. Comprehend?

BRICE: Copperhead.

FATHER: Very well.

BRICE: Wait a minute, Daddy.

FATHER: What is it?

BRICE:	I got a noisy feeling coming over me.
FATHER:	Snooks! I warned you!
BRICE:	It's gone now, Daddy. I'll be very quiet.
FATHER:	Okay. Hold on to my hand.
BRICE:	What's in the library, Daddy?
FATHER:	Books. Thousands of books.
BRICE:	Did Uncle Louie make them?
FATHER:	No, of course not.
BRICE:	Well, Mummy said that Uncle Louie was a bookmaker when—
FATHER:	Never mind that! Just don't snoop around so much! And don't repeat everything you hear!
BRICE:	Why?
FATHER:	Because that's gossiping! Leave that to your mother!
BRICE:	Huh?
FATHER:	Nothing! Trouble with all women—if there were just three women left in the world, do you know what they'd do?
BRICE:	No.
FATHER:	Two of them would get together and talk about the other one!

BRICE:	Why?
FATHER:	Because they would!
BRICE:	If there was three men left in the world what would they do?
FATHER:	I don't know. Come on in.
BRICE:	Would they get together and look for the three women?
FATHER:	Forget about the men and women. We're going inside now, so be quiet.
BRICE:	Who's that man behind the desk?
FATHER:	Shhh. He's the librarian. I have to talk to him. Er—excuse me.
RUBIN:	(VERY QUIET, MEEK MAN) Yes sir. May I help you, sir?
BRICE:	What's he scared about, Daddy?

One particular and typical *Variety* review (of the September 5, 1947 broadcast) summed up many Snooks reviews of the era: "As written by Phil Rapp, 'Baby Snooks' was more than simply a comedy show with an occasional laugh. It was pleasant listening and its characters were essentially likable people. Snooks was a mischievous moppet, with an incurable knack for turning a quiet household into turmoil and shaking the sanity of her parents, but she was not a brat. She was not nasty or mean, spiteful or sadistic. She was at heart a nice kid. Similarly, Daddy, as played by Hanley Stafford, was harried and desperate, and occasionally was driven to spanking his impish daughter at the sign-off. But Daddy wasn't ill-tempered or unkind with the kid. He wasn't a crab. And the show was amusing and enjoyable. It was fun, without offending good taste or anyone's sensibilities. Any listener could safely hear it in his home, whether the company included strangers or children."

Once Snooks evolved as a whole, bratty person, Brice found her own personality taking a back seat to it. When the little girl became a star, the woman in her forties began to do Snooks a bit too often in public, even giving interviews in the voice, and referring to Schnooks as a living person.

I first met Fanny Brice in 1932 after a session with her then husband, the late Billy Rose. (The eerie thought strikes me that all the people mentioned, with the exception of Bob Young, have passed from this vale of laughter.) The meeting with Rose took place in his impressive office in the Candler Building on 42nd Street. Young as I was, I had already made my mark as one of the two top radio comedy writers. The other one was the late David Freedman. We were to become partners and collaborators shortly afterwards. Our association was a long and happy one which, unfortunately, ended on a sad note, the circumstances of which I shall refer to in a later chapter.

At any rate, Mr. Rose engaged me to write a radio program for Miss Brice, who was then appearing weekly for Chase and Sanborn Tea. The question of salary arose (I was then earning in the neighborhood of three hundred a week between writing and acting) and on a sudden impulse I told Mr. Rose that the money was unimportant and I would leave the compensation entirely up to him.

He stared at me for a full minute, then said, "Young man, you completely disarm me."

I wasn't aware of it then, but for anybody to disarm Billy Rose would be like a midget armed with a slingshot capturing a battalion of tanks.

The program was duly written and performed successfully— so much so that I was summoned by Mr. Rose who handed me a rear masala [sic] check and offered me a permanent job as the writer for Fanny Brice's show. I have no recollection of the writer or writers who were supplying material before I took over, but since I was engaged on several other radio projects for the J. Walter Thompson Advertising Agency, it was two or three weeks before I could take the job.

As I mentioned earlier it was during this interim period I met David Freedman. I kept in touch with him, told him of my good fortune with Fanny Brice—four hundred dollars a week would be added to our combined pot—and arranged a meeting with David to celebrate our amalgam. As I recall it, we celebrated with four bottles of Perrier water, to which he was addicted, then he dropped the bomb. He was thru with Cantor for six months. I was numb with shock as I realized my weekly take would now be only two hundred, but a deal was a deal. David lit a cigar, a blonde cigar, the best Havana at two dollars a throw, studied me with a smile, then casually informed me that we had signed to write the *Ziegfeld Follies of '33* with a fine advance, made a deal with Sidney Matz, president of Ex-Lax, for thirty-nine radio programs, and had taken on Lou Holtz for Chesterfield cigarettes!

"Were you worried, kid?"

"Not for an instant," I lied.

"You looked worried," he said. My hands were still shaking.

"No, honest." I reached for my bottle of Perrier.

"Okay. Then stop drinking from the ink bottle."

"Ink! Oh, my God—what'll I do? I swallowed some!"

"Just chew on a blotter—then we'll get to work."

That was the first joke David ever hit me with.

Good News (featuring Snooks) continued through 1939 and was altered to a 30-minute format in March of 1940. When it became *Maxwell House Coffee Time*, Frank Morgan received the first 15 minutes for his comic windbagging, and Snooks skits filled the latter half. Hanley Stafford continued as "Daddy," Lancelot Higgins, while Mommy was played by Arlene Harris, "the human chatterbox" on *The Al Pearce Show*. Harris didn't get to chatter too much on the new series, however. Mostly the shows were, as always, a dialogue between father and inquiring daughter. Sometimes the crying of Snooks's brother Robespierre was heard, played by Leone Ledoux, but it wasn't a mainstay of the show. John Conte was the announcer, Meredith Wilson took care of the music and Mann Holiner produced the series.

As time went on, Brice relied more and more on her various writers (Jess Oppenheimer and others joined later) and Stafford, and in fact it became almost all-consuming to her career. She and Frank Morgan were very competitive for topping the other, but finally Brice received her own solo CBS series, *The Baby Snooks Show*, in 1944, with Rapp writing sporadically for it. For the 1944–45 season Snooks was sponsored by Post cereals on Sunday nights, then switched to Sanka Coffee for 1945–46, at which point Rapp was off the series. The show moved to Friday nights and ran until 1948 when television began beating at the door. Snooks continued on radio, now on NBC, remaining there until 1951, when Fanny died.

Separate from his partial Snooks chapter, Rapp also penned the following Brice story:

"He couldn't adlib fuck on a shithouse wall!" This immortal line was uttered by Fanny Brice during a rehearsal of the MGM-Maxwell House Coffee radio show in late 1938. Fanny and I and Carole Lombard (a guest on the show) were seated in the second row of the ———Theatre where we broadcast every Thursday. The lusty slur was directed at Frank Morgan who was reading (with Bob Young, the MC) the seven-minute spot I had written for them. Fanny made the remark entirely without rancor or intended insult. It was just in response to Carole's reaction to what appeared to be Morgan's astonishing gift for the extemporaneous quip.

Actually Frank was a highly disciplined performer, apart from his delightful offstage vices, who read the lines in his script each Thursday evening as though they were engraved in marble. The "adlibs" were carefully prepared and written in parentheses—a typographical device that added to his magnificent timing. His amazing laugh that started with a giggle and ended like a spring freshet so infected the audience (that direction was written for him too) that they became victims of mass hysteria, or *folie a deux* as the psychiatrists call it. Just why an audience will laugh harder at what they think is an adlib than a line that is far superior in comedic value is something I have never been able to determine. But, take it from 40 years of experience in writing comedy, it is unshakably true. I offer the proof in the very section of the script that provoked Miss Lomabrd's naïve wonder and Fanny's worldly reply.

The above referenced script excerpt was not found among Phil's writings, so the below is included as almost the anti-example: a usual start (this time from January 7, 1943) to comically contrive a way of saying the title to *Maxwell House Coffee Time*, starring Hanley Stafford as Daddy and Fanny Brice as Snooks.

BRICE: Daddy!

STAFF: What is it, Snooks?

BRICE: Can you help me with my homework?

STAFF: Not now. I'm clearing up my accounts for this old year and I have a few more checks to make out. Look at these doctor bills!

BRICE: We're a sick family, ain't we?

STAFF: Not any more than any other family. But the twins cost me a fortune last year. I've already made four payments—and this is the last.

BRICE: Then do we own them?

STAFF: Yes. What's this bill here? . . . Oh, yes—my lumbago.

BRICE: Did the doctor bring that too, daddy?

STAFF: No, I had it. And the doctor came to the house.

BRICE: How much does he charge?

STAFF:		It all depends. If he makes a house call the fee is double.
BRICE:		For what?
STAFF:		For my lumbago.
BRICE:		What's that?
STAFF:		It's a pain in the back. You remember when I had it—my back swelled up and I couldn't move.
BRICE:		Yeah.
STAFF:		Well, this bill is the fee for his house call.
BRICE:		Do you have to pay it now?
STAFF:		Yes.
BRICE:		Why?
STAFF:		Because it's back swell house call fee time.
BRICE:		Ohhh! (APPLAUSE . . . THEME)

As you can see, neither the exchange nor the prepared adlib are models of excruciating wit but the audience response was enormous. Of course, people who went to see radio shows, like today's live TV audiences, are prepared to laugh at almost anything that is delivered by a high-priced comedian, or non-comedian for that matter. And in my book most comedians are non-comedians. More about that later.

Again, Rapp also wrote Snooks notes to himself for this chapter of his autobiography; those are included here:

The myth of the funny girl. First met Billy Rose—Candler building.

Fanny going into radio. Wrote spot—didn't ask for money—you completely disarm me, young man. Then got the show. Freedman lost Cantor—my salary was immediately cut in half. Soon shows came rolling in. Wrote the first Baby Snooks after reading Burdette—Chimes from a jester's bells. Never said why daddy. Only why.

Played Mrs. Cohen. Lou Sorin was husband. Later Teddy Bergman—now Alan Reed—played Uncle to Snooks. Later, Daddy. Hanley Stafford.

Had large type—heavy cardboard, dropped them all. Too vain to wear glasses.

Wrote and directed her only TV appearance—Popsicle. Too grotesque. Never appeared again on TV.

Friday nights at her home on Faring Road. Used to make batches of potato pancakes for me—always asked what the show was about the night before. House full of grifters. Plenty of fags. Never gave money—always refuge and food.

Ann Pennington. Billy and Frances.

Adlib—Morgan—couldn't adlib fuck on a shithouse wall. To Carole Lombard.

Used to relieve herself in sink in dressing room at NBC.

One great love in her life—lack of judgment—John Conte.

Always pronounced it Baby Schnooks.

Haunted antique shops—gave me a spinet [small piano]—painting—and a book of Paul Geraldy's poems—all of which she knew by heart.

Died at Cedars in 1951—Bea Canterbury (wife of the late Fred Wile) then her secretary called me first.

Wrote "She loves a lot" for Follies of '33—round bed. Boston—Willie Howard got no laughs—she got them all.

Opened at Wintergarden in NY—tables turned. She read her lines to scenery as he quickened his pace around the bed. She chased him with a stage brace.

Soul-saving Sadie—take-off on Aimee Semple McPherson—couldn't remember first line opening night. Played it cool—sensation.

Sam Moore called it Baby Snakes—Laacoon—wrestling with snakes—literary pun.

I would rehearse her and play Daddy—then rehearse Stafford and play Snooks. Then together. [The process of the Snooks show began at 1:30 on Wednesdays in Studio 2 of the CBS Building in Hollywood: a reading, then two rehearsals the same day with Fanny whispering or giving dispassionate readings, which worried the writers. Conferences and run-throughs were on Thursdays. The cast gathered in Fanny's dressing room at noon on Fridays for last-minute changes. Two more rehearsals, the second one being a dress rehearsal at 3:30, and the show went on the air at 5 p.m. PCT.]

How is it this week, kid. Only other person I ever heard her call kid was Ben Hecht. It stinks this week, Fanny. Every other week I made you a hit—now you go out and make me one.

Given to lusty language. Always had trouble with her teeth but ate like a trencherman.

Married Billy Rose? Why? Well, it's like taking the dope cure. I was once married to a big gangster, now I'm tapering off with a little one. He couldn't stand her belching.

Never saw Barbra Streisand but cannot *imagine* her playing Fanny. [The one dame who could play Fanny in a movie would be Joan Davis, Fanny had told reporters. Talks about a film on her life were started by studios after the success of *Yankee Doodle Dandy*, but nothing came of it.]

Loved caviar—ate it with a soup spoon—twelve dollars an ounce.

Myth—she was able to detect a phony at fifty yards—surrounded by phonies. Paradox—also entertained intelligentsia—Huxley, Hecht, others—friendly and warm.

The great split. She didn't want me billed in the early part of the show. Probably her agent put her up to it because she couldn't care less. Anyway, she had no rights in the matter. Rather than continue at loggerheads I quit despite thousand-dollar-a-week raise, making me highest-paid writer in radio.

There was a single paragraph, separate from the above, also found among Rapp's papers:

I cannot find it in my heart to conclude this chapter with such a slur against Billy Rose. True, he was not universally liked, but I always found him a gentleman, a man of great wit and understanding, a tremendous feeling for things beautiful. Witness his collection of great paintings, all sorts of art, some will say he collected such things for profit. I differ. He truly loved his objects, never quibbled about price, and amassed a collection envied by every art lover in the world. As I have indicated, he was not a hard man to deal with, only sharp enough to recognize sharp practice.

CHAPTER 4
WAR & PEACE OF HEAVEN

During his writing for *Maxwell House Coffee Time*, Rapp purchased six acres in Encino, on Haskell Avenue, from E. A. Birdwell, who sold it to him for $14,500. The land was to be developed with a ranch-type house, stables and swimming pool, at a projected cost of $30,000.

During a newspaper interview, Rapp said, "It's fine to have a ranch and live off your own products. I figure, in view of my overhead, my pedigreed eggs cost me about two dollars a dozen and my home-grown steaks about five dollars a pound. But, just the same, it's nice to think they are all your own products—a nice comfortable feeling even if it is expensive."

They needed the room, now with another addition to the family. As Paul Rapp vividly recalls: "At Midnight, October 23, 1937, my parents were told that it was doubtful that I would be born alive. An emergency operation to save my mother's life was urgent. Two hours later I was born dead, but after two tanks of oxygen had been administered, I managed to survive. A special nurse was hired to see that I remained alive, since the first instinct, which is hunger, seemed to have escaped me. My first instinct was to want to sleep 24 hours a day. My parents and doctor had other thoughts, and they won. A few days later I was named Paul Winston Rapp. Paul, because that was my father's favorite name: Winston, because my mother admired Winston Churchill, and Rapp, because that was the last name of my father and his and my ancestor

The ranch was an exciting place to bring up a family. Paul loved it: "We got the ranch around 1942 or 1943, and we kept it up until the early 1950s. We also had a custom-made 1941 Woody made by

Packard. That car today would be worth over a million dollars. The Buick was their largest sedan model. It was black, with the roll-up window between the passenger and chauffeur. We also had a cook—David. My parents hired him on one of their trips back from New York and met him on the train. He was the chef. At the racetrack they found a man named Hubert (we called him Chappy). He worked in the Turf Club where my parents always went. He stayed for some length of time, as a handyman and helper, at the same time as David, in the 1940s. When he left, he went back to the track, he just couldn't stay away. But it was Sal who was in charge of the whole ranch.

"The ranch was walled-in, so you entered through gates when you drove up to the house. We had a large Victory Garden, growing just about everything you could find in the market. And during the war my parents kept a Crisco can on the sink with bacon fat, etc. in it that they would donate that to the war effort.

"We had a very large, fancy chicken coop housing the hens. Sal killed most of them, and I did a few by chopping their heads off with an ax. We had about three hundred chickens, and raised a lot of them in a giant incubator in one of the horse stalls. I hated having to clean the chicken coop, but I was so small and could get in there and stand up straight to do it, so I had to do that. What I *did* enjoy was collecting up the eggs in my basket. We used the eggs and other things to barter with the market for things like sugar, which was rationed. And we kept a lot of it in one of the first freezers ever made—the Kelvinator.

"We had this fabulous manure pit, with two big doors that closed down on it like a tornado shelter. We had to put the manure in there every day from the horse stalls. The pig pen was really neat—letting the pigs wander out into a corral. There were troughs where all the leftover food was tossed.

"Sal once took two big metal garbage cans, which had a fire underneath them. The cans were heating water until they got boiling. He took a big pig out there and put a bunch of loose corn on the ground, so the pig would start to eat it. Sal took out one of his rifles that he had in a locked enclosure, and put it to the pig's forehead and pulled the trigger. The pig was still eating while it tipped over and died. They used a rope winch and dipped the pig in hot water to make it easy to get the hair off. Sal took a tree saw kind of thing and two people sawed the pig down the middle while it was still hanging there. He took the blood and the intestines out for blood sausage. The whole thing was a hobby to Dad, resting his brain while doing things.

"Most things on the ranch were for trade or to use ourselves. Sal built a big brick smokehouse adjacent to the tool house at the rear of the ranch, and what pig meat we didn't smoke was taken to the butcher, trading it for other kinds of meat. Butter was impossible to get too, so we bartered for that, too. The smokehouse was overly elaborate, the way lots of things were done in Beverly Hills.

"We also had beautiful horse stalls, because this was Dad's true love. Back then, it was a competition of which neighbor or star had the best stalls. The horses would put their noses in a sink-like device on the wall, pushing down, and it would fill up with water so the horses would learn how to get it themselves. We had four (occasionally five) horses, one for each member of the family. We had five stalls. And in that area we had these big wooden barrels, filled with cucumbers, the pickling kind, so Dad could make pickles. Green tomatoes were in with them. Dad was a big hit with his pickles. He had these big glass jars and often gave them to friends.

"He used the ranch to impress people. And that's where he cooked a lot—primarily Chinese dishes. He taught Danny Kaye, who became a world-class chef. Danny was the most frequent 'name' who visited.

"Behind the stalls, each horse had its own corral. In the same area adjacent to the stalls was a feed room which housed the hay, and attached to that Sal had his room. The tack room was adjacent to that, with all the saddles and equipment. It was all very elaborate and costly, with custom and silver saddles, made by a famous saddle maker who also made them for Roy Rogers and others. One of my main jobs as a kid was to saddle soap the tack room, and anything leather, including the large rack of beautiful boots, to get my allowance.

"The horses had to be washed sometimes. Dad had a palomino (Old Gold, named after the cigarette sponsor), then a white horse (Fox—he was almost unrideable for anyone except my dad). I had a pinto horse (I named her Papoose, from *Red Ryder*), a small mare. When Dad bought her, unbeknownst to all of us, she was pregnant.

We all watched her baby grow, but they didn't wake me the night Papoose foaled, so I missed out on that. We called it Mystery because we didn't know where it came from. I once took Mystery in the house, wearing boots and a cowboy hat, and my parents were hysterical.

"During Christmas and Halloween, we didn't do anything at the ranch. Usually Mom would read or be at the pool, or cleaning in the house. Only in the summers would we live there. Sometimes Dad would go out for three or four days at a time just to write, but we did go out there on weekends, but never on weekdays. We'd have a couple hundred pounds of ice in the pool when it was really hot, like in August. Sometimes I'd get on Papoose and ride down to the movies for a collection of Western serials.

"Dad was a really good rider. Once in a while Smitty, an old blacksmith, came over. He was like something from out of the old movies, shoeing horses the old-fashioned way with a wheel and fire. I always looked forward to watching him shoe the horses.

"I remember riding up Haskell Ave., just a short distance away. No houses then, just a hill which is today known as Royal Oaks Estate. The only way to get around was on fire roads which were built for the fire engines to get through. I don't think I ever rode alone; I was always with either with Mom or Dad, and often all three of us would go. Mostly open land and oak trees. There were deer and coyotes and butterflies.

"I collected a lot of gophers, rattle and king snakes—I made belts out of them. The king snakes ate the rattlesnakes, being immune to them. And we had a lot of cats and mice and rats in our feed room. Dad had these fancy electric fly catchers, too. Imagine a box about one-foot high and three-foot square. You'd put manure inside and the flies would land on the wires and get electrocuted. The cats would run across these and burn their feet.

"It bothered me that Sal drowned kittens in a gunny sack in our elaborate fish pond which was up near the two houses. It had a waterfall and big goldfish and a perch. When you parked the car you walked by the pond which was about fifty feet long and ten feet wide. There were two large oak trees there which cast a nice shadow over it. The lawn was long and beautiful; the main one between the stable and the houses was about 1,000 square feet. Also, there was a formal English garden with all kind of nut trees, like almond. As you drove along the driveway you saw the Victory Garden and where Sal had put in a formal cactus garden. Dad was really into making things grow. There were a lot of black widow spiders around, too. I always had to hit my boots to make sure they were empty before putting them on.

"There was an enclosure near the front if they wanted to isolate the horses. That's where I first trained Mystery. I would put him on a long rope to get him used to being attached to something.

"In the large lawn part we had archery, with targets. Johnny and Dad would play baseball. They were close friends with Leo Durocher, the great Yankee player and later Yankees manager. Another friend who was there quite a bit was Tony 'Rocky' Graziano, the boxer, and Benny Rubin, the comedian. Dad didn't socialize with jockeys—that would be like socializing with your maid.

"My mom bought an 1,800-square-foot house, somewhere in the Valley, and had it brought over by truckers. The guest house was for Joel and me, and the main one was for Mom and Dad. The family pool was unusual—Mom said it was built by Paddock Pools, the Rolls-Royce of swimming pools. It was big and beautiful! Joel and I had a small 8x10 pool, a children's pool, connected to the big pool. Dad swam every day, so did Mom and me; Joel was already in high school. Every time Dad went into the pool at the ranch, he wore a rubber swim cap. He had a great head of hair!

"That ranch was about ten miles, as the crow flies, from Lockheed. There were constantly P-38s fighter planes, with two tails, flying over, because it was World War II. It always wowed me—always exciting to see. There were hundreds of those!"

War had come. Phil wanted to do more than just collect chicken fat. He wrote to Atherton W. Hobler, founder and Chairman of Benton and Bowles Advertising, which sponsored the *Maxwell House Coffee Time* and *Three of a Kind*, the show he was currently writing for Fanny Brice. Hobler's September 14, 1942 letter back to Rapp, read:

My dear Phil:
Your wire of the 13th was on my desk bright and early when I arrived this morning. It's really rather hard to answer this

wire. We don't want to stand in the way of anyone giving everything he has to this job of winning the war. However, a good deal could be said on whether or not a man in your position cannot do actually as much continuing to carry on as you are. You are writing one of the important shows; important because it is carrying various war messages to a great many people—important because of the opportunity it has to serve in furnishing relief and helping to keep up morale.

I think it is very laudable that you feel this way about trying to serve in the armed forces, but I am wondering, in view of your general health situation, whether or not the army can sufficiently waive this question and whether, therefore, you will not serve better by continuing to operate as you are.

For you especially this whole thing is quite a serious decision, and I am glad that you are proceeding carefully as you say.

Thought the show last week was quite good, and I know that everybody appreciated the fact that it was kept wholesome.

I want you to know I appreciate your taking this question of enlisting up with me so promptly and I think that you know you can count on me to help you do anything that is best in this situation.
Sincerely,
Hobe

The indecision continued, and Rapp continued to seek out friendly advice. From the Office of War Information in Washington, William B. Lewis, chief of the Radio Bureau, on September 18, 1942, wrote of his concern, calling Rapp a key man in radio. "However," he clarified, "I disagree pretty radically with the step you are taking, and I wish I could hold up your decision, no matter how firm it is, until I get a chance to talk with you on my forthcoming trip to Hollywood. I shall be there the latter part of next week."

Four days later Phil received the following letter from work-friend Chester J. LaRoche, Chairman of the Board of Young & Rubicam Advertising, possibly the most powerful ad agency in the country.

> Dear Phil:
> If I felt the way you did, I would certainly go into the service. A decision of this sort is one that must be made on the basis of which job will bring the most satisfaction.
>
> I feel that you can do an outstanding piece of work by staying in radio, but I wouldn't urge you to do that for one moment if your interest and your sense of duty made you feel you should join the armed forces.
>
> All we have tried to do here at Young & Rubicam, when a man is undecided, is to show him that a decision today should not be made on the basis of the last war—that this war is totally different and that it is fought on three different fronts—military, economical and *psychological.*
>
> Hitler, long ago, realized the great importance of the psychological front. We are just beginning to. Over half of Hitler's first victories were won on bluffs. Some of our victories are going to be won by disorganizing Germany, and at the same time, organizing this nation to a pitch and intensity that will cut the war days down and save millions of lives.
>
> My feeling is that the only practical group of psychologists in this country is our advertising radio men. In that group you stand at the top—that's why I feel that you will get a chance to do a real job—a needed job.
>
> All I can say to you is that I would move carefully and be certain that your decision is based on logic and not emotion.
> Cordially,
> Chester J. LaRoche

Rapp vigilantly decided to take that advice and stay on the home front, immersing himself in raising money for his country. For the time and effort he gave, he received many accolades of praise. On October 26, 1943 the Treasury Department wrote:

Dear Mr. Rapp:
Now that the Third War Loan Drive has been successfully concluded, I should like to tell you how much we in the Treasury Department have been encouraged by the generous and wholehearted response of the American people. The unprecedented results of this campaign will undoubtedly strengthen our united efforts for speedy victory.

A large part of this splendid achievement was due to the complete and patriotic cooperation of members of the radio and motion picture industries, who gave their time so generously.

Many thanks! Your willingness to stress the vital necessity of supporting the Third War Loan was a most important part in achieving our goal.

Such wonderful assistance is deeply appreciated, not only by myself and my co-workers, but also—and particularly—by our troops who depend on the contributions of the home front to bring about the victory we all desire.
Sincerely,
Ted R. Gamble
National Director
War Finance Division

Phil had found his patriotic niche, the "Rapp" way.

He received several citations from the Director of Press, Radio & Advertising, Vincent F. Callahan, "in recognition of your assistance in the War Bond Financing Program" for writing at least several 1944 episodes of the radio series, *Three of a Kind*. The United States Treasury Department's series starred Bert Lahr, Reginald Gardner and Shirley Mitchell, and Wilbur Hatch and his Orchestra. With such luminary guest stars as Charles Laughton, it was a zany, fast-paced show, much in the line of an early Marx Brothers' film. Says the announcer from the April 27, 1944 episode in which Orson Welles was the guest: "Good evening, ladies and gentlemen. I would like to read you a memo from the front office. It's addressed to Tobe Reed, that's me, and the message is quite pithy. It says 'Get the program off to a fast start, get off some persuasive remarks about the purchase of War Bonds, and get off.'"

And after a brief resume of cast: "As you may or may not know, Reginald Gardiner and Bert Lahr are two confidence men temporarily operating a psychiatric clinic and constantly on the lookout for a patient with a bundle of nerves and a like amount of cash. They are firm advocates of the bouillon treatment for neurotics—or, as Dr. Lahr so aptly puts it—soup to nuts. This is a high class variation of the old shell game."

Rapp once told a reporter, "We radio and television writers are no Hemingways. It's pretty much pick-and-shovel work—often tough going—but if you discipline yourself and organize your technique, it pays off. I can't work at all by daylight. I find the night most conducive, when I'm not distracted by anyone or anything. On the coast I'm a sucker for the California sunshine, but when it's dark, I find it easy to stay indoors.

"Sleep? It's overrated—largely a waste of time. I like my pleasures too much to waste hours either sleeping or writing. So I've trained myself to work fast and get the drudgery over with. Writing for radio, movies and television can be inspirational only to a limited degree. Since I've learned to write rapidly, I get the distasteful part over as soon as possible."

Paul Rapp states,

> I was forbidden to disturb him during the week. In our Oakhurst Drive house, he worked in a beautiful wood-paneled den. He had a wet bar and refrigerator in there. And he always wrote on a typewriter, then for notes and corrections used a brown pencil with no eraser on it, very soft lead, and a wider, heavier point. You see it all through his notations. Curiously, Martin Scorsese, who I have worked with, used the same pencil for his storyboards and laments that they

are no longer available. The den door faced the center hallway, and when the door was closed, I had to be quiet. When he came out, he had fun with us, and he always tried to make us laugh. I also tried to make him laugh by doing stupid things.

Oakhurst ran north/south and was the most eastern street of Beverly Hills, between Sunset and Santa Monica. The area was only half built around 1937, when I was born, with only a handful of homes there. Dad was 30 when I was born and that was the year the family moved into the Oakhurst house. Prior to that, he had been renting a house on Walden Drive in Beverly Hills since about 1934 or 35, when the family first moved to Los Angeles. They came from New York through the Panama Canal, when Joel was a baby. The Oakhurst home was a newer house that they could afford because of his work writing for Eddie Cantor. It was a great house. We always had a Friday or Saturday movie night—Dad would screen a movie which he brought home from the studio."

Along with radio work, Phil Rapp was working hard for MGM, punching up already-written scripts mostly, but preparing new projects as well. On April 16, 1943, he signed an MGM contract for $2,500 to provide "screenplay material" for a film to be entitled *Everything for the Army*.

As Paul explains, "When Dad was under contract to Goldwyn during the early Danny Kaye years, the average salary was $1,800 a year and the average car sold for $800. Dad told me a story of how he was sitting in Goldwyn's office when a writer was pitching a story, and Goldwyn became bored and asked the writer to take off his shoes. The puzzled writer unlaced them and took them off, then Goldwyn told him to take the shoes and set them outside the door of the office. The writer promptly did so and returned to his chair. Then Goldwyn looked the writer straight in the eyes and said, 'Please go get in them and thank you for coming.'

"Another time Dad was sleeping on the couch in his office while working with his partner on a screenplay for Goldwyn. Goldwyn came in—he liked to see if his writers were really working, and he went over to Dad and stood above him. With great intuition, Dad leapt up and pointed to his partner and said, "I've got it, here's how we do the scene!" And he was saved from a Goldwyn scolding.

"Dad was under contract with Goldwyn on a weekly salary when he first came west. He had writing assignments with other writers who ultimately got credit on the projects—just like I have with Roger Corman. When Dad was with Goldwyn, he worked on the *Up In Arms* film with Don Hartman, who received screen credit. I recall going to Grauman's Chinese theater with my nanny to see the movie. I was about seven years old.

While Phil kept busy in radio and film, Mariam kept the home fires burning. According to Paul, "She worked as a nurse's aide at the enormous VA hospital in West Los Angeles and while she was there she decided to raise a large amount of money from the members of Hillcrest Country Club to build a large and lovely nine-hole pitch & putt course which is still heavily used today. I played many rounds there in the passing years. And if that wasn't enough, she knitted sweaters and blankets for the Russian war relief. To say her plate was full is a gross understatement.

"My mother was a superb golfer. So was dad. Dad had one hole-in-one at Hillcrest in 1952. It was customary to buy everyone a round of drinks if you did that. He was doubly lucky that day because there were only two members there and neither drank.

"They entered a number of Hillcrest tournaments together, and won about three or four of them. She won a number of the women's trophies, too.

"If she had one failing it would be cooking. Blanche Bickerson was far ahead of her. This accounts for Dad's great skills in the kitchen: self defense. Another Bickersons similarity? My parents didn't sleep together in the same bedroom because of his snoring and his hours."

PHOTO GALLERY
SECTION ONE

Phil's birth certificate from England.

Phil Rapp's father, late 1930s.

Phil's mom, 1940s.

Phil Rapp and Bob Morris during their vaudeville days.

Out and about with Eddie Cantor.

Writing and clowning with Cantor.

Living the good life.

Phil, Mariam and friends at the Coconut Grove, Ambassador Hotel in Los Angeles in the 1940s.

Mariam Rapp.

Paul: "This picture is over 70 years old, taken in 1938, when I was probably six to eight months old. My mother cut my hair and put it in the frame. I think pictures at that time were colored by hand, though I can't be sure. You will notice I am wearing a pink outfit. I don't know who handmade the outfit for me, but I have been teased over the years that I was a girl."

PHOTO GALLERY: SECTION ONE | 95

Early days working on *Baby Snooks* with Alan Reed.

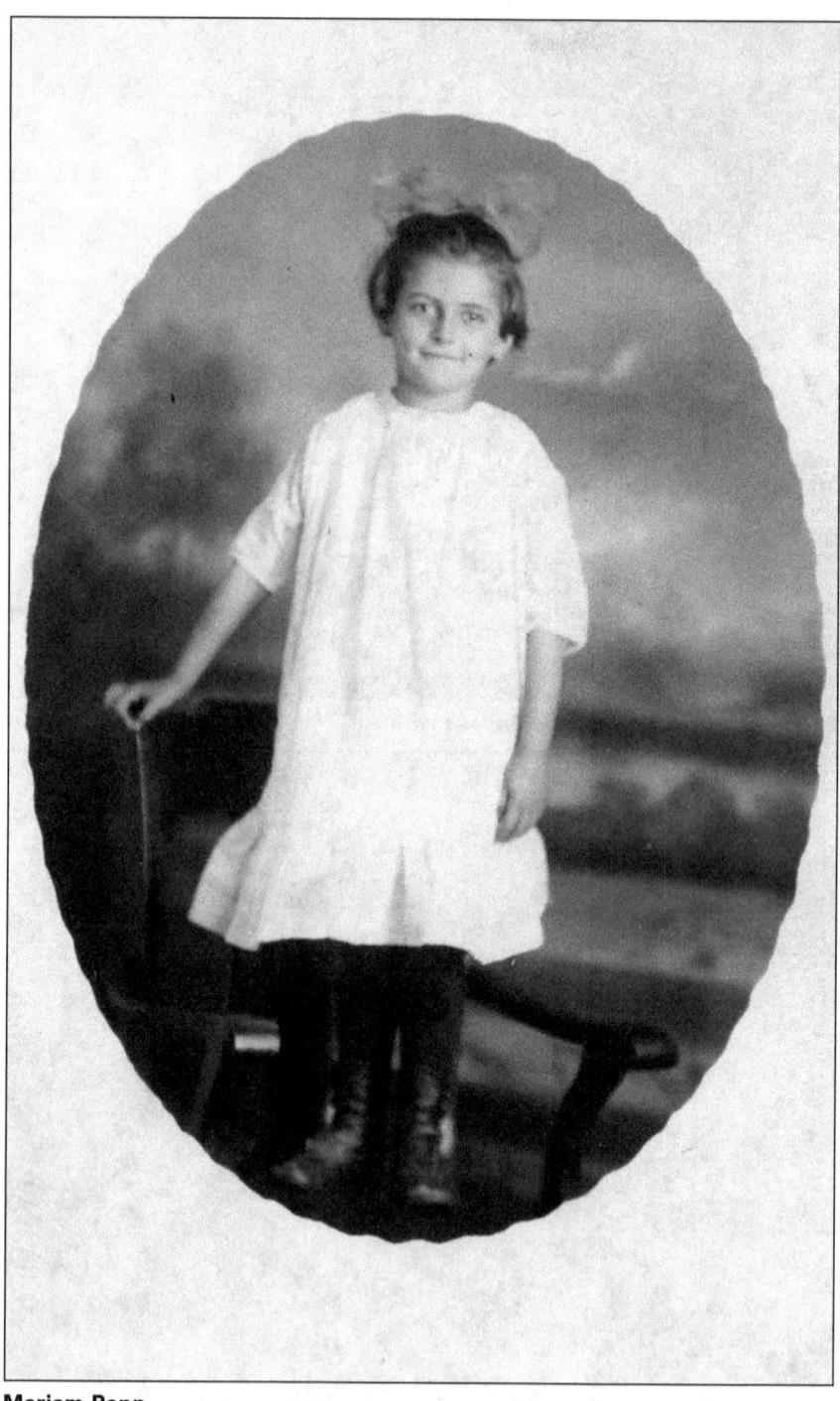

Mariam Rapp.

Phil and Mariam, circa. 1939.

The Philmar, **1939. Owners: Philip and Mariam Rapp.**

LOBERO THEATRE

SANTA BARBARA

ARTHUR J. BECKHARD

Presents

"OPEN HOUSE"

A Farce Comedy

by

PHIL RAPP and GEORGE BECK

Staged by MONTY COLLINS

Production and Direction Under Supervision of
MR. BECKHARD

Thursday, Friday and Saturday Evenings
AT 8:30
March 30-31, April 1, 1939

Motion Picture Relief Fund Testimonial

to

Phillip Rapp

This is to express our appreciation and our gratitude for the unselfish service you contributed in behalf of your Motion Picture Relief Fund on the broadcast of **March 19, 1939** over the Columbia Transcontinental Network from Hollywood, California.

Board of Directors Motion Picture Relief Fund

by *Jean Hersholt*
President

Phil and little Joel Rapp.

The Rapp family.

Paul: "That's Mom feeding the horses, at the Suzy Q Ranch in Hemet, about 1947. This may be one of the best race horses we had, named Big as Life. The baby is named Sweet Horty. The name comes from the lady who lived down the block from us. Her husband was an important producer named Sam Katzman, and her name was Hortense. She was widely known for her flaming orange hair and she loved horse racing. Unfortunately, Sweet Horty turned out to be another expensive toy that didn't work."

Paul: "The first picture is Aunt Blanche and me at the ranch, about 1943 or 44. Notice the pool on the right side, stables in background with hay wagon to clean stalls. We had a large dog run on the property with Dalmatians. They ended up killing all the chickens so we got rid of them."

Fooling around for the camera with brother Johnny.

Phil's father Maurice, always the class act in a suit, cooking on one of the many barbeques at the ranch, circa 1947.

An exhausted Paul riding his favorite horse, Papoose back to the barn. Papoose is pregnant in this picture.

620 N. Oakhurst Dr., Beverly Hills.

Phil cheering on the horses in Hurst Park, England, where he went to have the Bickersons put on a Royal Command Performance for the Queen.

Phil, bottom left, with a bottle of Haig & Haig scotch, and Johnny Rapp (far right) in Phil's Oakhurst house den where he wrote *Baby Snooks*, circa 1943.

Fun on the Snooks set with Joe E. Brown.

Fanny and Hanley, doing their schtick before a live radio audience.

ACTORS

The play was of the most wildly dramatic character, but the great scene is that in which the hero confronts the sneeringly triumphant villain:
"Sir Marmaduk," he exclaimed, "you have reduced me to beggary, broken the heart of my aged mother and eloped with my wife. But Beware!......Don't go too far!"

ACTORS

DIRECTOR: Mills wants $600 for playing the part of the Indian in our new film.
MANAGER: Offer him $300. Tell him it's only a half-breed.

ACTORS

A director and a casting director were looking for a girl with sex appeal.
"What about Ann?" asked the director naming a girl with whom the casting director had quarreled.
"Her?" he snarled. "Why, listen. If we cast her as Lady Godiva the horse would steal the scene!"

ACTORS

Is he a ham actor?
No - you can cure ham!

Cards from the infamous joke file.

Phil's massive joke file was kept in these boxes.

Celebrating Frank Morgan's birthday on the set of *The Old Gold Show.*

Paul: "Mom and Dad—the Bickersons, at the Ranch. The car in the background appears to be a '46 Oldsmobile, so the year would probably be 1947, right about when the Bickersons were created. The car would possibly be Uncle Johnny's or Aunt Blanche's. The building in the background is the elaborate tool shed and, ultimately, the smokehouse was placed right behind the car next to the tool house. The structure to the left was the room for Sal, the caretaker, and is connected to the stables and tack room. The garden right over my mother's head is a formal English garden with almond trees. The main house is directly down the walk behind Dad's back and the secondary house; he would be looking directly at it from his view here. The pool was made by Paddock Pools. The slide into the pool was just adjacent to the steps and to the right side of the pool was the soda fountain and baby pool. The lawn was of considerable size and required abundant maintenance. At this point, the ranch was still under development."

From a new movie "*Rhapsody in Blue*"	featuring life and music of George Gershwin
Rhapsody in Blue $2.62 Concerto in F 4.72 American in Paris 2.62 and many other Gershwin tunes	Latest Recordings by Victor—Columbia—Decca—Capitol **MOSHER MUSIC CO., Inc.** (Boston Most Convenient Music Store) 181 Tremont Street, Boston

BEGINNING OCTOBER 1st, 1945

THE MESSRS. SHUBERT

in association with

MONTE PROSER

present

MILTON BERLE

in

SPRING IN BRAZIL

A Musical Play

with

ROSE MARIE   BERNICE PARKS   CHRISTINE AYRES

JOSEPH MACAULAY

John Cherry • Jack McCauley • Mort Stevens • Roger Obardiene
Kent Edwards • Ray Long • Don Arres • William Quentmeyer
Wilson Woodbeck • Jesse Blakeley • Rita Angel • Charles Hart
Harry Klein • Harold Crane • Jack Kerr • Russo de Pandeiro

Walter Gonsalves

Book Written, Staged and Directed by

PHILIP RAPP

Music and Lyrics by

ROBERT WRIGHT AND GEORGE FORREST

Dances Staged by MARJERY FIELDING
Ballet and Native Dances by ESTHER JUNGER
Costumes by TED SHORE and MARY SCHENCK
Settings by HOWARD BAY
Musical Director — ANTHONY R. MORELLI

Production Staged by

JOHN MURRAY ANDERSON

Orchestration and Choral Arrangements by

ARTHUR KAY

The NEW **PADDOCK** *Cafe and Cocktail Lounge*

Bell Rings
3 minutes
before overture
and end of
intermissions.

255-259 TREMONT ST
(Next Door to Shubert)

On location filming *The Secret Life of Walter Mitty*. Phil is the bottom-middle guy.

CHAPTER 5
SNORING THROUGH IMMORTALITY

The Bickersons is undoubtedly one of radio's most beloved and lasting creations. Though not of the same timber as comedy teams Abbott & Costello and the Marx Brothers, John and Blanche Bickerson, as convincingly portrayed by Don Ameche and Frances Langford, are certainly radio's #1 marriage problem.

1946. The War was still real, and realism was swiftly creeping into even lighthearted family entertainment. The world had changed, and was changing. Audiences *identified* with the battling Bickersons, as first heard on *Drene Time*, yet they could easily distance themselves from the crazy antics of a lazy, nagging wife and a belabored, snore-blasting, trod-upon yeller who somehow managed to stay together without killing each other or the cat.

This is how it all began:

MILLER: (OVER MUSIC) The Bickersons have retired. Mrs. Bickerson tosses restlessly while her husband, John, lies in a profound, dreamless sleep composed of equal parts of bourbon and seconal.

(MUSIC OUT)

DON: (SNORES)

LANG: (SOFTLY) John.

DON: (A SUSTAINED SNORE)

LANG: John . . . John.

DON: (GRUNTS) Mmmmm.

LANG: Are you sleeping?

DON: Mmm.

LANG: Turn over on your side. You're snoring hideously.

DON: Mmm.

LANG: Why don't you get one of those snore balls at Eel & Conger's sleep shop? You've got everything else. Double thickness sleep shade, lullaby musical pillow, toe mittens, electric pajamas and an automatic sheep counter. I know you've got insomnia, but when you *do* fall asleep you snore so loud you sound like Hotchkiss reciprocating force pump draining a peat bog in Clonakilty. Why don't you get a snore ball?

DON: (VERY SLEEPY) Hmmm?

LANG: If you'd take those wax corks out of your ears you'd be able to hear me.

DON: (PLEADING) Why don't you let me sleep, Blanche?

LANG: Well, get a snore ball.

DON: (HALF ASLEEP) Wassa snore ball?

LANG: It's a rubber thing you pin to your pyjamas and when you roll over on your back it

	squeaks at you and wakes you up.
DON:	What do I need that for when I've got you?
LANG:	Don't be so funny.
DON:	Well, I wanna sleep. I have to get up in the morning and you know how long it takes me to fall asleep. I can't help it if I snore.
LANG:	But you keep me up half the night.
DON:	I don't snore anyway.
LANG:	(GASPS) John! How can you say that!
DON:	(DROPPING OFF AGAIN) 'S your imagination. All wives think their husbands—(DEEP SNORE)
LANG:	John!
DON:	Huh?
LANG:	Sit up. If you won't let me sleep I won't let you sleep, either.
DON:	Okay. If that's how you want it. Turn the lights on.
LANG:	The lights *are* on. Take off that sleep shade.
DON:	Oh . . . . . . all right, I'm awake. Now what do you want?
LANG:	I don't see how you can sleep anyway.
DON:	Who's sleeping?

LANG: I mean I don't know how you could have fallen asleep in the first place. I've been waiting and waiting for you to say something but you never did. Do you know what day this is?

DON: It's not day—it's night.

LANG: (TEARFULLY) You've forgotten.

DON: Blanche, that's one thing I will not be accused of. I have not forgotten how to tell day from night. Even if I do wear a sleep shade.

LANG: How could you, John?

DON: What's so terrible about it? It's just that I can't sleep if there's any light in the room—

LANG: Not that. How could you forget?

DON: Forget what?

LANG: It'd be different if we were an old married couple—but it's only been three years and this is the first time you've ever forgotten our anniversary.

DON: Anniversary?

LANG: Today is our wedding anniversary.

DON: (DEFIANTLY) Blanche, this is Sunday and our anniversary is Monday the sixteenth.

LANG: I know it is.

DON: Well, what are you beefing about?

Lang:	What time is it?
Don:	Time? It's twelve o'clock.
Lang:	It's one minute past. (TRIUMPHANTLY) That makes it Monday, and that's our anniversary and you completely forgot about it.
Don:	(CONTROLLING HIS TEMPER) How do you like that!*

Paul Rapp relates the origin of some on- and offstage Bickersons characters:

"John Bickerson was Dad's brother, Johnny, and his wife was Blanche. He trained Johnny as a gag writer in the beginning—I'm certain it was on *Baby Snooks*—and they wrote a lot of gags together. After coming back from the Army, Johnny soon got work with Bob Hope.

"I think Blanche was a very henpecking wife. She always thought she was dying, like she always had a week to live. And she was very meticulous. I liked her a lot, but she was kind of a mousy woman. She liked to be the take-charge kind. She was a bright woman and read a lot. Johnny was always sneaking out and doing things.

"There were *some* differences, of course. Like bourbon. My Dad chose the word *bourbon* because it's funny. Dad once told me he wouldn't drink bourbon if you put a gun to his head. He drank Cutty Sark Scotch whiskey, though he never drank when he was really working. And there were some of Mom and Dad in the Bickersons, too—like that gag where John takes the garbage, because it's neatly wrapped up, thinking it's his lunch. My mom wrapped the garbage.

"During the war Johnny worked on the Army newspaper, *Stars and Stripes*, when he was in Italy. My aunt Blanche was always knitting sweaters and blankets for the RWR, the Russian War Relief, at the same time Mom was working as a nurse's aid."

---

* Reprinted from *The Bickersons Scripts* by Philip Rapp. For a complete history of *The Bickersons*, see *The Bickersons—A Biography of Radio's Wittiest Program* by Ben Ohmart.

The Rapp family was living in a three-story house on Palm Drive—a house previously owned by Oscar Levant. According to Paul, "When we first got into that house, we noticed there were hidden microphones all over the walls. It seems the FBI was very interested in his activity."

Starting in 1972, Paul moved into a nearby home on Alpine Drive and lived there for the next 32 years. The family's previous residence, up until the mid-1950s, had been on Oakhurst Drive—right across the street from a real Bickersons character.

"Dr. Hersey lived across the street from us," continues Paul. "We were at 620 N. Oakhurst, and he was about five houses down the block, next door to Fred and Jesse Kahn. Fred was head of casting for 20th Century-Fox. Dr. Hersey was the real-life inspiration for the pivotal Bickersons character of the same name. He was large and imposing, and his wife was a little mouse, but quite attractive. He was Chief of Surgery at Cedars of Lebanon. It later dropped the 'Lebanon' to become Cedars-Sinai. Dr. Hersey saved my mother's life when he operated on her for breast cancer. He was a great man, and Dad spent a lot of time with him, knocking back a few."

Phil's best friend in the 1940s was Mel Shaw, legendary Disney artist who worked on the likes of *Bambi* and *Beauty and the Beast*. Bickersons aficionados will recognize the name as that irksome, never-voiced character that always sent John Bickerson into a rage whenever his wife dared to compare his affection quota to Mel's.

"I met Phil through my brother Frank who was a Navy pilot," states Mel. "The shows that Phil was writing were mostly through MGM at that time. Frank was going to UCLA then and was a pre-law student, also working in the mail room of MGM. He would deliver mail to all the various departments in MGM, including Phil's office. Phil was interested in Frank and heard that Frank was then the captain of the UCLA polo team. Phil wanted to come out and see the horses because he wanted to buy a ranch in Encino, which is where we had our ranch. We had six acres and I had my polo ponies out there where Frank used my horses when he played for UCLA. So Phil came out and met me through Frank and we became very close. At that time I was working at Warner Bros. with Loony Tunes, in the Harmon/Ising Studios. Bob Clampett was the guy sitting next to me doing in-betweens (drawings that go in between what the animators make) when I started.

"Phil bought his place, but I don't know where he got his horse. It was huge, 16 or 17 hands tall, and Phil was a little guy. He wanted to learn to ride but Frank was in school by this time so he called me and said, 'You know, I wanted to ride my horse, but I couldn't get the bridle on him. Could you help me?' Every time he would go to put the bridle on, the horse would lift up his head and Phil couldn't even reach his head! So I showed him how to do everything."

"We both liked horse stuff. Phil liked to ride at night. He was a last-minute worker before his radio shows. He wouldn't start writing until he was on the carpet for being late. Sometimes he'd call me late at night and say, 'How about going out for a moonlight ride?' We'd get our horses, being just a couple blocks away, and we'd start riding these trails right behind the Santa Monica Mountains. He'd ride along and eventually get an idea for a script, then say, 'Well I guess I've gotta get back. I gotta get this show done for tomorrow morning.' He'd write for an hour or two and he'd have the show done for the next morning's rehearsal.

"Down the street from us was Mickey Rooney, down from me was Bud Abbott. And at the end of the street Daryl Zanuck had a little private polo field on Valley Vista. I met Don Ameche quite a few times over at Phil's place. He was a very nice person. I liked Don.

"The thing about Phil was that he didn't mess around with many people. I was one of the few people that he would really seek out to do things with. He liked to go with me to this beachcomber's place, a place out in the Valley fixed up like a Hawaiian village with a little pool and sand around the edge and a treehouse for guests. And that type of cooking, with ribs and so forth. Phil loved that stuff, and learned a lot of cooking tricks from that cook.

"Frank Morgan came from a very wealthy family. They were the ones who owned Angostura Aromatic Bitters, a popular condiment back then. So he had a big yacht and invited Phil and me out a couple of times. I remember Phil fixing his usual barbeque and Hawaiian meal for Frank and others. Frank was a good actor and came across as a bit of a bumbler, but it was just an act.

"Phil was always asking about the horses, for tips. I don't think he bet on his own horses, though I think Mariam did. They went more by how the trainers thought the horses were going. I don't think they ever made any money on the horses though, I think it was all down the drain. Phil was very much intrigued with the jockeys. They were about his size and he used to go into the jockey room where they got ready and got to know quite a few of them. He decided he was going to write a story about the jockeys. One of the magazines paid him $25,000 in advance to do a story on them and their background. He really didn't want to do it and we kept talking about it but he never could do anything with it."

In fact, Phil did commit his mind to twenty pages of a manuscript entitled *The Jocks Talk*. As Phil explains in the opening page of his *Jocks* treatment:

We were sitting around at Romanoff's [a five-star restaurant for Hollywood's elite]**, chewing the fat. With the prices that Mike charges for his steaks a man's a fool if he doesn't chew the fat and eat the bone, too. The Santa Anita meeting was over and Arcaro was going down to Florida for some golf and fishing and it was a sort of a farewell party. Ameche was there and Jack Sullivan and Mike Romanoff and Dave Chasen (it was Monday night and Dave's joint was closed) and a half a dozen others, all licking their wounds from a disastrous season at the track. I listened, enthralled, as these great raconteurs, each of them wise in the ways of the turf, told stories about the bangtails. At the same time I felt a little inadequate because I couldn't contribute. It didn't really make sense for I was the only one in that crowd who owned a racehorse. As a hobby, you understand.**

Of course, owning racehorses doesn't make a man an oracle on handicapping and turf history any more than buying a hundred shares of Saltpeter Aviation makes one an authority on instrument flying. I got into the Sport of Kings purely by accident.

About seven years earlier an improvident friend of mine put the bite on me for a sum of money I could ill afford. I have never suffered from banker's heart, but my sketchy kind of business plus my thorough knowledge of this character's character made me ask for security. I should have suspected from his willingness

to put up collateral that I was in a fair way of being rogered. The security turned out to be an oat burner by the name of Orphan Cribber, a nine-year-old maiden gelding. I felt rather sheepish about accepting the horse because it was the man's only means of transportation. It goes without saying that I never saw my friend or my money again and I was left holding the nag. So I became an owner and have been ever since.

It was because of this fact that Paul Warwick, the advertising man, approached me with his idea.

Paul Warwick, as you may know, is head of a large advertising agency, Warwick and Legler, and a more energetic man never breathed. Ideas shoot from his fertile brain like corn popping in a pan. Corn also pops from his brain, but it seems to pay off in the advertising business.

Briefly, this is what he had in mind. I was to interview the jockeys in their natural habitat, i.e., the jockeys' room, and write an intimate piece that would disclose facts and facets of the little men that had never before been revealed. Not an expose' or a whitewash job, but a piece about jockeys practically by jockeys. Make them talk, said Paul, and I'll guarantee the public will gobble it up.

He had it all figured out. He would contact the Jockeys' Guild, get the necessary permission and make sure that a large percentage of the proceeds, if any, would go to that worthy organization. An okay from the State Racing Commission would give me open sesame to the jobs and room at four or five major tracks. At that time I didn't realize that it was easier to steal the bullion from Fort Knox than for an outsider to get into the jockeys' room.

At first I demurred, reminding Paul that, while I was an owner, my knowledge of racing was limited to paying feed bills. In fact, I almost never visit the track even to see my own horses lose.

Warwick didn't consider this any drawback. On the contrary, he pointed out that the virgin approach to the story would be infinitely better than the blasé reporting of a hardened aficionado. While I was mulling this over he was already on the phone getting the blessings of the Jockeys' Guild and the New York and California State Racing Commissions.

Well, here I was in Romanoff's telling the boys about it and Eddie Arcaro was shaking his head, skeptically.

"It's a wonderful idea," said the Champ, "and a wonderful title, *The Jocks Talk*, but I know jocks, and they won't."

"Won't what?"

"Talk."

But talks and contracts were well underway for Rapp to submit his horsey manuscript to Documentary Publications, Inc., six months from the date of a May 18, 1949 agreement. He could claim up to $1,000 expense money. But as of October 18, he hadn't finished yet; he would take weeks more, because of a variety of other commitments. By December 5, after a load of promises, Phil just couldn't seem to finish the work. By February, Jack Warwick (in charge of the project for DP) was feeling pressure from all sides, including the new twist of the Jockey Guild wanting to produce a radio program based on the final manuscript. Warwick may have been right—perhaps Rapp just couldn't get enough cooperation from the fellas.*

If Phil didn't know a lot about horses personally, he was smart enough to know who to hire to handle them. "Our trainer, R. H. 'Red' MacDaniel, became world famous," says Paul Rapp, "but when Dad found him he was in the gutter. He became famous for many years, and ultimately he had hundreds of winners. My mother bought him a suit and put him back together again. His wife was Evelyn, a sweet lady who stuck by him. Red started out as a jockey but he couldn't maintain his weight.

"My mom had a scientific way of picking horses—she could always pick which was the fastest horse. Whether it would win or not was another matter. She spent a great deal of time with me and loved the races.

"When Dad went to the racetrack in the Cadillac, we went to the Turf Club, and they would valet park the car in a special area. Over a period of time, he lost a *considerable* amount of money.

---

* For the full yet incomplete manuscript, including short interviews with Charlie Ralls and Melvin Lewis, see the appendix.

"Once, a bookie was pressing for his losses, almost $10,000. My dad typed something up, went to Louis B. Mayer. 'I have the synopsis for a great movie,' he said, and handed him the idea in a sealed envelope. 'But I need $25,000 right now. Just don't open the envelope until I leave.' He got the money. And Mom paid the bookie off.

Joel Rapp gives an even more colorful account of the infamous payout in his autobiography: "My father was an inveterate gambler. Horses, mostly—but he was known to pay an occasional visit to one of the illegal gambling casinos operating quite openly on the Sunset Strip—on this particular night it was the gambling-room upstairs at Ciro's, a famous Hollywood night-spot.

"It was the night of October 24, 1937. My mother was in the hospital, in labor with my brother-to-be, and the doctor had told Dad nothing would happen until at least morning, and most likely Mom would have to have a C-section if there was no baby by noon. So Dad decided to go gambling. After only a couple of hours at the famed nightclub/casino, Diamond Jim Rapp had lost $25,000—which he paid for with a check—from an account in which he had no money!

"Imagine his predicament—first and foremost, how would he ever explain such a tremendous loss to my mother, especially while she was struggling to have his kid—and how was he going to cover that check by morning?

"Ever resourceful and refusing to panic, my father dashed home and sat down at his typewriter. He'd had an idea for a screenplay for several weeks and had done nothing about it, but by eight o'clock in the morning he had finished a thirty-page treatment! He called the hospital and learned that they would have to do a C-section after all and it was scheduled for noon. He'd best be at the hospital by eleven. The clock was ticking.

"He showered and shaved and then he picked up the phone and called Harry Cohn at Columbia Pictures. Cohn was head of the studio and one of the most hated men in Hollywood. (When he died, hundreds of people turned out for his funeral. An actor who had a particularly sour relationship with Cohn remarked, 'Give the people something they want and they'll show up in droves.') For whatever reason, however, my father and Harry got along just fine.

Cohn agreed to see him at noon, but my father insisted it be no later than ten. He had a story he wanted Harry to read and he needed an answer right away.

"So, Dad showed up at the Gower Street studio at ten o'clock. By five after, Harry Cohn was locked in his office reading the treatment while Dad paced nervously in the outer office, preparatory to pacing nervously in the waiting room at Cedars. Fifteen minutes later, Cohn buzzed for my father to come in. 'Okay,' said Harry. 'I'll buy it. Twenty-five G's, take it or leave it.' My father fought back a grin of triumph. 'Well . . . . . okay. But I want a check right now.' At this point Cohn got a little miffed. What the hell was the big hurry? My father, having really no choice, told Harry the truth—he'd lost a bundle gambling and needed the money to cover a check before my mother found out. Basically sympathetic, Cohn had the check cut and my father made it to the bank and the hospital in plenty of time to welcome Paul Winston Rapp.

"My father had committed the perfect crime. Almost. A couple of weeks later, while Dad was out somewhere and my mother was still recuperating in bed from the surgery, she answered the telephone and found herself speaking to a man named Jack Hellman, who was one of the top writers at the show-business bible, *Variety*. 'What's up with that picture Phil sold to Columbia?' Jack asked. '*What* picture?' was my mother's reply, and Jack proceeded to spill the entire can of beans. I was only four years old, but I think I recall Mom waiting at the front door with a baseball bat when Dad came home.

"It all worked out, however. Mom forgave him when he convinced her there'd been no blood—he'd have never written that screen treatment if he hadn't gambled away the money, so nothing really was lost, when you thought about it. For whatever reason, my mother decided to buy that somewhat flawed logic, and as for the picture, it never got made. My father always suspected that Cohn's purchase was a 'mercy buy,' but whatever it was, it bailed him out of a tough one and for that he was forever grateful."

Paul states, "When his horses *did* win, Dad would never go in the winner's circle, for taking a photo of the owner. He considered it bad luck. My mother was in the pictures. So was Red, the trainer."

"One time Phil and I decided to take an adventurous trip out to the desert with our horses," says Mel Shaw. "Since I was playing polo, I had my trailer, so I took both our horses in it. We were just going to camp out. We had hobbles for the horses and everything else, and a couple of bags of hay. We found this one place so we parked the trailer, got the horses out and started to walk into the hills. We came upon an old teepee and Phil said it looked like an old movie set. There was a little pond, it looked like an oasis, and there was nobody around. He decided we should stay there that night, so we set up and put the hobbles on the horses and so forth. We sat around the fire and felt like we were in the wilderness. We went to sleep and when we woke up, the horses had wandered off a little bit so we started to follow them. His horse had found a place that had green grass, and we look up and we're right in the middle of one of those little settlements with little homes and little yards. The horse kept eating and pretty soon the people came out. It turned out we were in the early development of Palm Springs.

"I think Phil considered me his best friend. He'd call me up anytime, and anytime of the night, too. I probably moved away first. I kind of lost track of him after that, around the 1950s. There was one dramatic situation where Phil called me and told me that he wasn't well. He'd had one too many and called Paul to come over and help him up; that was pretty close to the end of Phil.

"I asked him to help me one time on a picture I was producing, *A Midsummer Night's Dream* in animation. He just said, 'You know, Mel, I've kind of lost it. It's hard for me to write anymore.' I wanted him to help me with the writing. Livingston and Evans were doing the music for it. It was pretty sad. Someone who was so alive."

With the Bickersons hitting it huge and film work steady, 1947 was a banner year. In May, Rapp was approached by NBC for "the development of new ideas, creation of packages and in general everything of an artistic and creative nature." He was to work on any show they sent his way, which "would also include his assistance in *The Henry Morgan Show* or any other show which Mr. Trammell or Mr. Strotz might think necessary. Salary for all such services to be $100,000 per year." At a time when the average house cost $8,000, this was amazing money. NBC would sell the packages with net profits to be divided evenly between the studio and Rapp. They also offered him a flat $200,000 for "all rights of any nature in his production of *The Bickersons*" so they would own it forever. Rapp said no—to that part—as he would for years to come.

Somehow he found time to become radio's jack-of-all-trades and still pen films for MGM, such as *That's Life*, during June. By November he'd signed yet another radio contract, this time with advertisers Lennen & Mitchell for his services of writing and directing an unknown radio series (possibly a Bickersons incarnation) for 33 weeks. It was to be broadcast on CBS in the 9–9:30 p.m. slot. He received $3,000 per week, with an option for an additional thirty-nine consecutive weeks at $3,500 weekly, with extra clauses for several further big-money extensions.

With so much income, Phil decided to legitimatize his racing hobby by incorporating Philrapp Stables, Inc., on February 9, 1948 "to raise, acquire, own, hold, sell, lease, breed and train horses of all types and descriptions." As well as acquire and maintain all the land and buildings that this would take. His off-time pleasure would at last be tax deductable. And it paid off, in various ways. Three years later, he leased one of his horses, Moderator, to W. D. Rorex of Glendale for $250 as a stud fee for three times with his mares, and Rorex would provide the upkeep. They would split any gross stud fees fifty-fifty.

Mariam Rapp took care of the money, as she always did, from every avenue. The war was over and everything was sunny. "In 1948 you could finally buy a car," says Paul, "because production was booming again. Dad went over to Beverly Hills to the Hillcrest Motor Co. and he bought a brand new four-door Fleetwood Cadillac, in very dark British racing green. I was so proud of it in the driveway."

"Mariam thought that she knew everything," says Mel Shaw. "She was in vaudeville, in the Pony Chorus, and was pretty much the one who took over the management of everything Phil did, the money and so forth. She made the wrong investments every step of the way. Phil should've ended up a billionaire, really, from the money he was making in those days and the kind of investments that he could've made. In the depression days, everyone had ideas and things to sell, there was so much *available*, and Mariam just picked all the wrong ones."

CHAPTER 6
WINTER IN BRAZIL

Schubert closed *Sping in Brazil* because
Milton did a lot of adlibbing.

—Paul Rapp

One stumbling block Phil had came in the early 1940s when he had the idea for a stage musical; an event which turned out to please no one, including the writer himself. After a draft of the show had been written and enough preliminary interest had been attained to produce it for the young comic Milton Berle (who specialized in improvisation), Phil penned the following outline.

SPRING IN BRAZIL

(These are rough outline notes and may not even be in their property sequence. The general idea is to indicate the production numbers, a little of the theme, and several of the black comedy scenes. It is also intended as an aid in casting and scenic designing.)

In a nutshell, this is the story of young HAMILTON BOYLE (MILTON BERLE), a likeable, fast talking, jack-of-all-trades, who has tried everything from selling hardware to being an M.C. in a nightclub, and who makes a soft dollar operating as a legman for a political grafter in Brooklyn. His glib manner enables him to garner votes, public offices and financial tribute for his unscrupulous boss—with Hamilton making very little out of all the transactions. To get rid of him the politician dispatches Hamilton on a wild-goose chase to Brazil with the promise of an important career. How Hamilton manages to get from Brooklyn to Brazil and what happens to him while he's there constitutes the basic plot.

The first scene will probably be a brief prologue taking place in the office of the politician in the Presidential election year of *1952*. Roosevelt has just been elected again and defeated his opponent Gracie Allen (the Republicans were hard pressed for a likely candidate). HAMILTON BOYLE is referred to but not seen during this interlude and the machinery for his departure is set up. This tiny scene should yield a good measure of topical comedy.

SCENE ONE:

The opening proper of the musical will be a lavish replica of the interior of a section of a *post-war* CLIPPER plane flying regularly non-stop between Miami and Rio de Janeiro. Naturally, this place will be designed with great imagination and only an estimation of its size will be indicated by the part of it shown to the audience. This section will be the recreation bar and salon. Through a huge plastic window upstage, running the full length of it, an occasional cloud is seen drifting by to give the illusion of flight.

Since all commercial planes today have a stewardess to attend to the needs of the passengers it's safe to assume that our post-war CLIPPER will go them one better and have a stewardess to cater to every passenger. Each stewardess looks like a showgirl (and indeed she is) and it's really surprising how much attention the male passengers need. They pay little heed to the television equipment, the stock ticker or the grand piano in the salon and the main attraction seems always to be the girls. This leads us logically into the first PRODUCTION NUMBER—a sort of combination between FLYING DOWN TO RIO and THE PASSENGER IS ALWAYS RIGHT by the girls.

In a short scene following this we meet the passengers, including PROFESSOR JUNE (HUGH HERBERT or BENNY LESSEE type). The professor is a chemico-botanical inventor traveling on behalf of his organization, the Procrustean Girdle Company (more about this later). They are about 60 miles from Rio when the FIRST OFFICER (JOHN CONTE) comes into the salon for a smoke—and also to have a few words with his sweetheart, the barmaid (ELLA LOGAN). When the passengers ask him who's flying the plane he answers casually that the SECOND OFFICER is at the controls, a new man on his first flight. Oh, yes—his name is HAMILTON BOYLE. While the FIRST OFFICER is reassuring the passengers that BOYLE is a hell of a pilot, the ship lurches, there's a momentary panic, the FIRST OFFICER rushes forward to the cabin and it's made clear to prepare for a forced landing.

We black out.

SCENE TWO:

The interior of the fabulous Brazilian night resort, CAFÉ DIAMANTINO. It is the first night of the traditional CARNIVAL WEEK in Rio and a spirit of great revelry permeates the club. People in native costumes and fancy dress jam the place and an AMERICAN RADIO ANNOUNCER is broadcasting the significance of the event to the people in the United States, and also making clear what is happening to the theatre audience. This should be a lively native number done in the best possible taste. At the conclusion of this number and while the ANNOUNCER is still talking, there is a grinding, alarming commotion from offstage. A report that the CLIPPER has been forced down a hundred yards from the club, in fact, on the golf course. This causes everybody to rush from the place to the scene of the accident.

We black out.

SCENE THREE:

Upstairs in the owner's luxurious office. The owner is a rich Brazilian, NINO BORBO (AKIM TAMIROFF) who made his original fortune from the prolific rubber plantations he controlled throughout the country. He is looking through the window with a pair of binoculars, and has a satisfied smile on his face. He turns to another man also watching and they both nod smugly, indicating that the plane accident was no accident. This is done in a few lines of dialogue. BORBO's companion is an unethical chemist from Argentina, CHACO DEL PAMPAS (LEO CARRILLO). The scene between these two men tells a great story. First we learn that in 1952 the rubber industry is virtually wiped out.

Nobody uses the stuff anymore—there are so many substitutes. The only commodity that uses rubber to any great extent is the ladies girdle. Thank heaven they still control the girdle market. But even this is in great jeopardy, due to the new invention of PROFESSOR JUNE who has discovered a way to make a perfect elastic girdle out of a secret formula not containing even an ounce of latex. If JUNE is allowed to get his girdle on the market, BORBO is ruined. It turns out that even his night resort is in hock. In brief, their plan is to get JUNE'S formula and destroy it together with the inventor. BORBO has engineered the plane landing in order to get the professor into his clutches before he reaches his branch in Rio. He arranges to introduce DEL PAMPAS as a member of the Argentine Legation.

We black out.

SCENE FOUR:

Lights up the club again. The occupants of the plane are being ushered in and it appears nobody was injured. When the FIRST OFFICER makes a check-up he discovers HAMILTON BOYLE is missing. There is a lot of confusion and they are about to leave on a search when BOYLE makes his entrance dragging a parachute attached to his can. He is slightly disheveled. By means of a joke he explains why he jumped and the ensuing scene will be played for full comedy value. It turns out that BOYLE is not an aviator and he got the job under false pretenses. All he wants to do is meet Professor June. His meeting with June results in a double entendre bit of comedy with each one referring to grafting in a different sense. This, thinks BOYLE, is the political job he was sent for. When he finds out the Professor is talking about botanical grafting and not political, things look very bad. Incidentally, one of the passengers on the plane will be an Eve Arden type of dame who goes for BOYLE in a big way. BOYLE doesn't return her affection. Maybe a comedy number right here.

BORBO comes down with DEL PAMPAS to greet his "unexpected" guests and offers them the hospitality of his place. The FIRST OFFICER demurs and says he can telephone Rio for company limousines to drive the people in. It's only 60 miles away. But BORBO will have none of this—insists that they spend the night there or Brazilian hospitality will be desecrated. All he really wants, of course, is Professor JUNE and his fabulous girdle. With the help of his beautiful daughter, MARIA, BORBO persuades the FIRST OFFICER and his charges to remain. The INGÉNUE doesn't like the way MARIA is devouring the JUVENILE with her eyes—but what can she do when everybody seems so agreeable?

At a signal from BORBO, DEL PAMPAS, the chemist, goes to work on the Professor after being introduced as a member of the Argentine legation. The questions he asks and his cagey manner causes the Professor to become suspicious and he clams up. DEL PAMPAS can't make much headway and time is short.

When the guests are being shown to their rooms the Professor asks BOYLE to come with him. He indicates there is some mysterious work afoot. BOYLE agrees to meet him in his room.

We'll probably have a short scene between the boy and girl right here, leading into a song that testifies he'll never love anybody but her. She's satisfied but still a little dubious. After all, that MARIA is plenty competition for anybody.

SCENE FIVE:

In the Professor's room. When BOYLE comes in he quickly locks the door. BOYLE is a little scared and can't figure out what the guy wants. The Professor wants to tell BOYLE about the girdle but feels that possibly he can't even trust *him*. So he goes about it in a roundabout way. The truth is that the Professor has never recorded the formula for his wonderful girdle and only made one, which he is wearing himself. He figures that's the safest place to carry it. Suspecting that DEL PAMPAS is after the girdle, the only thing to do is put it in a safe place—a place where they'd never dream of looking for it. Without telling BOYLE the reason, he makes suggestions that he would like BOYLE to try the girdle. He claims BOYLE is heavy in the waist and it isn't becoming to such a handsome fellow. You can well imagine what BOYLE is thinking when the Prof starts to undress. Finally, the Professor convinces him to wear the girdle, but insists on BOYLE returning it to him when they reach Rio. "What's so wonderful about this girdle?" asks BOYLE. Now the Professor explains to him why it's called the Procrustean girdle. (It goes without saying that the minute BOYLE gets into the girdle his life is in danger.)

NOTE:

This is the story of the Procrustean girdle. It gets its name from the legend of Procrustes. In Greek mythology, Procrustes was a bandit who waylaid travelers and put them in the notorious bed of Procrustes. He had some crazy idea that this bed would fit everybody. If they were too short he would stretch them to fit—if they were too long he would log their feet off. So the theory is that the Procrustean girdle fits every woman perfectly and gives her the finest degree of feminine perfection. (We may see a little of this feminine transformation working on BOYLE.) The telling of this legend might conceivably work into a real classy number based on Greek Mythology with the Gods and Goddesses. Good for BOYLE as Apollo, or any of the other gods. Perfect for a ballet.

SCENE SIX:

Back in the Café Diamantino, the exciting Carnival is in progress. Some people are masked and nearly all are in fancy dress. A Brazilian master of ceremonies functions at the microphone, dressed as Mephisto. He is about the same size as HAMILTON BOYLE and has a somewhat similar carriage. (This is important for later developments.) According to native tradition the best song of the year is to be chosen at the conclusion of the Carnival Week (this is authentic), and beautiful songs written especially by the talented natives are played and sung. This might possibly be the spot to do the WEDDING OF THE GAUCHO number. At any rate, all manner of diversion and entertainment will fit in very nicely here, anything from a magician to a tumbling act. The scene should be done with a great deal of excitement and spirit. Most of the occupants of the CLIPPER will be present through this and incidental dialogue necessary to the action will be picked up by special lighting.

SCENE SEVEN:

While the gaiety is going on in the café, BORBO and his

henchmen are searching the Professor's room for either the girdle or the formula. They find nothing. For a comedy scene it might be well to have them turn a beautiful dame loose on the Professor to get him to undress. They suspect he is wearing the girdle. The trouble is that he's already parted with the girdle and he undresses far too readily to suit the dame, who barely escapes with her honor.

HAM BOYLE is parading around in his new girdle, not mentioning it, of course, and we may find that its power of imbuing the perfect feminine spirit is working on him. We must be careful, of course, to avoid the nancy [homosexual] implication, but since the people are in fancy dress it would probably be all right for HAM to wear the outfit of a Carmen Miranda. He gets involved with a talkative dame who tells him the most personal things.

In the meantime, the Professor is growing more worried so he decides to put a call through to the manager of the Rio branch of his company. He wants to tell him that he thinks somebody is after the girdle. He places the call and we see that the telephone operator connects him with BORBO'S office instead. One of BORBO'S men gets on the phone and impersonates the branch manager. In the ensuing conversation the Professor voices his suspicions and the phony manager tries to get him to tell where he hid the girdle. This is done with as much suspense as possible, with the Professor hedging all the time and not wanting to tell. He insists it's in a safe place. "I know," says the phony, "but suppose something happens to you, how will we ever find out where you hid it." The Professor finally breaks down and says that HAM BOYLE is wearing it. At this point BOYLE opens the door to the room which is full of potential murderers and says, "Excuse me, where's the ladies room." Naturally, they can't kill him right there and their efforts to detain him are fruitless. This scene is played for full comedy value. We feel now that BOYLE will most certainly be destroyed in a very short time.

SCENE EIGHT:

In the café the revelry continues. Beautiful music, beautiful dancing and a progression of the boy and girl story. The Professor, feeling very secure, is getting loaded on the powerful native drink, cachaca. BOYLE enters and, tiring of his Carmen Miranda outfit, makes a deal with the Brazilian master of ceremonies to trade costumes. This is done. We build now to a first act curtain of BORBO'S men knocking off the M.C., thinking that they've nailed HAM BOYLE.

In the second act BOYLE will still be wearing the girdle so the danger is never lifted. The fact that he is oblivious to all the menace will greatly heighten the comedy and give it a Chaplinesque touch.

After the murder of the Brazilian M.C., HAM BOYLE will function in the investigation. He is also a bit of a detective, he claims. The re-enacting of the crime should be one of the big comedy scenes, with BOYLE almost getting shot.

The café cannot run without an M.C. and BOYLE takes over. He does a great job until he becomes involved with the Six Amazons in their adagio specialty. (This has been discussed.)

A dream sequence might be done with six midgets dressed exactly like the Amazons.

There are several other ideas for block comedy scenes, which are not ready for outlining just yet, in addition to the various musical and production numbers we discussed like the BOLAS number, and the BOUNCE on the trampoline.

I have purposely omitted most of the things we have already noted on paper before your departure, Harry, in order to save time. I have complete notes on everything.

That was the *first* draft outline. In the full-length script:

Walter Gribble, Jr. (Milton Berle), working as a librarian for the Magellan Society, an Explorers' Club, to repay his late adventurer father's debts, is sent to Brazil to locate an unknown Caucasian reported to have mysteriously emerged from a dense jungle where Walter's father died and in which explorers Colonel Roland Peoples and Justin Lake claimed their explorative discoveries revealed nothing but cannibals. Gribble and his search party revel in Rio's carnival where Walter is amorously pursued by the sensuous Carnival Queen, Anya Veranda. During their jungle mission Walter poses as a native medicine man to save himself from being the main entrée on the cannibals' menu. Walter learns from the white Amazon Queen that the mysterious boy, Jongo, is his brother, so Walter and his sweetheart, airline stewardess Katie Warren, plan to return to civilization with Jongo.

An early report in the *New York Times*, before the book was completed, stated that the title of the musical was *Needle in the Haystack*, and that Milton Berle was trying to convince Joan Blondell to come into the show with him. Once the book was written, the same paper announced that the producers were trying to induce Daryl Zanuck to release Carmen Miranda from her Fox contract for a bit to join the show.

Spring in Brazil opened October 1, 1945 in Boston, and closed, on January 12, 1946, in Chicago. Produced by the Shubert brothers and Monte Proser, the show had a lot going for it, with music and lyrics by Robert Wright and George Forest (*Song of Norway, Kismet*, etc.). But according to Milton Berle, "We should have opened in Brazil and closed in Boston! Business was so big we sent the whole audience home in a taxi!" The show cost $300,000 to produce, a huge Broadway investment at the time, but even lavish spectacle couldn't save this show.

Joseph F. Dinneen in his "Inside Boston" column, wrote: "I dropped in to a rehearsal of *Spring in Brazil*, the new musical comedy opening in the Colonial next Monday night, and came away with the impression that Monte Proser probably has another hit on his hands, not because of what I saw on the stage but because of the excited wailing and gnashing of teeth on the part of everyone in any way connected with the executive side of the production. It's usually the kind of frustration that presages a successful opening. Putting on a play these days poses problems that never pop up in normal times. It's almost impossible, for example, to find enough stage carpenters in Boston to build the sets needed for next Monday night. There's a painful paucity of painters in Boston, and a lot of work for those available to do on scenes. There aren't enough hotel rooms in Boston to house the 100 actors and actresses in the cast.

"Almost everybody was tearing his hair out for some reason or other. Shipments and express from New York are delayed. Equipment that is needed has not arrived, but that's always true of any opening. Somehow things are done. Shipments finally do arrive. Everything is ironed out and in spite of all forebodings the show opens on time and turns out to be a bigger success than anybody ever thought it would be.

"Philip Rapp, the director of the show, for example, was in a blue funk yesterday. Today he will probably be delightfully happy again, but with some reservations, because if a director is ever completely satisfied with a rehearsal the chances are there's something the matter with the show; so Rapp won't be completely satisfied. He's an entertaining companion at the dinner table, but making ready a show is wearing. He only works twelve weeks a year, anyway, he tells me, and takes it easy for the remaining forty.

"Rapp says that *Spring in Brazil* is an intelligent play turned into a musical. It is written for humor but to a great extent it is literate, and could easily be turned into a straight three-act play. After the play opens, Rapp returns to Hollywood to write the story for a picture, *The Bishop's Wife*, for Danny Kaye."

Problems ran deeper than mere "typical" musical chaos. *Variety* reported on November 8, 1945: "Phil Rapp is feuding with Milton Berle over the comic's treatment of his material in the Shubert musical, *Spring in Brazil*, and is threatening to lodge a complaint with the Dramatists Guild. Failing to get satisfaction there he will consult attorneys.

"Author of the show's book, Rapp is smarting under the criticism of columnists that the material in the show is corny. He contends that Berle's consistent ad-libbing and other liberties taken with the storyline and dialog have injured his reputation as a playwright and will have a deleterious effect on the play's sale to pictures.

"Representations have been made to the Shuberts and Monte Proser, who cut himself in for a piece of the show, with the suggestion by Rapp that Berle withdraw in favor of Danny Kaye or Ray Bolger, both of whom have expressed willingness to play the role. Rapp declares the *Brazil* lead was originally intended for Kaye, whose portrayal of the milquetoast character was more in line with his type. Berle's distortion of the role, Rapp charges, completely changes the character from one of timidity to that of a brass, flip wise guy.

"*Brazil* is now playing Philadelphia and makes a stand at Pittsburgh before moving into New York. If Berle doesn't play the character as written when it reaches Broadway, Rapp will file charges with Dramatists Guild or force the issue through legal action."

Lawrence Perry wrote an interesting account of *Brazil*'s final rehearsal in the *RKO Newsette*, telling of a bet Rapp gratefully paid off to a disgruntled Berle. As a comic known for his instant, sometimes constant ad-libbing, there was fear if Berle would stick to the script, the first show in which he played one continuous character (he was used to variety shows). As Perry explained the situation, "Rapp maintains that you could separate his book from the score and have a good three-act play. Let's give him any benefit of the doubt we may have until Boston passes opinion as to this. In any case it is enough of a book to warrant strict observance of scenes and dialogue as set down by the librettist. This is precisely what Berle—for whom the piece was written—has done."

Berle, according to Perry's article, tried hard to be "an actor now" and Rapp contradicted himself (probably in an effort to achieve good press just before the opening) to admit that "that's what he is. Never for a minute has Milton gone off on a tangent. Never for a moment has he been Berle instead of the character he has been called upon to play. And sooo, what with Berle and Rose Marie, a grand actress; what with lovely music, what with a swell book—yes, I'll say it's swell even if I did write it—what with everything, I think the show is going to knock 'em off their seats in Boston, and in New York, too. Of course I may be wrong. I had better say I leave the success of the piece to the good Lord and to the critics. I guess that's the correct billing."

In *Milton Berle, An Autobiography*, Berle admitted that this was a low point in his early career. "I hated *Spring in Brazil*, but starred in it. It flopped. Cy Howard, a writer whose best lines seemed to surface after Broadway flops, couldn't wait to get to the Round Table to tell me, 'I saw *Spring in Brazil* last night. Milton, you should have gone to Brazil in the spring!'"

Berle had just completed a tour of 387 military hospitals before the war ended on September 2, 1945, his adopted daughter Victoria Melaine Berle had just been born, and he had gone straight into rehearsing *Spring in Brazil*. But the show had misfortunes from the outset. The genius of the Shubert office, Harry Kaufman, had just died. He was supposed to guide the show smoothly. Also, the big names promised for the musical—Carmen Miranda, Xavier Cugat and his orchestra (which would help sales during the current South

American craze)—weren't coming through. To top that, Berle had been deeply insulted by Lee Shubert; upon enthusiastically showing Shubert a picture of his recently adopted daughter, the producer responded, "What are you so thrilled about? It's not actually yours."

On October 2, 1945, the show had its first and last standing room performance, on opening night at the Shubert Theatre in Boston. The reviews weren't kind, and immediately there were meetings on how to save the show. Berle suggested chucking the book out in favor of the songs and sketches, turning it into a revue called *Brazilian Nights*. "Phil Rapp refused to have his book tampered with, Wright and Forrest objected to having any other music with theirs, and Lee Shubert was certain the show could be saved. In other words, we were on a sinking ship and all hands aboard were busy polishing the fixtures."

On another night, Berle was outraged when he caught Rose Marie coming out of character during her "I'm Gonna Miss Him So" number. She was told to inject the ending with a bit of imitation of Jimmy Durante singing "Who Will Be With You When I'm Far Away?" Outraged, Berle went to Shubert to complain about the lack of continuity that was breaking the show down; for weeks Berle had had to learn new lines and bits of business, make daily changes and omissions and new material. But Shubert just glared at the actor, explaining that he was in charge of the show, and that it was *his* money. Berle followed him around to try to appeal to Shubert's sense of loyalty—he thought he made a lot of money for Shubert in his *Follies* and so, his opinion was worth something. But the seventy-two-year-old producer merely shoved Milton. Berle clenched his fists, but he later claimed he couldn't hit an old man. Instead, he spat on the floor in front of him, walked away, and the rift between star and management only widened.

The show picked up speed as it moved from Boston to New Haven to Philadelphia to Pittsburgh, always adding songs and new scenes, but never gluing together into any sort of hit. The Pittsburgh reviews came in with a blizzard during Thanksgiving week. Not only were the reviews bad, but Berle had just discovered that his first wife, Linda Smith, had been sent to a sanitarium because of a drinking problem which had canceled her studio contract. And Berle felt that Linda was his only link to seeing his son again. Seeing the heavy snow, the small crowds and the holiday decorations sent Berle into a heavy depression. He phoned his wife, Joyce, and begged her to join him in Pittsburgh. Because of their child and the weather, she demurred, and Milton Berle later claimed that he felt like jumping out of his hotel window.

He bit the bullet, and the show finally closed weeks later, on January 12, 1946. After Berle's final bow at the last performance, he held up his hand to quiet the limited audience and said, "Well, ladies and gentlemen, I hope you liked the show, and if you want to see the scenery you can go over to Cain's Warehouse later this week." This was followed by Peter Lind Hayes's imitation of a drunk crying "Author! Author!" Berle needed no further prompting, and went to find Joe Burns, still in his gorilla costume. He dragged Joe out, and introduced him as the author. Peter shot the gorilla with a gun full of blanks, and the "animal" fell to the floor.

"That's it, folks," said Milton.

New York Times critic Sam Zolotow reported optimistically near the end of the run that "business seems to be holding up splendidly" on the same day that Phil (after supplying "extensive rewrites" for *Brazil*) returned to Hollywood to resume his screenwriting work. He had stayed an extra week to help John Murray Anderson find his feet (and give gag advice) when he took over directing duties from Phil, redirecting most of it. Choreographer Marjory Fielding also walked away from the production, leaving a gap that had to be filled if the dances were to be reshaped into a whole new production.

Variety, covering the opening of *Spring in Brazil* in Boston, reported, "Many of what were intended to be its most striking attractions, both musical and comic, fell as flat as a tortilla before a house too deadpan to make possible a smash hit anywhere . . . . Music lacks inspiration and only a few of the songs have any chance of lingering in the memory of those who came with high hopes at $6.60 per head and who endured some boring scenes until the grand finale . . . . *Spring* took pride in having a book and what a book! It flew apart like a 30-year-old flivver." Boston critic Elliot Norton added, "The new Berle, as presented at the premiere last night at the Shubert Theatre, is not a comedian, as was the old one. The new one is an 'actor,' a fat, middle-aged giddy goon. In *Spring in Brazil*, two girls want him. They can have him!"

By the time *Brazil* reached Philadelphia, Milton Berle was placating the bored audience with quips during his performance like, "If you think this is bad, you should have seen us in Boston!" The show stumbled West instead of venturing toward Broadway. Mary Healy replaced Rose Marie; many other replacements came over the course of the trek. All the while persistent producer Lee Shubert kept insisting the Brazilian fiasco would improve.

Joel Rapp wrote in his autobiography, *Radio, TV, Mother Earth & Me*: "My father and Berle hardly spoke over the next forty years, although both were members of Hillcrest Country Club and saw each other on a regular basis. I played golf with Milton one day, and during the round, the now much-subdued comic told me he'd always felt very badly about the fate of the show, and asked me to pass along his apologies to my father. I told him it would be better coming from him directly, but unfortunately it never did."

Phil Rapp himself did not write much about his *Brazil* experiences, but there was one slight tangent, which he penned in his *Gripes*:

FUNNY BOY

Early in 1945 Milton Berle, for whom I was writing the musical comedy *Spring in Brazil*, took me to see a young performer named Jerry Lewis. It was in a downstairs café somewhere on Broadway and business was brisk. All I can recall about his act was that he had a mop on his head and was going thru the motions of conducting an orchestra while a phonograph record played in the background. He also walked on his insteps and imitated a spastic. I was not impressed.

A couple of years later, with the monumental flop of *Brazil* still rankling in my breast, Abby Greshler, a genius of a personal manager and talent discoverer, called me and prevailed upon me to go with him to Slapsy Maxie's in Los Angeles to see his new team, Martin and Lewis. Object: radio series. I had never heard of Martin and Lewis and never connected Lewis with the young man I had seen with Berle. If I agreed to write for them, Greshler assured me, a radio series was guaranteed. I went and I saw them. The audience, a first night affair, responded as they

do at nearly all first nights. People were rolling in the aisles at the simian antics of Lewis and were pleasantly appreciative of the singing of the attractive Dean Martin. To me they seemed horribly mismated. But they were to go on to bigger things with the expert guidance of Greshler and carve for themselves a career in which I played no part. For having seen them that opening night I told Abby they'd never make it in radio and I could be of no help.

Now the point of this confession is that when Martin and Lewis finally separated, Lewis pursued his course of calculated imbecility which made him a millionaire, a fact which speaks ill for American audiences, and Martin started on a career that has culminated in what I had always suspected was the case. Dean Martin is the funniest man on or off the American stage today. He is the true comedian, his charm and easy grace, with body movements like a ballet dancer, his happy delivery purveying a sense of enjoyment in his work puts him at the head of my list. He is Funny Boy!

CHAPTER 7
DANNY KAYE, MGM AND *THE BISHOP'S WIFE*

The report that Rapp was busily writing *The Bishop's Wife* while knee-deep in *Brazil* quicksand was true. By January 30, 1946, he and Lawrence E. Watkin had handed in an incomplete First Draft of the script to Sam Goldwyn, which differed infinitely from what would be the final product released to theatres in December of 1947.

The filmed story traces the off-kilter journey of smiling angel Dudley (Cary Grant), sent from Heaven in answer to Bishop Henry Brougham's (David Niven) request for guidance from God in getting his great Cathedral built. Well, the Bishop should've been more specific about guidance, because Dudley seems to spend half his time flirting with the Bishop's wife, Julia (Loretta Young) rather than helping Henry find the million dollars it's going to take to build a church no one seems to be interested in.

Watkin/Rapp's story only retained the characters and the semblance of story, rerouting the action thoroughly. Whereas the Bishop knew of Dudley's angel-ness constantly in the filmed version, the only one who knew of it in Rapp's version was Henry's daughter, who is the real instigator of the plot:

CLOSE SHOT — JULIET

JULIET
Please send Daddy an angel with a good head.

> (then an afterthought)
>
> And please send me one too, and if you do, you can tell Sammy Claus he needn't bring my sled, because the angel can get it for me and I would like an angel with a mustache, Amen.

She opens her eyes, and lifts them hopefully and a little fearfully toward the moon.

> LONG SHOT — SKY

A star breaks from its position in the firmament and streaks across the sky into the path of the moon.

> CLOSE SHOT — JULIET — WATCHING STAR WITH AMAZEMENT
>
> SHOT OF STAR

As it approaches the earth—gradually the star is growing larger and in its flight toward earth is accompanied by celestial music. It begins to resemble a man; hatless and coatless and zooming through space. Deftly, he lands on a moonbeam and slides down it backward like a little boy on a banister.

Dudley retained his heavenly wickedness in Rapp's version, and the much-loved skating scene remained, but the First Draft touched on elements of the war (such as it stopping production of the half-built cathedral) and other themes that perhaps made it too controversial as a Christmas movie.

The final result was nominated for Best Picture and four other Oscars, winning for Best Sound Recording, and proved to be a stalwart uplifting Christmas movie, though without the ultimate staying power of *It's a Wonderful Life*. It also contained one of Cary Grant's most memorable, restrained performances. Several other uncredited writers worked on *Wife* rewrites as well, such as Charles Brackett and Billy Wilder, but even though the studio passed on Rapp's rewrite he found himself pleasantly occupied with more Goldwin projects.

His long association with lively comic Danny Kaye the year the War ended with *Wonder Man*. As Phil Rapp writes, "*Wonder Man* in 1945 had Kaye starring as twins; one of them 'shy and bookish,' the other, 'a cocky nightclub performer who is slated to testify against a gangster. A few minutes into the movie he's murdered, and for the next hour and a half the ghostly twin slips in and out of the bookworm's body.' Released in 1945 and did great."

Paul Rapp has a different recollection of the Wonder Man: "For my memory, Danny was a tool that his wife, Sylvia, used for her songs. I remember going to his house in the late '50s with Dad. He lived only a couple of blocks from Dad, and seemed very strange and unfriendly. I know that I was very irritated by his attitude. He seemed to be very condescending to Dad and showed complete lack of interest in our visit. I came away with very bad feelings and they stayed with me."

Variety's June 7, 1945 review of *Wonder Man* called Danny Kaye's second film "a wholesale, complete and exhaustive demonstration of Mr. Kaye." And true enough, the film was a perfect vehicle for the plethora of Kaye antics: comedy, dance, singing, and plenty of gags for his dual role of outgoing performer and shy guy.

Rapp finished his final draft of this star vehicle on July 10, 1944 which kept very close to the filmed version. There were a few trivial cuts from the 111-page script, including this bit in which Edwin (Kaye) tells Ellen (the beautiful Virginia Mayo) why he didn't make it back to her apartment the night before, for the second part of their date:

CLOSE TWO SHOT

As Edwin catches up to her on the ladder. He reaches over and holds her ladder to keep her from pulling away.

EDWIN
Believe me, Ellen, this is my brother's suit.
I slept in his apartment last night!

ELLEN
I thought you said you hadn't seen
your brother in over ten years.

EDWIN
Well, I have and I haven't.

ELLEN
Oh, but you saw him last night?

EDWIN
I did and I didn't.

ELLEN
Well, was he there?

EDWIN
He was and he wasn't.

ELLEN
(getting sore again)
Oh, is he crazy, too?

EDWIN
(simply)
No, he's dead. So you can see you have
no reason to be upset.

ELLEN
Oh, of course not. After all, what did
you do? You lied to me that you worked in
a pet shop, policemen tore your clothes,
you went to bed blind drunk, and you
murdered your brother! What am I supposed
to do now—kiss you?

FLASH OF SCHOLARS
As they lean forward, open-mouthed, their books forgotten.

Next came *The Secret Life of Walter Mitty* (1947), based on a 1939 James Thurber story from *The New Yorker* magazine, in which meek Walter Mitty (Danny Kaye) is always daydreaming a better life than the one with which he'd been saddled. Sylvia Fine wrote the songs, such as "A New Symphony for Unstrung Tongue" and the great "Anatole of Paris." The film cost $3 million, and sources state that Thurber himself collaborated on the script with Ken Englund. Thurber hated Kaye's patter songs, especially "Anatole of Paris," which is a dream within a dream. The next-to-last script draft—containing additional daydreams from Thurber—ran 180 pages, which would have made it *Gone With the Wind* length. Later, in *Life* magazine, Thurber stated, "Almost everything I had written, suggested and fought for was dropped."

Thurber himself did not care for the first draft script he read, complaining to Sam Goldwyn on April 1, 1946 that there were simply not enough dreams in the picture. He didn't care about the construction of it or how close or far apart the dreams were: a daydreamer dreams when he gets the chance, he argued. He wanted more dreams in there, especially in the sparse and all-important third act.

The studio, with the exception of the Story Editor and a few others, were against this, calling the addition of too many dreams "too literary" and "too *New Yorker*." In fact, they were concerned that Thurber's timid literary creation was too stifling for Danny Kaye's manic showmanship. Goldwyn himself admitted that they were buying the idea, not the story.

After several versions of a script, including many hours of collaboration from Thurber (who admitted learning a lot about the problems facing a motion picture), Phil Rapp was called in by Goldwyn to "help funny up the Dreams." Thurber had already been working extensively with screenwriter Everett Freeman, an old friend of Phil's (they'd both worked on radio shows for Victor Moore, Mary Martin, etc.), so the great humorist wasn't keen on a gag writer coming in and giving Mitty a definite clown persona. But when it was reported to him just what Phil was doing, Thurber (slightly) eased off his worry (though when seeing the final result in the theatre, Thurber commented to his friends, "Did anyone get the name of that picture?").

TRIALS OF WALTER MITTY

(Phil Rapp's original outline for *The Secret Life of Walter Mitty*, quite different from the filmed version)

We open with Mitty's mother holding reveille on our boy . . . getting him down to breakfast . . . nagging him to do this, do that and to hurry! And incidentally he got a letter yesterday, which she opened . . . something about jury duty, but her mind's made up. He's not going to do it. He salvages the letter from the wastebasket . . . telling his mother about every citizen's sacred duty to serve on a jury when called. She tells him his sacred duty is to watch the bacon . . . while she squeezes the orange juice. With the best of intentions, and a spatula in one hand, he starts to comply . . . but the spatula becomes a scepter and our boy is good King John at Runnymede and his letter calling him to jury duty is the Magna Carta. By the time he gets back to earth, the bacon is burned and his mother is screaming at him for being an idiot.

Mitty tells his boss he has to report for Jury duty. The boss instructs Mitty to ask to be excused. Mitty says no. The boss says if he doesn't, he'll be fired. Mitty is temporarily cowed, but something springboards him into a kind of "Tale of Two Cities" trail where it's Mitty against the mob . . . leading to the guillotine itself. Just as the knife is about to fall, Mitty comes to . . . to realize he's due in court.

Mitty is almost too late . . . the jury has been selected from the panel . . . and Mitty just gets taken as an alternate juror. He calls his mother during his lunch break . . . is told to come home promptly at five o'clock. He pleads that he's on a jury. He can't come home until they are dismissed. His mother says she'll be down and see about that! And poor Mitty . . . the thirteenth man on the jury . . . is the most neglected guy in the court room. Even his fellow jurors treat him like a bench warmer. Of course, this doesn't keep our boy from projecting himself into the role of any and all of the participants in the case being tried. Alternately, he is Judge Mitty. He's a busy little guy. In fact, he's so busy he gets in the Judge's hair a bit . . . with a few questions of his own. Helpful questions, Mitty thinks . . . directed to the main prosecution witness. But the Judge warns him against more of these questions which upset the court and its calm procedure.

And then Mitty's mother shows up to see who would dare order her son to run counter to her commands. The Judge, after all, has to respect motherhood . . . can't throw Momma in the clink for contempt, but has to recess the case while he regains his judicial composure.

The jury, with Mitty, is taken across the street during the recess for coffee. Mother tries to corner Mitty there. He pleads with her to stop treating him like a small boy . . . which elicits a six-months' pregnant, "Well . . ." from his mother. Still smarting from this, Mitty rejoins his fellow jurors and is escorted back to the courthouse. In the corridor, they pass the defendant and his attorney. Mitty (and we) observe that they are in deep conference . . . they seem to notice Mitty especially as he passes.

We stay with defendant and his attorney . . . prototypes of a big-time gangster and his crooked mouthpiece as the latter is telling his client that it looks very black indeed. The only thing that could save him (the client) would be a lucky break . . . like having one of the jurors drop dead, so they could get that feather-brained alternate juror into the jury. Then he'd have hopes of a hung jury. Malone . . . the defendant . . . "Lucky" Malone to his friends and the press . . . proves how he got that name. If he needs that kind of a lucky break, he knows how to make it happen. He tells the attorney what he must do.

As soon as court reconvenes, the defense attorney comes forward with the demand that the jury be locked up for the duration of the trial. His client is being tried in the press and the radio . . . the jury must be protected from these opinion-forming media. The Judge grants this and the trial proceeds.

That night, one of the jurors is murdered at the hotel, where the jury is put up. And Mitty is found right in the middle of all the evidence available. He's charged with the crime. Lucky Malone . . . his plan having backfired . . . jumps bail and escapes from the country. Mitty pulls a jail break à la Willie "The Actor" Sutton and picks up the trail of Lucky Malone. Perhaps the trailer should be in the person of a luscious blonde. Anyway, the trail leads him to Rio and finally brings him face to face with Lucky on the cable car which goes to the top of Sugar Loaf, high over the city. As they are doing a cliffhanger type fight in the cable car . . .

. . . a voice keeps telling Mitty he is through. He can go home. He comes out of it to find himself back in the court room. He is still the alternate juror. Still the thirteenth man. Only his status is changing at that second. The jury has been charged and is filing out of the court to deliberate. And the alternate has been dismissed.

A bit wistfully, Mitty watches them go. Then turns to go home to his mother.

The above was far removed from what was filmed, and may even have been suggested as a sequel. During the filming of many of the dreams, *Mitty*'s script and structure went through many revisions, more dreams being added as some shot dreams fell to the cutting room floor.

Joel Rapp recalls, "Dad worked on several pictures at Goldwyn on which he didn't get screen credit—*Secret Life of Walter Mitty, Inspector General*, and a couple of other Danny Kaye movies. I do remember that on Mitty, Dad got a call very early one morning informing him that the director (I believe it was Norman Z. McLeod) was too hungover to come in so they wanted Dad to come and direct the day's shooting. I went with him and I'll never forget it. They were shooting a scene on a huge stage with Danny and Virginia Mayo on the deck of a boat caught in an enormous storm and it was fascinating to watch."

On April 20, 1948 Rapp signed a contract to write *The Inspector General*, but had a provision put in the Warner Bros. agreement that he should have every Thursday, Friday and Saturday off in order to assume his writing/producing duties for *The Old Gold Show*. He received $2,500 a week for writing the film, and $3,000 upon its completion. As of July 29, 1948, the title was known as *Happy Times*.

The classic comedy, based on the Russian play by Gogol, was a true star vehicle again for Danny Kaye who, as the illiterate Georgi, is mistaken for Napoleon's Inspector General in the tiny, corrupt town of Brodny. The thieving Mayor and government officials first think he's a beggar and have him arrested, but Georgi soon finds himself unwittingly in the seat of power where he is offered bribes galore. Poor, simple Georgi merely wants to do some good while he can, but his evil gypsy boss Yakov (Walter Slezak) plots to use the boy to take all the bribes for himself.

Of course, what Kaye film would be complete without some complicated patter numbers to round out a competent, sometimes hilarious film? Phil didn't touch the songs (Johnny Green won a Golden Globe for scoring the picture; lyrics were by Kaye's wife, Sylvia Fine), but he did team up with Harry Kurnitz to write the 100-minute comedy which was released on December 30, 1949.*

The *New York Times*' review of *General* was highly complementary, starting with "The Old Year can now exit laughing, thanks to Danny Kaye and the people at Warner Brothers." The film gave Kaye "one of the most congenial roles that he has played. Philip Rapp and Harry Kurnitz have written a script which is, in spirit as well as detail, in the modern slapstick vein. Indeed, the whole structure of this picture is carefully and cleverly designed to give unrestrained play and freedom to the talents of Mr. Kaye."

During this time, Phil also wrote an original outline for a Kaye picture called *Two on a Straw*, which was not produced. Kaye works in a Rexall drugstore in Hollywood, hoping to be discovered by his impromptu juggling, singing and general clowning. (Rapp's partial outline is included in the Appendix.)

After the big success of yet another Danny Kaye vehicle, on September 19, 1949, Rapp signed on with Warner Bros. to write and direct *Stop! You're Killing Me* for Kaye. The job began that day and was to continue for no less than 32 weeks. Phil was to receive $1,785.71 per week for the first 14 weeks, $1,388.88 per week for the next 18, and $1,562.50 per week for anything after 32 weeks. By October, contracts had changed. Now the studio wanted him to *direct* the picture at the rate of $1,562.50 a week, paid each Wednesday. The contract stated that Rapp was back writing for

---

* Since *The Inspector General* wound up in public domain years ago, it has had constant television play and has become Rapp's most popular video offering to modern generations.

radio's Baby Snooks for 39 consecutive weeks, so time had to be allowed for his other job, as usual. Phil hoped to get the bulk of the first $50,000 that year, but Warner Bros. was hesitant about making such a promise. Since the picture was ultimately scrapped, it's easy to see why.

The following February, after *Stop!* had stopped, Rapp signed on with Warner Bros. again, this time to author *Working Our Way Through College* for the bright sum of $2507.74 a week. Not content with yet another canceled film, on July 27, 1950 Rapp switched studios and signed with Columbia at the rate of $2,500 per week to write *Third Girl from the Right* . . . which also never materialized.

It was the end of Rapp's feature film heyday, but *The Inspector General* saw to it that he went out with a bang.

For the outline of his autobiography, Rapp wrote, "Do a whole chapter on Danny Kaye. Went to see him at the Mastbaum Theatre in Philadelphia. Sent by Goldwyn. Kaye was the quickest study in the world. He had to ride a horse in *Mitty*. Learned in ten minutes. He was moody—mistaken for rudeness—shy. Crew didn't like him. Fabulous success in England. Pictures were designed to be a Kaye tour de force. No acting required. He could imitate anything. Vastly interested in surgery. Watched operations. I'm sure he could have performed one successfully. Interested in flying."

If only Rapp had expanded on his comments . . .

During the Kaye years Phil Rapp found himself in the news for a whole other reason. Early in 1945 (as reported by *Variety*) radio and television correspondents were planning their annual dinner in Washington. The guest that year: President F. D. R. The "do" was always important, and only the best professionals were called upon for entertainment. That year Fanny Brice was chosen to recruit a special team. High on her list were Danny Kaye and Danny Thomas, whose names had to be set forward early on in order that they could be checked out thoroughly for security in these tense anti-Germany/Japan times.

After weeks of intense scrutiny by government agents into the stars' public and private lives, the two Dannys were okayed and hopped the east-bound Santa Fe Chief. The train was crawling with Secret Service agents, but Danny Thomas was especially thrilled about performing for the President. He didn't even mind being followed—he thought—when he went off the train for a walk at Albuquerque. It was when he returned that all heck broke loose.

A Western Union man had delivered some wires to the conductor just before departure, and messages were soon dispatched to the travelers, one being Thomas. His eyes nearly popped out when he read SCHULTZE YOU HAVE YOUR ORDERS signed FATHER. He had to sit down. Obviously the telegram was from some pranksters—and it was sent from Los Angeles. But who had sent it?

It had surely been read by the many nearby Secret Service men. They didn't miss much where the security of the President was concerned. But what to do? He couldn't destroy it—that would look guilty. He couldn't keep it, in case someone accidently came upon it and got the wrong idea. After much deliberation, Danny decided to hide the cable in his suitcase.

The comedian was nervous all the way to Washington, expecting trouble at any moment. But when the big moment came—meeting F. D. R.—Danny Thomas didn't feel like being funny. There was only one thing to do. Right there in front of the entire room, he read the telegram. SCHULTZE YOU HAVE YOUR ORDERS signed FATHER. There was a tense moment of silence. And then F. D. R. began banging the table and howling with laughter.

The wire, of course, had come from Phil Rapp. And it proved to be a great ice breaker to the gala evening.

CHAPTER 8
THE BICKERSONS VS. THE HONEYMOONERS

What did the Bickersons mean? The truth. I just put a tape recorder under everyone's bed and just reported the truth.
—Phil Rapp

Phil didn't limit his brain to radio, films and bogus telegrams. He penned his strong thoughts on humor writing in the following article on "Postwar Comedy" which ran in Thursday April 5, 1945's *Citizen-News* paper.

Will the comedy radio program of the postwar era differ from the present day form of air entertainment? Having spent the better part of 16 years writing for and directing the top radio stars, I feel qualified, at least, to hazard a guess that there will be some changes made. Radical changes.

I, along with the general listening public, have a profound respect and deep admiration for programs designed for cultural advancement—the educational forums, symphonies, opera, classic literature and the serious works of contemporary writers such as Norman Corwin and Arch Oboler. These programs are the pearls in the oyster bed and should attain an even greater degree of importance in the scheme of radio diversion when peace comes.

Still, it's an indisputable fact that, if we are to believe the figures of statistical organizations engaged in making national surveys of the listener's taste, the comedy program has ruled the roost, undisturbed since radio was in its swaddling clothes. And if the comedian would remain in power he must change his tactics, his ideas, and his program when Johnny comes marching home.

Rabid radio fans have begun to display an apathy toward the high-priced comedy program, and even a sporadic listener can detect a certain shabbiness creeping into the top-ranking shows. It is not at all unusual to hear the same jokes or situations on two or three different comedy programs in a single evening. Little or no regard is given to originality, imagination in most cases has been entirely dispensed with, and the theory seems to be that if the studio audience laughs, the program is a success.

It is astonishing to learn the number of tricks a comedian will employ to make a thousand people gathered in a radio studio roar with laughter at an otherwise dull and vapid remark. Unfortunately, these tricks are mostly visual and consequently they are completely lost on the home listener. You have my word for it, he doesn't roar with laughter. He doesn't roar with anything except rage and frustration.

This is not to say the comedian is entirely at fault. Laughter is as necessary to a comedy program as food is to an empty stomach. But forced laughter is no more pleasant than forced feeding. Obviously, the writing must be improved. Contrary to a widespread impression, radio comedians do not make up their stuff as they go along, no matter what you read in the fan magazines. They employ writers, and the comedian either contributes to the construction of the weekly program or he does not. Mostly not. Then the writers are to blame for the bad programs, ipso facto.

Before we condemn the poor, maligned, heavy-salaried radio writer, let us consider his case. In nine instances out of ten he is guided in his preparations by the tastes of the comedian, the fact that he is over-worked, and the necessity for sacrificing characterization and literate writing in order to get laughs. He, together with his collaborators, may be employed by more than one comedy program due to the manpower shortage. Hence, the repetition of jokes on the air.

But, you may say, and rightly so, we heard jokes repeated on programs long before there was a manpower shortage. True. However, it cannot be denied that the general quality of the comedy program was improving and the listener was more discriminating.

The article continued the next day:

The listener is no longer discriminating. He has no choice. He must accept what he gets because the level has dropped. The reason for the retrogression doesn't really matter. The important fact is that the postwar comedy program MUST be different. We're going to have a different audience.

The boys who come home will certainly have a great effect on the thinking and tastes of the entire nation. It is for them the new type of successful comedy program will be designed. Sure they screamed at those comedians when they entertained them in army camps. Those very private jokes about the sergeant and the K. P. and foot drills rang a bell with them. But they were mentally geared to receive that hysterical kind of corny comedy.

I have it on very good authority that it's different with men who've seen action. My young brother, John, on the Italian front, keeps me well informed. He speaks not only as a listener, but as a qualified expert, since he was one of radio's most talented writers before going into uniform. Add to that the fact that he is one of the tiny group who run the Fifth Army's only Mobile Radio Station, that heroic unit that keeps the boys entertained under shell fire, and you must agree he has his finger close upon the postwar public pulse.

When they come back the demand will be for warm, human, humorous characterization. Hoke and the joke, like vaudeville, will die. Vulgarity will not be tolerated. These boys have grown up and are not going to be easy to fool. Writers must use more imagination and comedians must use better taste and judgment. Radio comedy must emerge as a fine art instead of a slovenly chore. Everybody in the radio business, from the sponsor down, or up, as the case may be, must strive to provide our new audience with real, first-rate enjoyment.

It's the least we can do for them.

Rapp's opinions were strong, but they kept him focused, and successful. On February 6, 1947, *Variety* announced that he was taking over as director/producer from Glenhall Taylor on Frank Morgan's radio show. Rumors were flying that Morgan and his Pall Mall sponsor were to have a parting of the ways soon, so new life was wanted. Phil was also busily scripting *The Don Ameche Show* for

Drene Shampoo, for which he received $2,500 per show to write and direct the entire program. He would take on Morgan's show once his film commitments were taken care of.

On November 25, 1947 Rapp changed agents, signing with MCA Artists rather than renewing with the William Morris Agency. MCA took 10% of all monies (*Old Gold* was netting about $3,500 a week for Rapp, for 39 weeks a year) during his employment on *The Old Gold Show* which kept "The Bickering Bickersons" sharply on the air. *Time* magazine proclaimed John & Blanche's anti-marriage as one of the sharpest skits on radio, and praise (and controversy) kept coming.

The following March, Rapp answered a "complaint" issued by plaintiff Addison Smith, denying the charges that he modeled his Bickersons after *Two Sleepy People*, which Smith wrote and produced. As *Two Sleepy People* debuted nearly two years after the Bickersons arrived on Drene Time, it was clear who copied whom. It was even *sponsored* by Drene, clearly an attempt to secure a clone series with less of a writing budget. *2SP* differed from Bix in its passion and intensity, more like a darker *Thin Man* series, with Cathy (Virginia Gregg) and Neil (Reed Hadley) far more flippant in their sparring and more blatant bouts of love than John and Blanche ever exhibited, and a lot less *plot* driven.

Phil's lawyer requested they exchange scripts to see just what similarities there were. The suit was dropped when Smith failed to "state a cause of action," after Smith's attorney failed to render a legal opinion on the matter. Rapp must have not only proved his case well enough, but assumed the offensive by demanding that Smith no longer portray his characters in bed, which seemed to be the main issue at hand. A mutual agreement was signed by Smith and Rapp, which put the major onus on Smith to be good, with both parties releasing the other from plagiaristic liability. There was to be no cash settlement. The situation was closed.

The Bickersons was the *All in the Family* of its day, separating the radio camp into two distinct factions. Hate them, or love them. The haters (at the time) believed the quarreling was just far too realistic (regardless of the audience laughter heard) or, at the very least, did not fit in with other shows of the day. Sure, Fibber argued with Molly, but there was that Irish wistfulness behind her smooth complaints. The closest Bickersons equivalent might have been Jack Benny—that poor picked on man who seemed to have no redeeming qualities to his friends but nonetheless emitted an aura of "I like this guy, despite his faults."

The alternate camp included most reviewers of the time and can be best summed up by John Crosby in his "Radio in Review" column from 1948:

> The air lanes are aquiver with the cooings of contented husbands and wives (Ozzie and Harriet, Phil and Alice, Ethel and Albert, to mention only a few) but there is one young couple who couldn't have been more thoroughly mismated and who make no bones about it. They are John and Blanche Bickerson, who are heard at the tail end of *The Old Gold Show* (CBS, 9 p.m. E.D.T. Fridays), and who are a sort of contemporary Jiggs and Maggie. On second thought, I withdraw the reference. Jiggs and Maggie aren't in the same league with the Bickersons.
>
> Blanche, played very capably by Frances Langford, is one of the monstrous shrews of all time. She makes her husband (Don Ameche) take two jobs, a total of sixteen working hours, in order to bring in more money which she squanders on minks and the stock market. Meanwhile he can't afford a pair of shoes and goes around with his feet painted black. In the few hours he has to sleep, she heckles him all night with the accusation that he doesn't love her. Her aim appears to be to drive her husband crazy and she succeeds very nicely. The harassed John's only weapon is insult, at which he's pretty good. I have here a sample of John and Blanche's conversation culled from a couple of scripts. Bear in mind that this is two a.m. and John is trying throughout to get to sleep.
>
> JOHN: I don't care. I've been doing it all week.
>
> BLANCHE: What for? I left you enough food for six days. I cooked a whole bathtubful of rice. What happened to it?

JOHN: I took a bath in it.

BLANCHE: Why didn't you eat it?

JOHN: I've told you a million times, I can't stand the sight of rice.

BLANCHE: Why not?

JOHN: Because it's connected with the saddest mistake of my life.

Just how pretty Miss Langford contrives to transform herself so convincingly into this venomous witch is her own little secret. She nags with the whining persistence of a buzzsaw, a quality that can barely be suggested in print. Mr. Ameche responds in accents of tired loathing which could hardly be improved on, though they may well cost him the women's vote.

At the risk of losing the women's vote myself I'd like to go on record as saying I think the Bickersons are very funny. In a medium which strives so desperately to spread sweetness and light, in which every wife is an angel of tolerant understanding and every husband dumb but lovable, the bickering Bickersons are a very refreshing venture in the opposite direction.

As of September 1948, Phil signed a contract for his Bickersons to appear on the Charlie McCarthy Program for 13 weeks, commencing October 3, 1948, at $1,500 per week, with options for 39 and 52 weeks more. Edgar Bergen was such a fan that he altered his radio format to include the Bickersons as his neighbors. Again, all rights Bix remained with Rapp.

Phil wrote, in his autobiographical notes, about Edgar Bergen: "The truth is that Charlie was the live one and Bergen managed to submerge his personality in the dummy. So much so that Bergen actually moved his lips more than the dummy. His technique was execrable but his characterizations were pure. This was the result of his radio days."

Because of incompatible commitments, Frances Langford was not available for Bergen's series and film actress Marsha Hunt assumed the role as a much less demanding Blanche; more whiny and needy than domineering. They were still the same ol' Bix, with each skit running at the same length (about ten pages of material per episode—nearly equaling the amount of time for the rest of the show) as on *Old Gold*, with few cuts and changes discernable from their *Gold* incarnation. The October 10, 1948 broadcast began:

CARPENTER:	**(COLD) The makers of Chase & Sanborn Coffee and Instant Chase & Sanborn present the Charlie McCarthy Show!**
CHARLIE:	**Heh, heh, heh.** *Love* **that coffee!**
MUSIC:	**THEME (UNDER TALK . . . DOUBLE TEMPO)**
CARPENTER:	**This is Ken Carpenter, ladies and gentlemen, greeting you from the Los Angeles Times-Mirror Auditorium, where today our broadcast comes to you as part of the dedication ceremonies for the new Los Angeles newspaper, The Mirror, on behalf of Edgar Bergen, Charlie McCarthy, Mortimer Snerd, Don Ameche and Marsha Hunt in "The Bickersons" by Phil Rapp, Ray Noble and his Orchestra, and Pat Patrick and Ersel Twing.**

It was unusual for a writer to be singled out for one skit in a series, though it had happened before, with the likes of Norman Corwin and other "names." Marsha Hunt also played Charlie's secretary, with Ameche coming in (he was a regular on the show for years) to give Charlie trouble. But when the Bickersons theme music began, 13 pages into the script . . .

ANNCR:	Now here are Don Ameche and Marsha Hunt as John and Blanche Bickerson in "The Honeymoon is Over."
THEME:	SOFT AND PLAINTIVE
ANNCR:	Ten minutes past midnight finds the Bickersons in a deserted railroad depot waiting for a train. Poor, exhausted John has been left to guard the luggage as his wife, Blanche, engages in a spirited telephone conversation with her sister, Clara. Listen . . .
MAR:	But I did try to get you, Clara. I called six times and the line was always busy.
CLARA:	(FILTER) I don't understand it.
MAR:	Maybe the phone's been out of order.
CLARA:	Couldn't be. I've been using it myself half the night.
MAR:	Oh. Is the lawyer still there?
CLARA:	Yes, he's here. But he hasn't read the will yet.
MAR:	Good. Our train'll be in any minute. And listen, Clara—
CLARA:	Yes?
MAR:	Don't let that lawyer start giving out the money until I get there. Goodbye, dear.
CLARA:	Goodbye.

MAR:	(HANGS UP) I knew we should have left earlier . . . (PHONE BOOTH DOOR SLIDES OPEN—FOOTSTEPS) Now where did John go? . . . This is the locker—I'm sure it is. (FOOTSTEPS OUT) Where's John? . . . He *would* run off and leave me to get the luggage out! (KEY IN LOCK . . . DOOR OPENS)
DON:	(LUSTY SNORE AND WHINE)
MAR:	John Bickerson!
DON:	Mmm.
MAR:	Get out of that locker! Come on!
DON:	Come on, Blanche . . . Wassamatter? . . . What time is it, Blanche?
MAR:	Get off that hook—and take the bags out.
DON:	(GETTING OUT) All right, all right—don't pull! Just closed my eyes for a few minutes.
MAR:	The very idea! Now, be careful with that stuff—don't pile those bags on my hatbox!
DON:	I don't know why you needed all this baggage, Blanche. We're only going to stay overnight and you brought 30 suitcases!
MAR:	Five suitcases—and some of them are yours.
DON:	*One* of them is mine. All I brought was my overnight bottle . . . Gotta have my Vitamin B shots.

MAR: Vitamin B?

DON: Bourbon.

MAR: You wouldn't travel six inches without that overnight bottle, would you?

DON: No, I wouldn't! I wouldn't travel anywhere if you didn't drag me!

MAR: With your money-grubbing mind I should think you'd be interested in seeing how much of a legacy my poor Uncle Thurmond left me.

DON: Poor Uncle Thurmond.

MAR: (SNIFFLING) He was such a sweet person—full of joy—always had a little joke for everybody—(SHE SNIFFS BACK A SOB)

DON: Oh, why don't you stop that! You never saw the man in your life and you know it!

MAR: Is it my fault if I never saw him? I still loved him.

DON: Go on! You wouldn't know he was alive if he wasn't dead. Loved him!

MAR: You just have no feelings, that's all.

DON: I got plenty of feelings.

MAR: Then why don't you show a little grief?

DON: I'll bust out crying in the morning.

MAR: You say it but you won't do it. Do it now!

DON: What?

MAR: Go on—stand up and start crying!

DON: Are you out of your mind, Blanche? Here it is one o'clock in the morning, I'm in a railroad station—no sleep—no dinner—and you want me to start crying for your uncle!

MAR: Well, you never displayed the slightest emotion when we heard the terrible news. Poor, dear man—taken away in the flower of his youth.

DON: Flower of his youth! He was a sexagenarian!

MAR: He was not—he wasn't even married!

DON: Huh?

MAR: He was one of the wealthiest bachelors in Canada! How do you think he got his title?

DON: What title?

MAR: You know as well as I do my uncle was knighted for his operations in the stock market.

DON: It was in the black market! And he wasn't knighted—he was indicted! . . . Knighted!

MAR: What's the difference? He made a lot of money—that's more than you did.

DON: Yep.

MAR: I don't know what's come over you, John. Before we were married you had plenty of ambition.

DON: Yep.

MAR: Whatever happened to your get-up-and-go?

DON: It got up and went. And I wish I could do the same.

MAR: Why don't you just say you can't stand the sight of me?

DON: I can stand it fine! What do you want from me, Blanche?

MAR: Well, I get to worrying about things—especially since this business with my uncle and everything.

DON: Stop worrying.

MAR: Tell the truth, John—if anything ever happened to me would you ever marry again?

DON: Never! I hope a rock falls on my head if I ever marry again!

MAR: Don't raise your voice like that. The ticket seller is staring at us.

DON: Let him stare! I'll punch him in the nose if he doesn't like it! Why isn't he looking after his broken-down trains, anyway? Where's our train?

MAR: It's a few minutes late.

DON: Not even a restaurant in this crummy depot. I'm dying for a cup of coffee.

MAR: There's some food and things in that brown paper bag. What do you want?

DON: What have you got?

MAR: How about a nice rhubarb and leek sandwich?

DON: Rhubarb and leek! What kind of a combination is that?

MAR: It's supposed to be very healthy. I got the recipe out of the Fernando Feed Journal.

DON: I don't want any.

MAR: They wean baby goats on it.

DON: I don't want any, I told you! What else have you got?

MAR: (RUSTLES BAG) Here. I spent half the day baking it.

DON: What is that!

MAR: It's a fudge nut strawberry marshmallow whipped cream cherry tuna-fish meringue cupcake.

DON: Holy smoke!

MAR: Do you want anything on it or will you eat it plain?

DON: Plain! I won't eat it at all! Who ever heard of a cupcake four feet high! Blanche, I wish you'd stop cooking for me.

MAR: Don't worry—I won't after tonight! As soon as I cash my uncle's will I'm going to hire ten servants.

DON: Hire 20 servants. What do I care?

MAR: You don't care about anything. You just wait till I get my inheritance. I'll be loaded and you'll be sorry.

DON: You'd *better* get it!

MAR: Why do you say that?

DON: Because if you don't *I'll* be loaded and you'll be sorry!

MAR: So! It's finally coming out now.

DON: What's coming out?

MAR: You married me for my money.

DON: What are you talking about? You didn't have a cent when I married you! I even had to lend you the two dollars for the wedding license ... I always knew it was bad to lend money!

MAR: John Bickerson! How can you talk like that, after I gave you the best years of my life?

DON: Were those the best?

MAR:	Keep it up. Torture me, go on. If my disposition isn't what it used to be, it's because of you.
DON:	Oh, dear.
MAR:	Never a kind word—never an ounce of sympathy. All I've ever asked from you is a little attention.
DON:	Nobody gives you as little attention as I do.
MAR:	How well I know it! It's been ages since you helped me on with my coat or opened a door for me.
DON:	Do it every day.
MAR:	You do not! And when you drive the car up in front of the house you might be a gentleman and help me in.
DON:	Help you in?
MAR:	No—I have to fling open the door and throw myself onto the seat.
DON:	Well, I slow down, don't I?
MAR:	I'd like to see you do that to Gloria Gooseby!
DON:	Now don't start with Gloria Gooseby!
MAR:	You'd sure be a gentleman if you had *her* in your car.
DON:	I've had her in my car plenty of times and I've never been a gentleman! I mean, I hate

	Gloria Gooseby and I wouldn't let her ride on my running board! Listen, Blanche—if this train doesn't get here in two minutes, I'm going home—will or no will!
MAR:	Oh, sit down.
DON:	I swear I almost wish your uncle Thurmond was still alive!
MAR:	How can you say such a horrible thing!
DON:	I thought you loved him so much.
MAR:	That's beside the point. What's happened has happened and it's not—(SOUND OF TRAIN ARRIVING) Oh, there's our train! Get the bags together, John.
DON:	Never saw so much luggage in all my life ... (GRUNTING) Suitcases, shoe boxes, hat boxes. There!
MAR:	Is that everything?
DON:	Yes. Let's go.
MAN:	Red Cap—carry your luggage?
DON:	No—she can manage. Move along, Blanche. (FOOTSTEPS) I'll get on first and you can hand me the stuff. The big grip first.
MAR:	Here—be careful, John. Hurry.
MAN:	(CALLS) Booooaard!
DON:	Come on, Blanche—grab my hand! (TRAIN

MOVES OUT AND GATHERS SPEED)

MAR: Well, there are plenty of seats, anyway.

DON: Let me get near the window. I gotta get some sleep.

MAR: Put your feet up here. Loosen your tie, John.

DON: I'm okay. Just let me rest.

MAN: Tickets, please.

MAR: Oh. I have them in my bag, conductor. Just a minute . . . . What time do we get to Temecula?

MAN: Temecula? You're going the wrong way, ma'am. This train doesn't go to Temecula.

DON: Doesn't—go?

MAN: No, sir. This is nonstop to Cleveland.

MAR: Oh, John!

MAN: I'll have to collect two fares, please. Ninety-one dollars and seventy cents.

DON: (A DEAD VOICE) Would you mind coming back in five minutes, conductor?

MAR: No—stay here!

DON: Please! I'll have the money when you come back.

MAN:	Whatever you say. (FADING) Tickets, please . . .
MAR:	Don't look at me like that, John. I couldn't help it. Anybody can make a mistake, can't they? How did I know it was the wrong train!
DON:	Ninety-one dollars and seventy cents! I don't save that much in a year!
MAR:	Oh, don't be so dramatic. When we get to Cleveland I'll wire Clara and she'll send me the will money.
DON:	Will money! Will money! How do you know you'll get anything at all?
MAR:	Because I know! The only thing that upsets me is that I have to spend the next two nights on a train with such an irritable, argumentative man!
DON:	Listen, Blanche, do you think I enjoy sitting up for two nights fighting with you? Have you ever asked yourself the reason why we argue so much?
MAR:	I can't understand it.
DON:	Well, just think for a minute. Why is it that an easy-going fellow—a guy who would run a mile to avoid a fight—why is it that I turn into a screaming, raving demon every night of my life?
MAR:	You've got me, John.
DON:	That's the reason! Goodnight, Blanche.

Mar:	Goodnight, John.
Music:	THEME
	(APPLAUSE)

The following week Blanche learns that she, in fact, inherited not a penny, and has to break the sad news to snoring John.*

The Bickersons was immensely popular, but radio was dying. The new road was television.

So, on September 25, 1950, Rapp signed an agreement with Stellar Enterprises to furnish his Bickersons as an "independent contractor" for use on *Star Time*, one of television's first successful variety programs, which was broadcast from New York City over the Dumont Television Network on Tuesdays from 10–11 p.m. Rapp would receive $1,800 per week for nine weeks, with options to extend the agreement for several 13-week periods at $2,250 per week. He would write, direct and produce the 12- to 15-minute Bix skits, which soon led to Rapp directing *Star Time* and providing additional material. As Don Ameche had other commitments, Lew Parker (later known for his role as Lou Marie on Marlo Thomas's late-1960s television series, *That Girl*), became the usual John Bickerson substitute. Lew was more of a downtrodden workhorse Bickerson than an Ameche-type shouter, but he still knew how to snore up an ice storm.

Young Paul Rapp accompanied his dad to New York. "We kept rooms in Essex House and the Waldorf Astoria during *Star Time*," he recalls. "Every morning I was picked up by a taxi—Mom would take the cab's name and number first—to go to school. Jimmy Blue Eyes, a bodyguard and professional killer, accompanied me to school. Dad would frequent Toots Shor's 21 Club and the Copacabana in his off hours.

"During *Star Time*, it wasn't uncommon for the crew to hold up the producers for more money at show time. They did it to Dad, and he got incensed because it was out of his realm. But Dad had

---

* The script to that episode can be found in *The Bickersons Scripts Vol. 2*, published by BearManor Media.

friends in the mob—even during the *Spring in Brazil* days—at the 21 Club who were very menacing; one time a guy lined up the crew and threatened them with a big knife. They told the crew that they shouldn't bother Phil anymore. Being Dad's friend was a big deal, and the mob liked to hang around celebrities, so it was lucky for him."

A promo sheet from October 1950 stated that only something very important and close to his heart was able to extract Rapp from the mild climate of his beloved Southern California. And getting the Bickersons on television was worth it.

Variety reported one week that *Star Time* was the top video program in San Francisco, according to the latest Tele-Que survey, beating out *The Long Ranger, Tru-Pak Movie Time* and *T-Men in Action* respectively. A Senior Productions budget showed that the two highest paid performers of the show were, of course, Frances Langford (gross $1,125) and Lew Parker (gross $750). The three others in the cast—Peter Leeds, Benjamin Rubin and Doris Singleton—received $80 a piece, while the total cost for writers was $500. The show's total, with many music bills to pay, came in at $5,045 per episode, a far cry from the millions it takes today.

On December 12, 1950 *The Hollywood Reporter* stated that *Star Time*'s sponsor was Grand Union Stores and that the series was planned "for extension" to the West coast after the first of the year. Reginald Gardiner and John Conte had just been added to the show's cast. His new contract allowed Phil Rapp to write in California for five out of his contracted thirteen weeks, and he could choose his own director.

In Sid White's syndicated "Main Street" column he wrote, "Nobody—but nobody—will ever get a Pulitzer Prize award for observing that Frances Langford can sing with the best of them—but we would like to go on record with the statement that the lovely Frances has outstanding talent as a comedienne, too. Catch her on DuMont's *Star Time* during the 'Bickerson Family' skits and see what we mean. She and her video partner, Lew Parker, do full justice to Philip Rapp's brilliantly penned skits." Another review bubbled that "Frances and Lew are so successful at this that I can say without hesitation that 'The Bickersons' is not only that high point of *Star Time* but one of the high points of all of television" and that Rapp's scripts were "clever, intelligent, funny, blisteringly realistic, loaded with viewer identification and a new and welcome contribution to the American TV scene."

Another New York paper was less complimentary to the surrounding components of the show, citing that the Chef Armando bit with Conte "could easily be dispensed with. It's not very funny the first time you see it, and just changing the recipe from veal cacciatore to picnic basket lunches doesn't make it any funnier." It called the Bickersons far superior to the rest of the package and urged someone just to extract those fifteen minutes out. It praised Lew Parker, claiming that he "gets more out of the character and situations than Don Ameche got out of them on AM." Frances was called perfect as the nagging wife, though they wished that when she sang her numbers, she would "wear gowns not quite so tight." They complimented Phil Rapp's writings as being largely responsible "for the bit's wow qualities."

Al Morton in his *TV Roundup* column didn't mind Frances's evening gowns and also praised the Bickersons as the bright light of the musical comedy hour. "Numerous other comedy skits are interspersed throughout the show but emerge hopelessly overshadowed by the saga of the battling Bickersons." But he concedes that John Conte, Reginald Gardiner and Katherine Lee "round out a cast that will give you a consistently good hour of entertainment."

The latest Ross Poll cited *Star Time* as one of two "most steadily improved" attractions for TV. News soon followed of "a deal in the making" for The Bickersons movie, with Rapp as writer/producer. Even Louella Parsons happily announced in her column that Frances would star in the Bickersons film, with Rapp directing and producing. But it was never to be.

At the same time, and perhaps because of *Star Time*'s popularity, The Bickersons finally got their own radio show. *At last*, there was no sharing time with another comedian; no 15-minute skit. This time, the focus was just man and wife—going at it.

It became a short-lived, half-hour radio show with Frances and Lew on June 5, 1951 over WCBS (originating from Station WNX-CBS, California), as a summer replacement for *Truth or*

Consequences. Critical praise was just as heavy, with regular fan the *New York Herald Tribune* again giving a significant rave for the Bix contrast to the usual type of family entertainment. Though the paper couldn't recall "a single likable character" in the show's short career, the *Tribune* thought the reason the series worked so well was because "you can feel both sorry for and superior to the Bickersons, which is a very pleasant emotional mixture." It likened Rapp's attitude to women, children and people in general to Al Capp, the *Li'l Abner* cartoonist: all humor is sadistic.

Weekly Variety's June 13, 1951 review of the new Langford-Parker series thought there was "real bite" in the fighting dialogue, but wished there had been more situational humor combined with it to keep the series from becoming too repetitive and stifled in one setting. It liked Frances singing "Blue Skies" but thought it slowed the opening and wished numbers could somehow be integrated into the story line. It praised the fine casting, yet thought Lurene Tuttle, Lou Lubin, Benny Rubin and John Brown were underused (this being a two-character play, essentially, they were indeed underused). Also the reviewer complained that the Philip Morris commercials were starting to lose their impact due to constant repetition.

The July 7, 1951 issue of *Cue* magazine wrote that "Lew Parker ... is every bit as good as Ameche—in fact, we begin to believe that almost any actor-comedian with expert time sense and a loud, fast and belligerent delivery would be pretty satisfactory in the role. Parker has all three of these, and he's swell.

"Miss Langford, we'd like to wager, is the indispensible one. This role of Blanche Bickerson started a whole new phase of her career, and brought her a new public. She's even won a couple of top comedienne polls, which is as it should be. She has a wonderful way with the nagging, complaining lines, and also that necessary time sense that has to be a part of top comedy."

Meantime, without it interfering with his Bix, Rapp found himself with a profitable part-time job. He signed an agreement with Wald-Krasna Productions on June 30, 1951 to write *The U.S.O. Story for RKO*, at the salary of $2,500 per week. Again, there was a clause included, giving Rapp time off for the Bickersons, and he was allowed to work from home on it.

Around this time, CBS made an offer to buy The Bickersons from Rapp for $1 million, but as the creator stated, "CBS President William F. Paley kept me waiting 15 minutes in his outer office, and anyhow, I had a horse running at the track, so I walked out on him." It's difficult to believe Rapp would have sold, however, even for a million. The Bickersons was and still is his trademark baby; he held the reins to it tightly during his lifetime. During which *no* one else ever wrote or directed it.

No wonder CBS wanted claim to the characters. The '50s was the Decade of the Bickersons. The feuding couple even appeared before the Queen of England in the mid-1950s for an evening Royal Command Performance.

Frances and Don (and more often than not these days, Lew Parker in Don's shoes) appeared on a lot of early television shows, such as *The Ed Sullivan Show* and *The Steve Allen Show*. John and Blanche also more than influenced the most beloved and influential series of the '50s, *The Honeymooners*, starring Jackie Gleason and Audrey Meadows as a working-class married couple filled with argument and woe.

Joe Cates, producer for *Cavalcade of Stars* (1949–1952) told Jeff Kisseloff for his book, *The Box: An Oral History of Television, 1929–1961* (Viking, 1995), "*The Honeymooners* started the second year of *Cavalcade* when Joe Bigelow and Harry Crane were the writers. Even the truth of that has never been told. Jackie [Gleason] had a friend, Lew Parker, a vaudevillian. Lew had just spent the summer touring with his wife, doing Phil Rapp's Bickersons sketch. Gleason promised Lew he would put it on the show, so we rented the sketch from Phil Rapp. The Bickersons were characters on radio played by Don Ameche and Frances Langford, a husband and wife who bickered. We did the sketch, and at a meeting two days later, Jackie said, 'We could steal that. It's perfect for me.'"

Harry Crane, also interviewed in *The Box*, claimed that the Bickersons had nothing to do with The Honeymooners, and that he wrote a sketch called "The Beast When the Honeymoon Is Over" because they needed more characters. He says that he thought up the notion of a bus driver and his wife who were constantly quarreling, based on his parents. Jackie Gleason loved it, and it evolved into *The Honeymooners*.

But the *Honeymooners'* origin was more than just a difference of opinion. Even Mel Shaw admitted, "I always knew Jackie Gleason's show was a take-off on the Bickersons." Many others saw the similarity right off, including Rapp himself.

It wasn't an isolated incident.

On August 14, 1953 *The Hollywood Reporter* informed the public that Gordon W. Levoy and Stanley Fleishman were filing a suit in Superior Court on behalf of Rapp against NBC, emcee Hoagy Carmichael, Eddie Foy, Jr., and director Sidney Miller to restrain them from using comedy sketches (four of them were broadcast in 1953) starring Foy on NBC's *Saturday Night Revue*, which Rapp alleged were based on his Bickersons. "There were two different sets of performers," he explained. "The two who played the just-married couple who were all affection and love played a short scene to show how wonderful it is when you are just married, and then that set blacked out and the lights went on to the couple, Eddie Foy, Jr. and Sara Berner, to depict how it looked several years after marriage."

The suit was for $750,000 actual damages and $500,000 punitive damages. Rapp estimated the value of the Bix property at $1,500,000, especially now that he had his "four movie shorts" made at a cost of $100,000, which he was presenting around Hollywood as pilots for a proposed Bickersons TV series. Several networks had bid on TV rights for the Bickersons, and NBC had once taken an option on it. But the value of the property wouldn't be worth much if the sketch was continued to be shown on another network, and in burlesque form at that.

Rapp had a few good facts on his side. The Foy sketch had been written by sketch writer Sidney Miller who had actually played minor parts as an actor in The Bickersons on previous shows. Not only did he had an intimate knowledge of the Bickersons charm, but had once requested, and been refused, rights to the series.

Then, in the first week of November 1953, Phil finally filed a $2 million infringement suit in New York Federal Court against CBS, Jackie Gleason Enterprises, and Jackie Gleason for his *Honeymooners*. Rapp had submitted his *Bickersons* at CBS at the request of the network, implying it would pay "reasonable value" for the show. Instead the skit was burlesqued in another Gleason skit on *Cavalcade of Stars* (which was canceled in 1952).

Meanwhile, *Variety*'s November 27, 1953 front page reported, "NBC SETTLES PHIL RAPP'S PIRACY SUIT OUT OF COURT ON 'BICKERSONS' BEEF." Though NBC paid off an undisclosed amount for the *Saturday Night Revue* suit, the Gleason case was still pending. Phil called it off a few days later and took a small payoff from NBC, with the network agreeing not to run anymore "take-offs."

Rapp was still trying to sell his Bix series. A December 29, 1954 wire from advertisers Kramer & Jordan told of the great reaction the fourth Bickerson episode produced for McAvity and other big shots at NBC. They were hoping Imogene Coca would do the Bix bit in her live show that season to help sell the series.

Unfortunately, when *The Honeymooners*' regular series began the following year, it became hard to sell a similar show. Rapp immediately slapped Gleason with another suit, and though *The Honeymooners* lasted a mere thirty-nine episodes (from 1955–56), the case seemed to drag on longer.

Rapp felt that even the name of the series was an affront, since he had always called his Bix skit, "The Honeymoon Is Over," as stated by various announcers on radio and television. A letter from Gleason's attorney Kupferman included several copies of reviews of *The Honeymooners* and expressed concern that they could find no copyrights for Rapp under the name "Honeymooners."

"The Honeymooners," they wrote to Rapp's attorneys, "was presented as a feature full-length sketch with Jackie Gleason, Art Carney, Audrey Meadows and Joyce Randolph over Channel 2 (CBS) on *The Jackie Gleason Show*, on January 16, 1954; also on the same channel on November 13, 1954; November 27, 1954; and April 16, 1955. On October 1, 1955 those four actors returned over Channel 2 for the fourth year. At present it's still on Jackie's show on Channel 2 on Saturday nights.

"CBS was considering a weekly half-hour *Honeymooners* and an audition program was to be recorded on May 6, 1954 with the four cast members and Ray Bloch's orchestra.

"With $10 million in TV ad time to invest, General Motors settled on pushing its Buick and bought *The Honeymooners* to do the job in the fall of 1955 on CBS."

Kupferman's associates dug up facts in which the title "Honeymooners" had been used on other programs: in 1935 there was a sustaining program entitled *The Honeymooners* with Grace and Eddie presented over WJZ in New York; Jane Bisher was the author of a radio series entitled *The Honeymooners* in 1940; and several television scripts entitled *The Honeymooners* by Angela Langford (copyright 1955) and Kaye Phyllips (also 1955). Also copyrighted was the humorous short cartoon from 1955, *The Honey Earthers* featuring script and voices by Daws Butler.

A December 8, 1955 letter from Rapp's attorney Gordon Levoy was sent to Kupferman along with a wealth of correspondence that would affect the case:

> You will note that some of it, for example, is fan mail addressed to Phil at CBS or even directly addressed to the station when the [*Bickersons*] program was last on radio in 1951. This is selected at random, and Phil says he has 'tons' more than CBS delivered to him at the time. It is quite obvious that the sentiments indicated therein influenced CBS ultimately to make its Gleason move.
>
> I cannot help but feel that even if 'bickering' per se has gone on since Adam and Eve and is the motivation in *The Taming of the Shrew* and other significant works, that insofar as this medium is concerned (radio and television) it definitely brought a new and original format.
>
> P.S. I am also enclosing a copy of a report of a *Variety* item in 1948. When this occurred, Phil's attorney (at that time) called the network and asked to hear the transcription, whereupon the show [*Two Sleepy People*] was cancelled and Phil was sued. The outcome of the suit was favorable. It may be, however, that this type of proceeding would add to the proof of the establishment of 'The Bickersons' at that time.

At the end of 1955 Levoy was still pushing for a trial against CBS. There was talk of subpoenaing John Crosby to testify to the originality of the Bickersons. Kupferman was worried and wrote, "I am afraid that if we do not have a witness of Crosby's caliber to testify on the originality of the Bickerson characters, we may not even get to the jury."

In a January 25, 1956 letter from New York attorney Theodore R. Kupferman, he states, "Jack Denove, producer [of *It's the Bickersons*, the unaired TV pilots], claims—and he would so testify—that he was unable to sell the series because of the Gleason program and the pending law suit."

Sixteen days later Gordon Levoy wrote to Kupferman: "Phil's present plans are to arrive in New York sometime next week, but he will not be available for the continuance of the deposition until next Friday, February 17th. He has been advised by his doctor that he should not tax himself to the point of spending more than four hours on this deposition.

"I am of the opinion, however, that we should not pass this information on to counsel for the defense, because if they feel that they are securing tangible results by badgering Phil, they might continue to use such tactics now and at the time of trial. It is my belief also that we must continue to maintain a completely nonchalant attitude toward their questions, so that they know we are absolutely in earnest about going ahead with the pursuit of our litigation."

He believed there couldn't be much more to ask, unless they wanted to concentrate on minutia, and believed the deposition was pretty well now complete. Phil Rapp, however, had not said all he had to say.

On February 13, 1956, Rapp's doctor, Julius Kahn, signed a notarized statement: "This is to verify that Mr. Philip Rapp has been a patient of this office for many years. He is afflicted with high blood pressure and is an extremely tense individual.

"If he is to testify in a court session the period should be less than four hours."

When questioned by the defense during a pre-trial examination on the crux of the matter—"Could you tell me in what respects the radio program that you allegedly created and originated was novel and unique?"—Rapp responded, "Well, to my knowledge it was the first time that the concept of marriage as an institution was presented in a rather unfavorable comic light. Heretofore, marriage and married couples had been presented in various humorous and pathetic situations where all seemed to be sweetness and light and affections.

"I contend that I developed and pioneered a new concept in the presentation of married life for fun. I think the things that made it novel and unique was, naturally, that it had not been presented before and, secondly, that my two characters, the husband and the wife, were drawn very realistically. In fact, one could say almost reportorially."

"In other words," the defense attorney asked, "you would say it was a mirror of the listeners?"

Rapp: "To a certain degree, but projected a little farther for comic purposes. We have to paint with a little broader brush when we want to make anything funny that borders, really, on the tragic.

"John Bickerson, I would say, is the eternally over-worked male; suffers a great deal in his work-a-day world; limited to very few real possessions; subject to the whim and caprices of a rather illogical wife, and is endowed with most of the vices and virtues of man. He has a passion for sleep which seems constantly denied to him, which in the early days of 'The Bickersons' was the motivating factor of each sketch.

"John Bickerson gave the appearance, although he was never seen to take a drink, of being a drinker. He was forever in love with his bourbon but at no time on any program, even though he referred to it lovingly and Blanche might have accused him of tippling too much, did he ever actually take a drink of liquor.

"Among the minor vices was his apparent shiftlessness. He was unable to hold a job very long, but he more than amply made up for that, I think, by getting two and three jobs at once.

"Blanche Bickerson is the wife of a man who apparently does not profess his love and affection often or audibly enough to ever please her. She is rather illogical in her perspective and she's guilty on many occasions of a slight nagging quality to achieve her ends.

"I think it was evident and apparent that a certain amount of affection existed between the partners, but I couldn't find any comedy in warmth, and if you can show me anybody who has, I'd be very appreciative. [John] would be forgiving of Blanche's trespasses and her rather illogical carryings on, and while he didn't leap into her arms and cover her with kisses, he said in so many words that he forgives her for it and all he would like to do now is get his sleep.

"There was a high degree of *violence in emotion* in the Bickersons. Not insulting dialogue, but rather, caustic repartee."

The entire history of the suit is printed *The Bickersons* biography and can't really be elongated upon here. Needless to say, the Gleason side decided to settle with Rapp for an undisclosed amount before it ever got to trial.*

---

* Phil's testimony is included in the third section of this book's Appendix, and gives a detailed overview, in Phil's own words, of his career up until 1954.

CHAPTER 9
TOPPER, JOAN DAVIS AND THE GANG

Rapp then wrote, directed and produced Ed Wynn's second hour-long show, the *All Star Revue*. A review of the NBC-KNBH show stated that the only two times the show came to life was during the "Punch and Judy" bit, and of course the Bickersons with Lew Parker and Virginia Grey: "No one can touch [Rapp] when it comes to bringing 'The Bickersons' to life and he and Parker and Miss Grey could easily make an outstanding network quarter-hour out of it, but that particular brand of comedy just isn't Ed Wynn's cup of tea."

Phil wrote: "Ed Wynn was a man who was clumsy, spoke with a lisp, had a bad speaking voice, couldn't sing or dance, yet insisted on appearing in public. Freedman said he made a brilliant career out of his defects."

Though Wynn didn't care for the Bickersons, that didn't stop them from again appearing on *The Toast of the Town* with Wynn, but by the mid-1950s Rapp was busying himself with a lot more than Bix, though much of his work seemed to stem from it.

Since everyone wanted the Bix for guest spots, Phil thought now was the ideal time to get a pilot made to push The Bickersons as a regular series. He made four half-hour pilot films, with Lew Parker again as John and the (almost too) beautiful Virginia Grey as Blanche.

Phil made *It's the Bickersons* in June and July of 1952 for himself, while Jack Denove helped with the financing. "A long period elapsed during which time I tried to sell my films," explained Rapp. "I had various representatives. At one time the William Morris agency represented the films, at another, Bernard L. Schubert, at another, MCB, and I personally devoted a great deal of time [a year and a half, through December 1953] in New York among the advertising agencies in an effort to secure a deal for them. Actually, I never stopped trying, you know." He sought to make a package deal with himself as producer and packager of the series, with all residual rights, $25,000 to $30,000 per film for a one-time showing, to be his. "I held myself open to deliver the writing and directing of these pictures in the event of a sale for as long as I was financially able, and then I made a deal with John W. Loveton and Bernard L. Schubert to make a pilot film for them on Thorne Smith's *Topper*."

Topper (1953–55) was the altered television version of the three popular screwball comedies of the 1930s starring Roland Young (based on the Thorne Smith book, *Topper*). For the small screen it was Leo G. Carroll playing the part of Cosmo Topper, vice-president of a Los Angeles bank, who is haunted by the fun-loving George and Marion Kerby (Robert Sterling and Anne Jeffries), once clients of Topper's, and now dead from an avalanche. Still, the eternally happy ghosts have fun with the *only* person who can see them, thinking their lack of heaven is due to their need to do a good deed: namely put the pep and oomph back into this square fish's life.

One significant television addition to the classic film, which starred Gary Grant and Constance Bennett as the ghosts, was that of a large St. Bernard named Neil; he also perished in the avalanche, while trying to save his beloved masters.

Rapp stated, "Apparently Loveton and Schubert had the rights to the Thorne Smith property *Topper* but were allowed to use only the main title and the main characters, but not allowed to use incidents from the book. Therefore, I was forced to create a new set of incidents and employ the three basic characters in *Topper*: Cosmo Topper and George and Marian Kerby, who played the ghosts. I did add one more element to it. I created a ghost, an intoxicated St. Bernard whom I called Neil." He served as director and writing supervisor of the first dozen or so episodes, then as supervisor in charge all writing, with an occasional directing credit. George Oppenheimer was brought in as a regular script writer. The deal was made in February of 1953 and the pilot film was shot in middle of the summer, for CBS-TV. The sponsor was R.J. Reynolds, makers of Camel Cavalier cigarettes. It was a deal for 26 weeks, with the first 13 to be repeated; *Topper* was set to replace *My Friend Irma* in October.

The 78 shows that were made before the series was canceled in April of 1955 were actually more popular in repeats decades later than they had been in their original airing.

Though Phil is credited with writing at least 19 shows, script editing on several episodes, and directing the premiere episode, almost nothing exists in his vast collection of papers, not even a single script. So it's uncertain to what extent Rapp was involved with the series' run. Even Joel Rapp, who wrote a few of the episodes, didn't have many memories of *Topper*, but explained, "Dad and Jack Denove bought the rights from the Thorne Smith Estate and made a pilot with Leo G. Carrol and Bob Sterling and Anne Jeffries. They added a St. Bernard named Neil, after my cousin." Paul states, "It played over ten cycles in Japan alone. It had a birthday in the U.S. market on the Fourth of July, where they would play every episode for 24 hours on various independent stations."

Variety loved the pilot written by Rapp and Oppenheimer and directed by Rapp, calling it "a slick cast paced into an ectoplastic winner by the Phil Rapp staging" and admitted it had "nonstop laughcades." Carroll was called "the most logical successor" to Roland Young, and Jeffreys and Sterling were named "a charming couple." It had high hopes for the series: "If it can maintain the level of the teeoffer, here's one of the most diverting skeins of the year."

The Hollywood Reporter wrote: "This television adaptation sticks pretty closely to the movie but the new faces and new settings reeled off on a smaller screen give one a feeling of newness and novelty.

"Leo G. Carroll, enacting the role played by Roland Young, is very reminiscent of Young—his accent, his expressions and his mannerisms. Robert Sterling is no Cary Grant, but nevertheless adds a nice amiability to Grant's wraithlike creation. Anne Jeffreys seems a little strong and real for the gentle, mischievous ghost originated by Constance Bennett with the help of author Thorne Smith. Lee Patrick, playing Mrs. Topper, is pleasantly irascible.

"The lines are often amusing and clever. An intoxicated dog, Neil, is pointed out as the first St. Bernard that couldn't hold his liquor (laugh track). 'Now that we're dead,' says Kerby after an avalanche, 'let's live it up a little (laugh track).'" When Kerby becomes a transparent ghost, the Mrs. comments, 'Now anyone who always wanted to know what I saw in you will find out (laugh track).' One dissenting comment—the artificial laugh track is distracting, annoying, unbearable at times and there are some laughs on it that could only have come out of a Coney Island side show."

The pilot involved the Kerbys' dying in an avalanche, after which Mr. and Mrs. Cosmo Topper buy their home, now haunted by the Kerbys. Lyle Talbot was the real estate agent.

Variety later wrote that Rapp has "a sharp comedy mind with just the right touch for such airy goings-on. The script is bright and frothy and has a direct approach in the best ghostly tradition." Unfortunately, Rapp found he couldn't devote himself fully to *Topper* with his most important children, the Bickersons, constantly in his mind. Also there was some dispute between different signed agreements which gave very different powers to Rapp. One contract placed Loveton in the producer's seat, with power over Rapp's abilities to write and direct—and when he could do either. This conflicted with another agreement which quite simply stated that Rapp was to be in charge of production and writing. Also Rapp was to do his work in the Los Angeles area, and his services weren't supposed to be so exclusive that he couldn't work on other projects, like the Bickersons, if a good opportunity arose. Loveton, of course, wanted exclusivity and reserved the right to send Rapp anywhere for filming. Phil did not like that, nor did he appreciate the difference in money between the two agreements. He understood that he was to receive a 10% gross of all income from every series he worked on over his $2,000 per show. Loveton understood that Rapp's $2,000 figure was all-inclusive.

Unable to "understand" each other, Rapp wanted to sell his residual rights to all the 78 *Topper* TV shows for $600,000. John Loveton responded in a letter dated July 26, 1955: in addition to his original directorial compensation, Rapp was to receive 10% of all grosses returned from the series, not counting the $4,000 owed to him for writing two of its scripts. Lopping off a 0, Loveton countered with a $60,000 offer, which Rapp accepted. $10,000 was included with the signed contract, the other $50,000 to be paid before September 30, 1955. These payments were to be separate from the 10% still owed Rapp from the then currently airing summer reruns. If the gross figure exceeded $800,000, Phil would receive 10% of all amounts over and above that figure.

During the run, John W. Loveton started giving Rapp 16mm prints of the episodes, and by the series end, he had the full set. It is unfortunate for viewers everywhere that he later sold the set to an unknown collector. Unfortunate, because many of these episodes are considered lost and very few have ever shown up on DVD.

Today, one of the most significant facts about *Topper* is that it had Broadway songwriting genius Stephen Sondheim (*West Side Story, Company*, etc.) on its writing staff. Lucky young Sondheim had met TV writer George Oppenheimer at a dinner party in Bucks County, Pennsylvania, after Oppenheimer had just sold the *Topper* pilot, and he needed another writer for it. Oscar Hammerstein II suggested Sondheim. After reading some scripts he'd written at Williams College, Oppenheimer offered him the job, finding Sondheim "an incredibly amusing guy." They had to get out 29 episodes in six months (some episodes had to be shot within *three days*), so he needed the help. Sondheim wrote ten episodes and they collaborated on another ten.

Sondheim worked hard for his $300 a week but quickly had his fill of this style of writing, and left after five months, having written eleven scripts. He didn't deal with Phil Rapp; it was almost always Oppenheimer. "My memory is strictly of sitting in my apartment on McCarty Drive and turning out scripts," says Sondheim to this author, "then meeting George in the production offices and editing the material together. I wasn't even on the set more than a couple of times, something I regret, as I would love to have talked to the actors, but I was too shy."

Paul Rapp also only visited the *Topper* set once. "I am very short of any memory. Dad was always talking about how difficult it was to do the trick shots. Today's directors would consider it a picnic. I can't imagine how fantastic the show would improve with modern computer graphics.

"*Topper* was a huge hit both in the U.S. and Japan, the reruns were in double digits. It would be #1 in these times. Dad sold his residual rights for about $500,000 and if you do the math it would have amounted to more than a million if he had held them—but with taxes, time, investment, etc.—it may have come close to the same as if he kept the rights. Dad didn't need the money, but he didn't want Mom to know so they wouldn't fight about the money—see Bickersons.

"For most of *Topper* I was in high school and early college. I was in high school from 1951–55, and my attention was mostly focused on school and getting laid, so my *Topper* history is not good. I was given my first car in 1954, an MG-TD that was super. It was stolen from me in late 1954 and my next car was a brand new 1955 Chevy Bel-Air convertible that cost $2,400. On today's market a restored model would fetch $30–50,000. My senior year at Beverly Hills High (just like the TV series *90210*) was so easy that I started classes at USC night school where Joel was going. And by the time I graduated Beverly High in 1955 I had finished an entire semester at USC.

"I took a couple of classes with Joel. USC is very expensive. Today it is something like $75,000 a year and much of the student body is Asian. Today, USC's film school is widely known for huge endowments from George Lucas and Stephen Spielberg, to name a couple of alumni. By the way, Joel graduated Beverly High in 1950, and Brian, my son, graduated in 1976, and was captain of the football team. Both my niece Lisa and her sister Danielle also graduated from Beverly High in 1976. USC football is actually in the top five teams in the country and my Mom was a really big fan and even went to some games with me. *Topper* money was being spent very well at this time.

"In an aside, in 1952 we moved to 601 N Palm Drive, Beverly Hills 90210. It was a fantastic three-story Spanish house. Mom had an addition added onto the six-car garage for Dad's private study with kitchen and fireplace to do his writing, overlooking a beautiful garden.

"When I finished USC I started working in show business as an assistant director. I joined the Directors Guild of America when I lied about my age, telling them I was 21 when I was 18. I met my wife, Jenny Maxwell, who was Deb Star of the Year 1959, when she was doing a part on *Father Knows Best*. She was 16 (I thought 17) and was the hottest starlet in Hollywood. The school teacher on *The Donna Reed Show* introduced me to her and Sandra Dee in the same day. Jenny and I married soon after, and likewise Sandra Dee and Bobby Darin were soon married. I was smitten by Jenny and we married and she became pregnant immediately with our son Brian. Shortly after giving birth, Jenny landed a large role on Elvis Presley's *Blue Hawaii*. I went to Hawaii with Jenny and Brian when he was six months old. The fame got to her very hard and we were divorced right after the film was released. I found myself having to care for Brian fulltime as Jenny wanted stardom and felt that a child held her back. I was the first single father in California to be given custody of a tender-age child and I raised him totally for the next 20 years.

"I was at times like the characters on *Two and a Half Men, Courtship of Eddie's Father,* and a dozen other father-son movies and TV shows. This lifestyle—being single, having a great looking athletic son—helped me to attract all the single girls who wanted to play 'mom' with me. I was a making a generous amount of money and had access to all the studio parties, etcetera, so there was no shortage of girls to date. In fact, at one time, when I had three girlfriends named Susan, Dad made a real *faux pas*. There was a time when I told Dad my current girlfriend was named Nancy and he inadvertently called her Susan. When I corrected him he said it was easier to call all of them Susan since the odds were in his favor.

"I lived the life that Hugh Hefner would envy. Brian and I to this day remain best friends. Raquel Welch sent a lovely gift when Brian graduated high school along with her son. I had seen to it that she got her SAG card in a film I produced for Roger Corman entitled *Girls on the Beach*. In the past I have done things like writing, etcetera, without credit to have a job and make some money, just as Joel did.

"I remember when Dad would bring Brian to the movie sets for small parts: *The Trip* and *The Wild Angels* (opening scene) and *St. Valentine's Day Massacre* (Brian played Bruce Dern's son) in 1966 at 20th Century-Fox. Roger Corman was very cordial to him. It was during St. Valentine's Day Massacre that Roger asked me to begin writing a script that had the feeling of J.P Donleavy's *The Ginger Man*. He reasoned since *St. Valentine's* was a major studio shoot that I had extra time from my associate producer duties to work on something for Roger's company. I tried and tried to get a handle on the story but no matter what I did I just couldn't figure it out. A damaged soldier from the Vietnam War that slowly went further and further down the road to self destruction—it was a real black comedy. I told my father I was really stuck, and stuck bad. At that time (1967) Roger said I was America's angriest young man. Dad kept critiquing me and that only made things worse. Simply put, it was out of my league. I begged Dad to write a treatment. In exchange he could sit on my '50 Hatteras in the marina with his typewriter and give me a fabulous lesson. I would in turn take him to Mexico in the summer with the big bucks I knew Roger would pay me. He laughed, 'Knowing Roger we'll be lucky if we have enough fuel to get out of the marina.' I countered that the good side was that all of the family will have worked for the legendary Mr. Corman. By year's end he had a 30-page treatment that would be the last thing he was ever to write, and it was fantastic. *P.O.P* or *Prisoner of Peace*. I am still very hopeful I can make it before I close out my career."

Paul also worked as Assistant Director on episodes of *Lock Up*, *The Donna Reed Show* and as second unit director in 1977 on episodes of *Happy Days*. For his feature films, he was assistant director on, among others, *Boxcar Bertha* (1972, directed by Martin Scorsese), and the Roger Corman films, *The Little Shop of Horrors* (1960), *The Terror* (1963) and *The Haunted Palace* (also 1963).

Meantime, Phil was keeping busy with writing projects and leasing out his beloved Bickersons. On November 21, 1956 he signed an AFTRA contract to supply the talents of Betty Kean and Lew Parker on *The Steve Allen Show* in NYC at the Hudson Theatre. He would receive $3,000 out of which he would pay Betty and Lew their fees. The performance would be on November 25 at 8–9 p.m. EST. The couple returned for a December 9 performance.

In April the following year Rapp signed with B&R Enterprises as Head Writer, and to write four programs (May 9, May 20, June 4, June 13, 1957) for the series *Washington Square* starring Ray Bolger, in New York City. Phil was to furnish the services of writer Richard Powell as well. Together they were to receive $5,500 per program. Then, on November 10, 1957 Rapp penned *The Chevy Show* for NBC, sponsored by the car maker. The hour-long musical-variety-program starred Tony Martin, Vera-Ellen, Nat "King" Cole, Red Buttons, and "special guest star," Joan Davis.

Phil and Joan Davis had had a stormy relationship a few years before when he had signed on to be "director for an audition television motion picture of a Joan Davis television program, including all preparation and rehearsals thereof" which was scheduled to start shooting on May 21, 1952. Rapp received $1,500 and, in effect, worked for Joan, as it was her production company. Rapp's contract included an option to produce 26 more shows, if the series sold to a network. The series was sold and Rapp's option went into effect, but he chose not to exercise it, due to the harsh demands of its star. And to have more time to devote to selling The Bickersons as a series. The series was *I Married Joan*.

Phil's official reply to Al Simon of Desilu Productions (where *IMJ* was being filmed) bore no trace of animosity:

August 19, 1952

It is with sincere regret that I advise you that I am forced to forego the direction of the Joan Davis TV series.

Since the sale of "It's The Bickersons," which, as you know I write and direct, is imminent, I feel it would be inimical to both our interests to carry the burden of the two shows. In all conscience I feel I could not do justice to Joan while I have any outside problems which might militate against giving my very best to her.

I'm happy to think that I was in some way responsible for making the picture that resulted in the sale of her show, and may I wish you and Joan a long, happy and successful life on TV.

Phil alleviated the stress between Bix pitching sessions by golfing. In April he had received a certificate from his beloved Hillcrest haven: "This is to certify that Philip Rapp is a member of the Walter Hagen Hole-in-One Club, having played in one stroke Hole Number 12 . . . 190 yards on the Hillcrest Golf Club Course, April 13, 1952."

By November, there was still No Sale. *Variety* announced, "Jack Denove, former TV production veepee at BBD&O, and Phil Rapp, writer-director, are in Gotham peddling the half-hour video series, THE BICKERSONS. Pair recently completed the first four of the series, a telefilm version of the show which had a long radio career and which recently was a segment on an hour-long DuMont variety stanza. Lew Parker and Virginia Grey are starred."

According to Paul Rapp, "A man named Jack Denove, whose occupation I do not recall, put up the money for the four pilots, and why four, I don't know. They were shot at the same studio that Desi and Lucy were shooting their pilots, both shows using the three-camera technique. Don and Francis did not want to do them, so Dad used Virginia Gregg and Lew Parker. They were filmed before a live audience and used an additional laugh track, which Dad hated. Dad and Jack peddled the pilots a number of places, but you must remember that TV in the U.S. was not even five years old at the time. The pilots were seen in Canada, and as far as I know, the fourth pilot was lost somewhere between Canada and the U.S.A., and we did not have any protection copies. One of these pilots, I illegally smuggled into England to Lady Weinstein, who was a producer of *Robin Hood* and offered me a sizable dowry to marry her daughter, Hannah Weinstein, a big producer in Hollywood today. We finally released *It's the Bickersons* ourselves on DVD (see bickersons.com), with other pieces which came from variety shows like Startime, Steve Allen, Ed Sullivan, etc."

One interesting bit of television history is the fact that *It's the Bickersons* was one of the first shows to use the three-camera, or multiple-camera, technique before a live audience, which covers the two most active characters plus a wide-shot of the entire room, each with its own camera. The set-up was less expensive to use, because it reduced the need for individual shot set-ups. Of course the technique had been around nearly since film began, but Desilu Studios was the one of the first, if not the first, to implement its use for live TV.

"I wrote a master's thesis in 1957 on the use of the three-camera technique in comedy TV," says Paul. "At that time, the only samples I could show were Dad's *Bickersons* pilots and *I Love Lucy*. Dad clearly understood the use of it. If you want to know, multiple cameras were not anywhere near new in the motion picture industry—going back to Cecil B. DeMille, as many as 19 cameras were deployed.

One of the big drawbacks was in the editing room, cutting all that footage together. Today with digital production, that problem is readily solved."

PHOTO GALLERY
SECTION TWO

Rapp the sportsman.

Phil and Frances Langford, October 1966.

Phil and Joel, relaxing over ukulele and cards.

Paul Rapp, 1954.

The Adventures of Hiram Holliday.

Contact sheet for *Deputy Seraph*.

Photo Gallery: Section Two

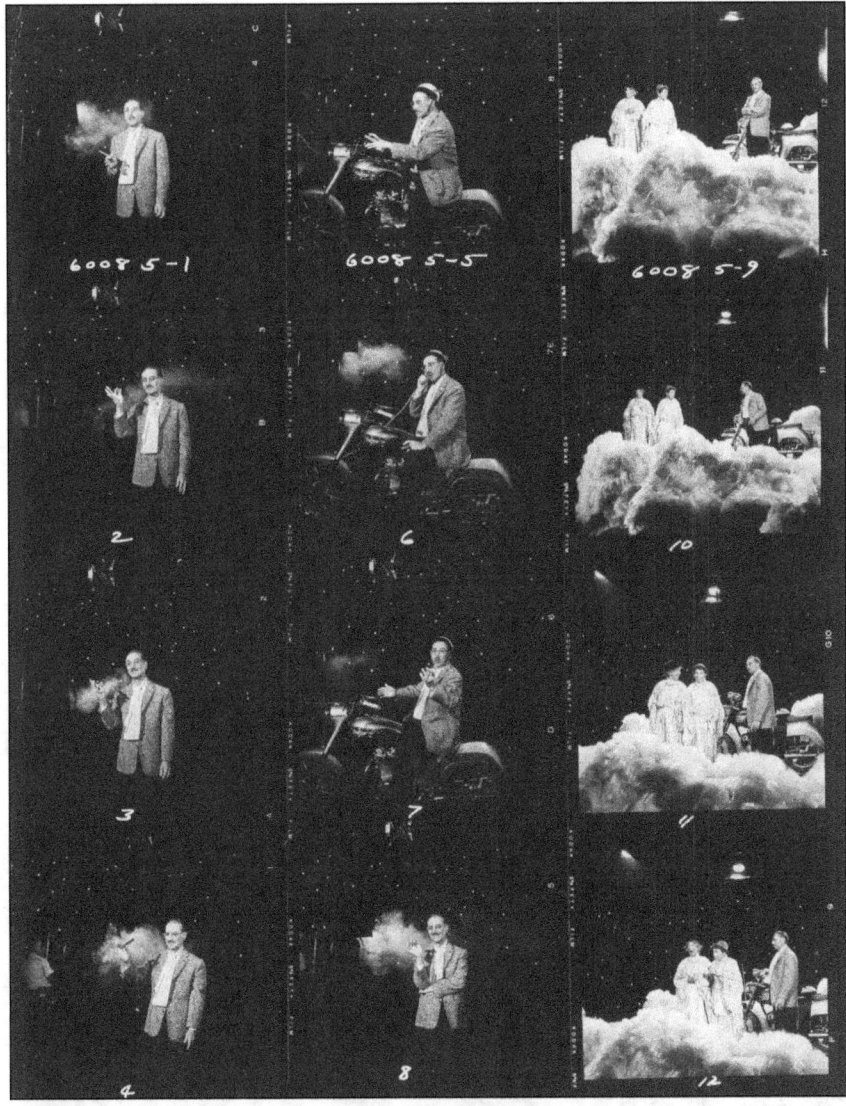

Ditto.

Phil directing his *Man of the House*. Assistant Director Paul Rapp is on the right.

Joel Rapp, ready for the prom, in the Oakhurst house, mid '50s.

Phil, Mariam and Joel at the Oakhurst house, all dressed up for Joel's high school graduation, circa 1950.

Writing *Match Please, Darling*, with Joel.

30th Street studio in New York, which was set up as a playhouse with a capacity audience for the occasion. Before the session got underway, Don and Frances warmed up for their roles by yelling at each other to get in character. With a promise from his wife that his favorite dinner (champagne and cold chicken) would be served after the session, Don Ameche went to work with his mouth watering. Here are a few highlights from the session:

You don't even know the meaning of the word matrimony, John Bickerson.

It's not a word, Blanche. It's a sentence!

Why don't you kiss me, John?

I can't. I'm not facing that way!

Where's my hat, Blanche?
In the ice box.

Where's my lunch?
In your hat!

A promo sheet for the Columbia Records recording of *The Bickersons* album.

CHAPTER 10
HIRAM HOLLIDAY

With *It's the Bickersons* being so uncertain, Philip Rapp kept visible and busy with a host of side projects. A contract between Rayben Television and Oil Company, Rapp, and comedian Ben Blue was drawn up on February 24, 1955 for Rapp to direct and produce a Blue TV pilot script for $2,800, the fee to be deferred until the property was sold to a network. Phil wrote a script called *Squeegee**, the name of Blue's character.

A budget was submitted on March 16, 1955 for "the Ben Blue pilot," which included a $1,500 payment per script, between $500 and $1,000 for an associate producer, $350 for canned music, and $1,650 for three days of stage space at Goldwyn Studios. If the series sold, Rapp would make a royalty of $850 per episode plus 10% of the net profits.

Rapp admitted, "Ben Blue, like Wynn, was a truly funny man, but could not handle dialogue. He moved like Chaplin."

Rapp was contracted to produce and direct the pilot, and to write one script with the assistance of another person "presently designated as Dick Powell [not the actor, but Richard M. Powell who would later pen a great number of *Hogan's Heroes, Gomer Pyle*, etc.]." Rapp was to receive $2,800, all deferred, with Powell to receive $1,500 cash. The script had to be delivered no later than April 1, and if the pilot was not produced within two years, or the filmed pilot was not sold within two years after its completion, all rights were to revert back to Rapp. If the series were sold, he could then go on to write and supervise the next twelve episodes for $2,500

---

* see *The Television Scripts of Philip Rapp*

each (which included his royalty). He would, however, have to get past the hurdle of making the pilot for $30,000 or less. His own budget sheet submitted to the studio brought it in at just less than $2,000 short of that.

Negotiations continued well into the next month, where budgets were slashed for cast, insurance, the associate producer, canned music and other necessities.

Richard M. Powell stated, "Phil and I worked together on other pilots, other projects. But it's hard to deal with the networks, hard to get a pilot on when you bring them an idea, but it's not quite what they want just then. They don't know, of course, exactly what they *do* want. That hasn't changed very much."

Indeed, *Squeegee* failed to sell, though the pilot was filmed.

Ben Blue call sheet

April 6, 1955

Shooting Call: 9:00AM
Stage 2

Squeegee — Ben Blue
Secretary — Phyllis Coates
Skinner — Jonathan Hole
Selby — Howard Wendell
Financier — John Banner
Young Man (night club) — Jack Richardson
Paulette — Monkey
Stand-in for Ben Blue — W. J. Thomas
Stand-in — Larry Mancine
Stand-in — Mary Jane Carey

Director — Philip Rapp
Asst. Director — Willard Reineck
2nd Asst. Director — Jack Doran
Production Manager — Herb Stewart

To supplement work, Rapp was back writing briefly for Eddie Cantor on *The Eddie Cantor Comedy Theatre*. A "Birthday Greetings" telegram sent by Eddie on March 25, 1955 told the same old working problems:

Dear Phil,
Mr. Platt and I are worried because it is getting quite late and the Pebeco script has not arrived. Certainly with Eddie Davis and Matt Brooks helping you should be able to get out 14 minutes of dialogue. And I think in the future we should cut out some of the Ida-No Son jokes [Eddie had only daughters]. May I suggest too that we put one or two original jokes in the script as I find Phil Baker & Beetle and Bottle are using the same jokes a week earlier than our Pebeco show. I suppose because this is your birthday I won't be getting the script until Sunday. Remember we have a preview at 12 noon so please be there so we can mark off the laughs. I was going to send you a present for your anniversary but if you are so negligent in not having the material on time to check with you. Congratulations nevertheless.
Eddie Cantor

Television was and is a hard business, even for the most seasoned professional. "You're only as good as your last picture" was/is an optimistic phrase that needs a rewrite. "Keep proving you're good enough" is the wisest unfair adage to apply to TV decision makers, when writers continue to get older and thick layers of new executives and directors continue to grow younger. Of course, Phil found himself in the uphill struggle of the former category, never without a new idea or pitch, but with much less patience to prove himself to foundlings who weren't eager to watch the old stuff. They wanted surefire hits, they wanted *modern*; ideas to appeal to cross-demographics and notions and scripts already based on proven formulas and recognizable laugh-getters. Phil found himself tired and weary in this new-old business since it wasn't the creative side that counted. You had to be a full-time salesman—and *full of energy.*

Once, long ago, in 1939, there was an adventure novel by Paul Gallico called *The Adventures of Hiram Holliday,* about a mild-mannered newspaper copywriter who, having saved his paper a bundle in a libel case, goes off to see the world with his handsome bonus. There, in the world, he has amazing escapades: sword fighting on the Appian Way, saving a princess from Nazis, and many other exploits, proving himself a heroic thrill-seeker.

It was a strange idea for a TV series, which is probably why Phil Rapp was so keen on it. As he told interviewer Ted Newson, "It began with a short story by Paul Gallico, which was rather downbeat. I bought the rights from him for $750, which is what you give for a tip nowadays. We expanded the idea and made it more whimsical and even Paul wrote and said he liked the series. We won an award with it, too—the very day NBC canceled the show. They had us on opposite *Disneyland* and Arthur Godfrey."

According to Phil's agent, George Gruskin (writing to Tom McAvity of NBC on June 9, 1956), the sale of *HH* went thusly: "When I took over Phil's representation again last fall, after a hiatus in our relationship of many years, I encouraged him to concentrate on the *Hiram Holliday* project with NBC; and because I thought the treatment of such a project in the hands of his unique talents would result in an outstanding series, I did nothing at all to distract him from this pursuit—although there were many independent projects, including his own packages which he could have taken advantage of with equal success, that were available to us.

"When Phil's pilot was completed I returned to the coast for a short trip and then went back to New York for a while. While some members of your company seemed enthusiastic about the series, I found that saleswise nothing was happening at all. As one of your close associates put it, 'The selling of the show had simply reached *dead center.*" I finally was able to secure a pilot from NBC, and went to work on the sale of the show myself, because in view of its freshness and obvious appeal and strength, I felt it would be a crime against nature if the show was not pushed and exposed to all possible sponsors who had or could have time on NBC.

"I returned to the coast when Rod Erickson of Young and Rubican, and John Brady of General Foods, came out here 'to find a show.' I pursued *Hiram Holliday* with them avidly, but had great difficulty in interesting Brady because Wally Cox was absolute anathema to him. He didn't want to look at the pilot at all because he told me frankly a half a dozen times that he literally *hated* Wally Cox as a performer.

"Finally, because of Rod's belief in my description of the show, and in my opinion of Rapp's tremendous talent and experience and the fact that this was a different Wally Cox than the public had ever seen, I was able to corner Brady with Rod's assistance. Brady and Erickson agreed to view the pilot at our office and to meet with Phil at the same time in order to discuss the scope and plans for the series beyond the pilot. I had had Phil prepare several dozen exciting story springboards.

"When Brady saw the film and listened to Phil's presentation of future planning, he changed his attitude completely and before he and Rod left our screening room they both said this was the best show they had seen for their purpose and the one they definitely wanted."

The half-hour comedy series starred Wally Cox, fresh off his starring role in/as *Mr. Peepers*, as Hiram, a timid-looking newspaper man who could seemingly do *anything*: sword fight, box, ride horses, speak any language, clout ruffians three times his size. Joel (Ainslie Pryor), his faithful sidekick, was also a reporter. Together, they circled the globe (always filmed in an NBC studio) for twenty-three episodes, finding villains to thwart and beautiful damsels to rescue, proving you just can't judge a nerd by his glasses.

On July 9, 1956, Rapp signed on as freelance director for thirty-nine half-hour television films to be made as *The Adventures of Hiram Holliday* at a salary of $750 per film. By Halloween, Rapp was already fighting over the use of the laugh track, which they originally insisted on. Now, the powers that be felt that "this predominantly action series is slowed up by the laugh track," and that "forceful music would do more to hurry the plot along and to punctuate the action." They (Rod Erickson, Vice President of Young & Rubicam, and others) contradicted themselves by wanting Rapp to start experimenting with the use of canned laughs: inject more in at strategic moments or eliminate the device entirely. They were also seeking to "sharply reduce the prologue so that we can get into as much action as quickly as possible."

Joel Rapp recalled, "I have very few memories of *Hiram*. I wrote three or four episodes, I think. A blacklisted writer named Richard

M. Powell was my father's partner, writing most of the shows, and I remember my father had a lawyer named Martin Gang who made it possible for Dick to get Screen Credits on the show. Dick eventually served a couple of terms as president of the WGA.

"Wally Cox was a quiet little guy. Marlon Brando was his best pal and we spent a few lunches together. One of the regular 'shticks' on the show had Hiram dueling someone or another, using his umbrella. Two of Hollywood's greatest fencers that taught him how, and one always stood in for his opponent."

Phil loved Wally Cox, calling him "articulate, literate and athletic. He could handle any stunt. He was a tireless worker who knew his lines to perfection and needed very little direction, but questioned almost everything. He learned to fence with the skill of a *master*."

The New York Herald Tribune's review of the premier episode stated: "Although it told an incredible story, *The Adventures of Hiram Holliday* on NBC last night (8–8:30) provided humorous Wally Cox with a TV showcase that far exceeds the appeal of the beloved 'Mr. Peepers' characterization. It is a charmer of a show which gets right down to the business of dispensing wholesome entertainment." After a description of the character and pilot, it concluded: "The show generously serves an entertaining blend of sparkling dialogue, fine direction and a disarming character. It is pure unadulterated fiction (courtesy of Paul Gallico) and one of the most refreshing half hours of the season."

Another reviewer commended Rapp's smoothly flowing direction and "while no individual scene caused any extreme heights of hilarity, the entire half hour was loaded with chuckles, a situation which seems to typify the entire series, one which we hope will be around for a long time." The *New York Times*' Jack Gould, was also highly complimentary, citing that Rapp did a fine adaptation and stayed true to Gallico's original character, and that Cox did indeed look mousey enough. But "from the standpoint of the more addicted Holliday fan there is a rub or two. It was a little hard to escape the conclusion that Mr. Cox was portraying Mr. Cox somewhat more than Mr. Holliday." Gould wished there was a more childlike essence to the character, as it is in the book, and wanted more surprise rather than the usual bold confidence with his every move. He also didn't care for Joel Smith's character having to step out of character to give the middle commercial. "It is really an intrusion on the viewer and on the play."

Critic John Lester wrote advance praise for *HH* because of his admiration for Wally Cox and even greater admiration and respect for Phil's show business know-how and writing talents. It was a rave in his February 22, 1957 syndicated column which later turned to eating his words when he began *viewing* the series. He had to write the truth, regardless of his friendship with Rapp.

Still, the series had a lot of positive media going for it, and NBC was rigorously campaigning for more viewers. Their November 16, 1956 advertising report for *HH* showed that on October 2–3 there were 25 on-the-air announcements, 12 the following day, and 20 on September 27. Since October 3 there had been 74 network on-the-air announcements with an estimated 302,000,000 ARB Viewer Impressions worth $306,000. A 400-line ad was placed in New York, Chicago, Los Angeles and Philadelphia newspapers on October 3, and the same in 100 other papers. "On October third," the report read, "HOLLIDAY had a 600-line Wednesday night block ad in New York, Chicago, Los Angeles, etcetera, papers. In addition, NBC offered to co-op this 600-line ad with all stations carrying the show. Six film trailers have been prepared for both network and individual stations. *HH* is included in weekly announcements of all major nighttime shows, over and above regular on-the-air spots."

People were aware of the series, and they watched it. A week before Christmas Phil received a congratulatory telegram proclaiming that *HH* had been voted "one of the top three most unique new programs" and in the "top three best comedy film series" from a poll conducted by *Television Today*, comprised of television editors and columnists.

But not *enough* people were watching. The Advance Nielsens ratings had come in, showing the series to have one of the lowest ratings of the Christmas season. *HH* was 101 out of 150 nighttime shows. It was the beginning of the end, but no one was giving up without a fight.

In a December 19 letter to Rapp from the vice president of Young & Rubicam (the ad agency behind *HH*), Rodney Erickson, wrote, "Let us assume for the moment that professional people, intellectuals and industry leaders have enthusiastically accepted everything you are doing with 'Hiram Holliday.' Let us also assume that the basic premise of this series is potentially tops—the little man who, self taught, can accomplish great physical and mental feats, should be the idol of everyone. We must, therefore, conclude that the show has been too good. The satire, the subtleties, the play on languages and names, will go down in the annals of telecasting as a superb bit of writing, but the show, as it stands now, will go down in the rating books as a commercial failure."

The suggested appraisal for an overhaul, however, was more disheartening. "First, most of the scripts lack enough humorous physical action distributed throughout the body of the shows. Let's use the 'Swiss Titmouse' as an example.

"Second, there is an overwhelming amount of repetition of pattern and plot from show to show." Rather than continuous jokes, the ad man took exception to sword play in the final scene as becoming too monotonous in the series. "Variety and mass audience appeal" is what he wanted, to compete with Arthur Godfrey and *Disneyland*.

The third problem was with the "contrived nature of the plot structure. When the policemen suddenly appear from nowhere the audience doesn't see this as burlesquing the formula, but rather contributing to it."

In short, broad humor and situations were sought to survive with clients, and compromise was needed if Rapp were to salvage anything. Erickson suggested Rapp forsake the writing and directing and concentrate on being executive producer "in order to give you ample time to develop a new version of a great idea." Regardless, it would certainly mean starting over from scratch, something Phil Rapp had absolutely no desire to attempt. Erickson promised a substantial publicity campaign if he could put in "more boxing and gymnastic feats of the Douglas Fairbanks type, in a familiar locale."

Fan mail poured in and was shared with Rapp directly. A January 8, 1957 report from the Radio-TV Mail Dept. of Young & Rubicam Advertising showed 67 praises, 70 photo requests, six critical comments, five mentions of the product (Sanka, Jell-O pudding and pie filling—General Foods Corp.), and 31 letters to Wally Cox. One letter from a Mrs. Stoner of Clinton, Tennessee, states, "It's hard to tell which one we enjoy most. Your TV program or your Instant

Coffee. I'm not much of a TV fan, but I drop everything I'm doing, no matter what, to watch *Hiram* (we like Joel, too)—that Hiram, so sweet looking, that innocent stare, and he always wins out—no matter what he gets into—that look on his face is what gets me—where in this world did you find such a guy—he's perfect for that part."

One executive from Young & Rubicam, Inc., *Hiram*'s advertiser, was concerned that more press was going to Wally Cox than "Hiram," the character he was playing. "If one were to cast this role ideally, it would probably be with someone who is physically more robust and possibly better looking." But, they'd agreed before the series started that Wally was perfect for the role. "Since his physical equipment is certainly adequate, you may want to show more scenes with Wally indicating his actual strength in order to further the believability of his exploits."

Ratings didn't improve—and being on opposite *Disneyland* did *not* help—but things kept going, and in January of 1957 Rapp and Powell were contracted to write "The Adventure of the Invisible Man" episode of *Hiram* ($2,500 to Powell, $500 to Rapp who also received $1,500 for its direction). Phil usually received $1,500 per episode for producing and directing, and a royalty payment of $250 per show. One such episode, "The Adventure of the Amontillado," filmed over February 12–14, 1957, had a total submitted budget of $37,926. This was the era of the 39-episode season, not the usual 12 or 26, which it is now.

The problem with filming an adventure show was that it always had to have new sets and characters. That and the sliding ratings were the deciding factors in *Hiram*'s demise. When budgets for the next ten episodes were submitted on November 16, 1956, the writing was on the proverbial wall. The costs of the productions had nothing to do with the length of time involved or footage shot, but with the number of set-ups (scenes, set construction) that had to be filmed, plus a large cast. The average shooting time took approximately 32 hours per picture. Five hours overtime would cost the production around $1,500. Show #2602, titled "The Adventure of the Lapidary Wheel" cost $7,985 for the cast, $3,580 for the story, $1,325 for supervision, and a mere $750 for direction. The total cost came out to $42,575.

"The Adventure of the Hollow Umbrella": $46,403.
"The Adventure of the False Monarch": $39,027.
"The Adventure of the Gibralter Toad": $36,768.
"The Adventure of the Sea Cucumber": $39,093.
"The Adventure of the Monaco Hermit Crab": $38,171.
"The Adventure of the Hawaiian Hamzah": $40,325.
"The Adventure of the Dancing Mouse": $35,953.
"The Adventure of the Romantic Pigeon": $36,751.
"The Adventure of the Swiss Titmouse": $43,867.
"The Adventure of the Wrong Rembrandt": $33,006.

The series was just too expensive to maintain, and the network did what all the villains in the world couldn't: they killed Hiram Holliday.

At its cancelation, Donald Freeman of the *San Diego Union* ran a tribute to the hard luck of the show. Quoting Phil Rapp, it stated that the show didn't have a chance due to its placement up against rival networks' *Disneyland* on ABC and Arthur Godfrey on CBS. "In any other time spot," said Rapp, "I'm convinced *Hiram Holliday* would have doubled its rating." *Mr. Peepers* had followed the same curse, being up against Jack Benny and *What's My Line?* at various times. Still, both series kept a resolute, dedicated following.

"Actually," wrote Dave Freeman, "when such shows are choked off, it is television itself which suffers the most grievous loss because its scope, which could be so vast, becomes that much narrower, its potential that much less fulfilled."

A series of letters poured in expressing the regret of the show's demise. One viewer wrote: "We also wept for *Mr. Peepers* departure, too. With all the 'junk' on TV why do they have to go and cancel this fine show? We're going to trade our set in for a record player. Growl!" Another wrote, "I also regret the demise of Wally Cox's *Hiram Holliday* show because it was different albeit following a sameness of plot. Cox is good. He is head and shoulders above the rock 'n' roll artists that are legion . . ."

There were also quite a number of "please don't cancel Hiram!!" letters sent to Phil Rapp by fans through the studio, which he kept.

The official letter from NBC confirming the cancelation came on January 31, 1957. Just 21 days before, Phil was paid $1,500 for producing and directing "The Adventure of the Surplus General" episode. It was estimated that it would cost $54,025 (not counting financial obligations to Rapp) to stop production of *HH* after the initial 26 episodes. The biggest cost, at $32,500, would be for stage rentals already contracted. These costs were estimated on previous costs: $60,000 for the pilot show, and $983,355 for the remaining 25 shows. The estimated cost to complete each remaining show was a mere $800.

Advertising man Rod Erickson still believed in *Hiram* enough to set up meeting between Rapp and Hannah Weinstein at Sapphire Films in London in June of 1957. He called Hiram "probably ahead of its time in television, but would make an excellent vehicle for Alec Guinness in a fast-moving feature movie." Also pitched to Hannah was Rapp's "hilarious" Merlin the Magician treatment, and, of course, the Bickersons, which Phil had hoped to have done at the Palladium Theatre. Rod emphasized Phil's native Britishness and the fact that he had access to capital in England.

Around 1967 *Hiram* was sold for a run on the BBC to be broadcast in London, Germany, and Switzerland. On August 25, 1967, NBC issued a distribution report on *HH* for the period ending June 30th of that year; the show had lost the network $353,388.39, even though it had earned $245,089 in cumulative sales ($69,271 domestic and $175,818 international).

Perhaps the series *was* cursed. Following the cancelation, on May 27, 1958, Ainslie "Joel" Pryor died from cancer at the young age of 36.

Paul Rapp states, "I thought Hiram was one of the best series of all time in that it was a highly intelligent James Bond. Wally Cox was a unique character. I think that today it would still make a great series or motion picture. I always felt that the time slot was its downfall. Plus, it cost so much money to make it as a TV show then, since the sets and locations had to change every week. Wally was able to be so many different characters, and, in fact, there was one show where he played seven parts. It shows how clever my father was in being able to pull that off visually."

George Gruskin at the William Morris Agency was very eager to get Rapp working on new properties for the coming television new year (1957–58). A lot of cancellations were rumored and more pilots would be wanted for screening. Phil was in England at the time and George wanted to set up meetings with some people about the number of English production deals cooking. He also wanted any other series ideas Phil might have.

Phil had plenty of them.

CHAPTER 11
JOAN DAVIS AND THE MARX BROTHERS

Early in 1956 Phil had exchanged letters with a writer who wanted to do a film of Mickey Spillane's second Mike Hammer novel, *My Gun Is Quick*, to be shot in Paris, but when rights to do the property fizzled, nothing apparently progressed with it. There was talk by director Victor Saville of making the story a "non-Spillane" script with Robert Mitchum in the title role of a renamed Hammer, but it seemed there was little point of doing Mike Hammer without the name Mike Hammer.

At this time in his life, Phil Rapp just wanted to write. He was bursting with ideas and treatments after (and during) *Topper*, but like most properties, more ideas fell through the cracks than were picked up by Hollywood producers. After the huge success of *I Married Joan*, Joan Davis was eager to have another go at a series, this time trying her hand at that cross-demographics which the producers were targeting. One of Phil Rapp's most celebrated projects was the pilot for Joan's new adventure-comedy series, *Joan of Arkansas*, written and directed by Rapp. It was a mixture of outer-space picture and comedy, starring Joan as an unlucky dental assistant who is drafted by her country to become the U.S.A.'s first female astronaut. She was chosen by a very stupid computer, and as a result has to endure the most harrowing, weirdly sophisticated aeronautical tests ever devised by NASA in order to get into shape to go *up there*.

The NBC budget for the pilot was put together two days before Christmas of 1957. Rapp's "supervision" credit (which included story and direction, but not a producer's fee) was inked in at $6,540, with the cast to receive $6,035. Total cost, with music, camera, props, insurance and everything else: $60,011.

Rapp and Davis enjoyed working together more this time around, but it failed to hit with the network.

Phil's November 22, 1957 outline of the *Joan of Arkansas* pilot read as follows:

> History is replete with legends of courageous women who saved a city, a nation, or a continent—but here's the story of one such heroine whose destiny was to save the world. Her name is Joan Jones, and she was born and has spent most of her life in Hot Springs, Arkansas. She is a dental nurse, the adoring right hand of Dr. Ferguson, a steady, good-looking but humorless, confirmed bachelor.
>
> Most of Joan's pay goes to help support her indigent father, a very attractive rogue who is no better than he should be, loves to eat and take an occasional nip, hates work, and, in short, has all the vices that make you fall in love with him. Joan is the second child in this motherless family, has a genuine affection for her older brother, John, who is fiftyish, fat and fussy, and loves her younger sister, Jane with an almost maternal passion. It is quite possible that none of the aforementioned people, with the exception of Joan, will ever appear in the series. It is important, however, to know our heroine's background, her family and her attitude towards them.
>
> Some fifteen hundred miles away, in a town which must be nameless for security reasons, a huge and complicated machine that makes Univac look as primitive as a Chinese abacus, is electronically shaping the destiny of Joan Jones of Hot Springs, Arkansas. For over two years, under the watchful eyes of three of America's leading scientist-psychologists, the infallible thinking machine has been at work, incessantly sifting, sorting, separating, taking apart in infinite detail each and every American adult.
>
> The electronic brain, specifically designed for this purpose, is eventually going to arrive at the name of one person who can be considered *completely* normal, according to the requirements and specifications laid down by the three scientist-psychologists. The search is constantly narrowing, and the one selected will then begin an intensive five-year training and conditioning program preparatory to becoming the first human to make a

trip to the moon, the subject, of course, being willing to engage in the project. The fateful moment arrives and the computer wearily discharges the name of the selectee—the *absolutely* normal adult. The scientists had never heard of Joan Jones of Hot Springs, Arkansas, naturally, but Joan now becomes not just a huge index card, but a living martyr to science and very possibly the protector of the peace of the world. Plans are made instantly to contact this most normal of all American adults.

At the very moment of decision we find Joan, the most normal of American adults, at lunch in her cubby-hole of a dental lab. She is eating her usual chow mein sandwich, and cracks an occasional walnut in the modeled uppers and lowers reposing on the bench. Whatever else she is engaged in will give silent testimony that the infallible thinking machine goofed. But that's neither here nor there. She has been selected, and therein lies the series.

Bribery, cajolery, promises of fame and riches fail to impress Joan when she is conducted to a top-secret meeting at the Pentagon, and despite pressure from her scamp of an old man who has been promised tons of loot and servants, Joan remains firm. She has no desire to go to the moon, no taste for the training and conditioning program—all she wants is to go back to Arkansas and live her own normal life, in an abnormal sort of way.

As a last resort she is ushered before the President, who makes a personal plea. She is assured that at no time will she be in any danger, she will be accompanied at all times during the five-year period by a scientist-psychologist who will record her reactions, and even a bodyguard in case there is some unforeseen emergency. Also, it is made quite clear that she will not be sent to outer space until experiments have proved that her return to earth can be accomplished with ease and no peril. She wavers, and a direct appeal to her patriotism makes her capitulate.

This is the launching point. It now becomes the design of the series to show day-to-day incidents, tribulations, and involvements in the life of Joan of Arkansas as she is groomed for the momentous trip. Like Pavlov's famous dog, long before Laika in Sputnik, she has to submit to some mighty strange conditioning. Let it be noted that the scientist-psychologist who is appointed to accompany her and record her emotions, reflexes, and reactions to any given situation, whether the situation is designed or accidental, is a skeptic who never did quite trust the selection of the electronic brain. Time and again, of course, he is proved right, but he is constantly overruled. During some of the wilder episodes he will wish he had never been born.

In an early test to determine her resourcefulness under trying conditions, Joan is placed on a deserted island with little or no provisions. At least, everybody *thought* it was a deserted island. What Joan comes up with baffles science and almost scuttles the entire project.

Thrust into a situation where she must pose as a waitress in the United Nations dining hall to supply the scientists with data regarding her diplomacy, Joan creates enough havoc to start the third World War.

Another test for shock reactions calls for Joan to be accidentally found in the locker room at the Army-Navy football game. Needless to say she winds up carrying the winning touchdown for Army.

Each incident created will probably have to start with the scientific group outlining the experiment or assignment for the day, week, or month. This gives us a sustaining set of characters and a focal point from which to operate.

Sooner or later Joan will have to be introduced to the weird vehicle that will eventually take her to the moon. Her experiences in the dry run can provide pretty funny stuff.

On March 19, 1958 Phil signed a contract as writer for two *Joan of Arkansas* scripts: "Joan Joins the Army" (probably the pilot), and "The Five-Minute Brainwash," signing as an employee of Joan Davis, to be paid $750 per delivered story treatment. A separate contract signed him up to direct for $1,500 per episode.

A month before, Joan snagged Phil's old friend Dick (that is, Richard M.) Powell to write two more episodes of the series: "The Undeserted Island" and "Introducing Renard" for the sum of $750 per story (to be completed within 14 days), and, provided the options were exercised, $750 for the first draft teleplay and $1,000 for the final draft teleplay. Joel Rapp also signed up to pen "The Changeling" for Joan under similar specs.

From the start there were money woes. NBC revised the series' budget and submitted it to the William Morris Agency. It cut corners on "the supporting star" by $500, the supporting cast and extras by $500 and set construction by $1,000 "on the basis that the standing rigged sets at U-I would be used to advantage through script control." Now the entire cast was to receive $4,850, with story and supervision budgeted at $75 and $840. The complete budget this time was a mere $30,569 per show.

However, just a few short months later this budget was nearly doubled. The cast shot back up to $6,025, supervision to $7290. The total: $58,628, with $52,543 already having been used as of March 3, 1958. Two days later a three-week report to NBC indicated the budget at $60,986.60. The budget was for three days of shooting per picture for ten hours per day; three pictures were to be shot in two weeks followed by a one-week rest.

Only the pilot was filmed, which NBC bought.* Phil did write an outline for the follow-up episode (included in Appendix 4 of this book), but tragically, no further plots were filmed, and Phil and Joan would never work together again. Joan Davis died of a heart attack in 1961, at the young age of 53.

As one of the famed members of the prestigious Hillcrest Country Club, Phil knew Groucho, Harpo and Chico Marx from their many hours of playing cards, drinking and swapping stories. He loved Harpo the most, and told interviewer Ted Newson, "Groucho, a knife-edged wit, would walk into the dining room to me and my wife and say to her, 'Oh, sitting alone again, are you?' Chico, the lovable rogue, would sit around the Round Table, lively and a born gambler. He'd say, 'Give me $100 to make a bet for you at the track—it can't lose!' It was like giving a cabbage leaf to a rabbit: forget it, he's going to eat it. But you did it anyway, he was such a sweet guy."

Having so much talent in front of him, Phil knew it would be

---

* The script for the pilot was reprinted in *The Television Scripts of Philip Rapp*, in 2007.

wise to try to get the guys together one last time. Chico needed the money, and Harpo was such a genial soul, there was no trouble getting him on board. Groucho was the key, and the lock. But first, he and longtime collaborator Richard Powell needed a pilot script.

Phil came up with notion—*Deputy Seraph*. The Marx Brothers in heaven. He and Powell structured the show so that very little would be required of the aging comedians. Phil explained, "The basic idea was, the other players in the story would become hosts for the spirits of Chico, Harpo and Groucho, and act in their manner. If I had a dowager in a fine restaurant or something, she's suddenly take a cigar from somebody, wiggle her eyebrows, and walk with a lope, and you'd know Groucho was there. You'd see a stuffy concert pianist suddenly shoot the keys with his finger and you'd know Chico was behind it, or somebody handing someone else their leg like Harpo."

A pilot script was written—and nearly filmed—in which Angel Second Class Chico, Able-Bodied Cherub Harpo, and Deputy Seraph Groucho, are given an assignment: to ensure that beautiful Linda Pavane and her American suitor, Paul MacDowell, are married by 8:30 that evening. Looking down at the couple from their clouds, it seems like an easy-enough project. But wait! She must have the permission of her temperamental piano-virtuoso Uncle Caesar first, and fortune-hunter Andre Lazar is blackmailing Uncle into letting *him* marry Linda. All three Marx brothers involve themselves in this dilemma, which includes angelic inhabitation of mortals' bodies now and then, with hilarious results. At the very last minute and against all odds, the marital feat is accomplished as Linda becomes Mrs. Paul MacDowell.

Phil described the series' hook this way:

DEPUTY SERAPH
(WRITTEN MAY 1, 1958)

This, I believe, is a brand-new approach to a serio-comic anthology series. It was expressly designed for, and has the complete blessing of, Groucho Marx as the un-cherublike seraph.

As the title implies it deals in part with fantasy—but even the ethereal portion cannot help but take on an earthy quality when

we meet the brazenly flippant Groucho lolling on his private cloud casing the workaday world below . . . his puckish observations orchestrated by his eloquent gestures with his ever-present cigar coupled with his inimitable sly manner.

The viewer soon learns he isn't a full-fledged angel—this with a raffish flexing of the Marx eyebrows—he is sort of probationer getting on-the-job training. Hence his title, Deputy Seraph—no relation to the current crop of Westerns.

He flashes his badge of office—a small pair of angel wings—and delivers an expository monologue, liberally peppered with Grouchoisms, explaining the nature of his work. At times he is pulled up short by a violent harp arpeggio, a constant reminder that he is under surveillance by the Boss. He shrugs off these musical admonitions quite inoffensively, for Groucho's stock in trade is his wonderfully insane, bold effrontery, and pretends momentarily to see the business at hand. In a confidential aside he lets you know that Henley, the author of "Invictus," didn't know what time it was. "I am the master of my fate—the captain of my soul" says the post Henley. "Horsefeathers," says the irreverent Groucho. "You have no control over anything. We pull the strings up here."

His work is laid out for him by the Chief Seraph, for the most part humdrum, routine stuff, guiding the lives of a set of dull people. Inevitably, Groucho's roving eye, his inability to keep his mind on business, and his general roguishness cause him to become involved in problems not on his beat. By the time he's through man-handling the earth-bound puppets, the strings are so hopelessly tangled that all seems lost. Somehow or other each episode reaches a denouement that is satisfactory, if a little rough on all the characters concerned.

During the course of each story, as Groucho himself makes it known, it will be necessary for him to appear down below—not as himself, of course, but nonetheless he will be the prime mover in many schemes. How will we recognize him? Simple. He will flash, quite surreptitiously and for the viewer's attention only, his pair of angel wings. This badge will identify him even though you'd swear you were looking at a suave French Croupier in Monte Carlo, a beautiful chorus girl among her lusty, busty fellows, or a tired racehorse plodding towards the starting gate at Santa Anita. Naturally the bearer of the wings will be endowed with all the character facets so closely identified with Groucho. Notice how the croupier leaves the roulette table after a remarkable coup—where before have you seen that crouching, leering walk? And to your utter astonishment the lovely chorine lights a cigar you could row a boat with. Was it an illusion or did you see that racehorse flex his eyebrows in a typical Marx fashion? You're quite right—Groucho will appear in many forms, inhabiting all types of bodies, animal and human. Curiously, this gives one a feeling that Groucho is actually playing these greatly diversified roles, even though common sense tells us it cannot be so.

Each story, peopled with fine actors, will establish its premise and be launched from the cloud through the extra-curricular intervention of Groucho. It will no doubt be imperative to cut back to him at times during the action, either for furtherance of plot or to find him defending himself against the onslaught of the irate harp.

I realize this merely is a skeletal structure, but I'm confident that if the stories are topflight, the actors ditto, and Groucho's picaresque character is adhered to closely, the general effect will result in a thoroughly novel presentation.

Groucho, a rather unhappy man according to Phil, was not pleased with having to do a second series during his hit show, *You Bet Your Life*, and needed a lot of convincing from Gummo, the agent of the group. Groucho knew all of Chico's money would go to bookies, and therefore wanted his salary placed in some sort of protective custody, to save Chico from himself. Harpo was just eager to work with his brothers again, even after having suffered a couple of heart attacks. The thirty-nine-episode series would be harder on Chico and Harpo, with Groucho only appearing in every third episode, for a total of 13 episodes. Groucho's bits would be short calls from heaven to the people in the plots (coming through on the other end as the voice of whatever character Groucho was inhabiting that week). Phil promised Gummo a Rolls-Royce if the series sold to the network. And Phil was a great salesman.

Just in case, however, he wrote up further notes, just in case Groucho proved too difficult to sign:

Deputy Seraph — now combining the talents of Groucho, Harpo and Chico Marx.

The original machinery as outlined in my synopsis dated May 1st, which is in the possession of James Swann, and later revised to suit Chico and Harpo without Groucho can now be easily made to function for all three brothers in the event it is your wish to add Groucho.

All three will be discovered in some celestial area, Chico with his little pointed hat, black curls and long white robe—he plays a piano that isn't there—Harpo, a ludicrous angel with his blonde wig, battered high hat, horn on a stick, also clad in a flowing white robe—he plays the instrument usually associated with heavenly figures, but we can see the harp—and Groucho as his raffish self, his leering walk and roguish flexing of the eyebrows punctuating the expository dialogue necessary at the opening of each film. While Groucho is the only one wearing a business suit, all three wear their badge of office, a small pair of wings, and flash it officiously as any policeman. On earth, in the body of the play, this badge will serve to identify them to the audience when they temporarily occupy the physical being of another person. It is quite conceivable that all three may have to descent to earth during any given story—their individual characteristics, that is, as portrayed by capable actors—or it might only be Harpo, or Groucho, or Chico. We will endeavor to keep this as flexible as possible, depending on the demands of the story.

I have been given to understand that if we add Groucho, he can only participate in thirty-nine pictures for a total of about an hour—some appearances naturally being longer than others—but it is my considered opinion that I can get across to the audience all that is necessary to maintain the illusion that all three run thru the entire series all the time.

The Marx Brothers' scenes were to be shot in Hollywood, with the bulk of the series to be shot in J. Arthur Rank's Pinewood

Studios (soon to be the fabled James Bond stage) in England. For a percentage of the show and overseas rights, Phil financed the show easily now that all three brothers were on board. But Rapp kept things quiet about the project until he knew a hit was forthcoming. "Too much of advance publicity and they piss on you when you fall down," he later stated.

The simple set in California Studios (which Phil partly owned) was lit by stars in the background and a cotton-covered stage to replicate a rather cheap looking heaven. Chico and Harpo appeared in white silk angel's robes, with halos for each, Harpo's being made of cake dough so he could eat it on camera.

Phil seemed to gravitate towards fantasy: *Walter Mitty*, *Topper*, etc. He had completed a script by April 30, 1959, so the brothers' scenes—the only ones shot (18 minutes' worth)—began filming in late June of 1959 while *You Bet Your Life* was on summer hiatus. At first, even though Chico was ill, Groucho insisted on having his scenes (usually separate from his brothers) filmed first. Rapp explained, "Groucho was difficult to direct. A tough man. For instance, I had a wind machine going while he was sitting on a stationary motorcycle, arriving in Heaven from somewhere out in space. He wouldn't permit the wind machine to give the illusion of flight. Luckily, I had some experience with trick photography. Johnny Fulton helped out on the early *Toppers*, and you can't get better than that. So I tied the scarf on his neck and had a man off-screen pulling it with a string to give the illusion of whipping in the wind."

Though desperate for the chance at a new series, Chico just wasn't feeling well enough to capture the magic of his character this time. Rapp stated, "There was one particular line that Chico kept blowing. He didn't seem extremely alert. And I remember Groucho really getting pissed. In fact, I don't remember Groucho talking to his brothers on the set at all, except during a take." Paul also recalled the communication problem: "I was assistant director and I had to speak for Groucho to his brothers. I found this despicable, but it wasn't the only time I had to act as interpreter on a set."

It wasn't this lack of harmony that would kill *Deputy Seraph* from becoming a series. While Phil went to England to show off to Rank what had been done so far, Chico had failed to pass the physical that would insure its stars with the studio—insurance was needed so that the studio could recoup any loses in case production had to be halted and all that work wouldn't be wasted. The 18 minutes wound up being wasted anyway, and Phil's biggest chance at another—what would have been his final—original TV series was gone.

Phil told interviewer Ted Newson, "You know what kind of a blow that is? All my own money, nearly $50,000 out of my pocket, gone. I said, 'Isn't there some way around this? Couldn't somebody piss in a bottle for him? Something?' No. His medical man assured me before shooting that he was fine, and he was always active around the club. Maybe something happened in the meantime. I'd never even thought of it. If I had any brains at all, I would've made sure. And I suppose I would've had grounds to sue the boys, but I didn't have the heart."

There was a suit anyway. By April 28, 1959, Marvin B. Meyer, representing Phil, Harpo, Groucho, Gummo and Chico, was preparing to file suit against Sol Lesser Productions and Sydney Box Television Limited for breach of an oral contract. Each of the defendants was to receive $1,000 of the $40,000 budget for each episode of *Deputy Seraph*. Also Rapp was to have received $3,000 for each new picture as executive producer and story supervisor for the entire series, plus 25% of the profits. Groucho was to have been in thirteen of the thirty-nine films in sequences not longer than 1.5 minutes per film; for this he would have received $3,500 per picture, plus a new Rolls Royce for use in America or England for the duration of the series. Harpo and Chico would have received $4,000 jointly for each film plus 25% of the net profits from any and all sales, with the stipulation that they would not appear in any other television series, except guest appearances approved by Rapp. Gummo was to have received $2,000 for each film. The scripts were budgeted at $3,500 each, with directing inked in at $1,250 per episode. Groucho had script approval on his 13 films, to be shot at California Studios in Los Angeles (as were Chico and Harpo's scenes). The remaining scenes were to be filmed at Pinewood Studios, Iver Heath, Buckinghamshire, England; the Marx Brothers were contractually obligated to travel to Pinewood Studios once for make-up shots. Groucho's 13 shows were to have been written first.

Rapp's suit was for $42,250, Groucho asked for $45,500 (plus $2,000 for no Rolls Royce), Chico and Harpo together filed for $195,000, and Gummo for $78,000. The law offices of Beilenson, Meyer, Rosenfield & Susman were to take one-half of the total recovery fee.

On August 29, 1960, Rapp wrote to his attorney Peter Cohen of the Beilenson, etc. offices to give him a detailed history of the agreements behind *Deputy Seraph*.

Dear Peter:
Here is the chronology, to the best of my recollection, of the events relating to the *Deputy Seraph*-Weintraub-Hayutin-Swann-Box deal:

Late in October 1958, George Gruskin, then head of TV at the William Morris Agency and my personal representative, introduced me to James Swann. Mr. Swann, representing Sydney Box, a division of J. Arthur Rank's organization in England, was in America to finance several TV series to be made abroad.

At our first meeting, in Gruskin's office, I told Swann of my format for a series called *Deputy Seraph*. Mr. Swann was immediately enthusiastic and arranged a second meeting with his American partners, Sy Weintraub and Harry Hayutin. This meeting took place a day or two later in Gruskin's office. My series idea was accepted unanimously and we agreed upon the casting. We selected Chico and Harpo Marx to play the leads. Negotiations were then started with Gummo Marx and Larry Beilenson. During the next week or two there were several meetings with regard to the project in Beilenson's office. Chico and Harpo Marx agreed to do the series. General terms acceptable to all were worked out.

In the middle of November I gave a dinner party at my home, on Maple Drive, for the Weintraubs, Hayutins, Swanns and Gruskins to celebrate the consummation of our deal.

The following week Weintraub asked for an early morning meeting at his home, 618 No. Rodeo Drive. Gruskin and Hayutin attended and it was then that Weintraub suggested that we strengthen the series by adding Groucho Marx. Once more we negotiated with Beilenson, Gummo, Groucho and NBC, since Groucho was under exclusive contract to NBC. We secured permission and agreed upon the terms of the deal.

Weintraub and the Swanns left for London late in November to set up studio facilities, crew, et cetera.

Shortly thereafter I met with Sam Sachs, of the William Morris Agency and Gummo Marx at Hillcrest Country Club to discuss final details relating to the deal. Sachs drew up a letter of agreement containing the terms.

Early in December I took Mr. and Mrs. Hayutin and Mrs. Weintraub to the Coconut Grove in Los Angeles.

A few days later, in response to a request from Mr. Weintraud in London regarding cast insurance, I met with Hayutin, Arthur Stebbins and David Stebbins, both insurance company representatives, at Hillcrest Country Club. Suitable terms for insurance were agreed upon, OK'd by Hayutin, and a binder was taken.

Hayutin talked to Weintraub on the phone, told him what had been accomplished, then suggested that I leave for London with the necessary insurance papers to close the deal there. I left on the 13th day of December 1958, and was met in London by James Swanna and his wife. They drove me to the Dorchester Hotel, where I registered, and they then took me to the Berkeley for dinner. The following morning I had a breakfast meeting at the Dorchester with Swann and Weintraub. The insurance question seemed settled and they arranged for me to meet with them and Sydney Box for lunch at Les Ambassadeurs. The series was discussed and there seemed to be no problems.

That evening we all met in the lobby of the Dorchester and a unit manager of Sydney Box's looked over my proposed budget for the series and pronounced it realistic and satisfactory. We had tea and cocktails and Box left. It was about an hour later that Weintraub told me that the treasurer of the Rank organization, John Davis, didn't like the Marx Brothers' deal. That was the first time I had heard his name. Weintraub suggested that I re-cast 'Deputy Seraph' with other performers. I refused.

On the 16th day of December I met once again with Weintraub and Box and they offered cast suggestions to replace the Marx Brothers. I couldn't accept them since we were all committed to Chico, Harpo and Groucho. I took Weintraub up to my suite and called Gruskin in New York. Weintraub spoke to him and explained the situation. I then took the phone again and Gruskin told me not to enter into more discussions since we had a firm deal. He advised me to leave for home immediately. I left London on the 17th of December, 1958.

Phil received several letters of congratulations on the "original, hilarious, and of course highly marketable" project from advertising people, after they read the script and before filming began. NBC had been first opportunity to schedule the pilot, but Groucho's contract read that *Deputy Seraph*'s "sponsor may not be one who is in any way competitive to the sponsors (or their products) of the current Groucho Marx *You Bet Your Life* series."

Deputy Seraph became the penultimate appearance of the three Marx Brothers on film together, though Phil had two further ideas for the Marx Brothers, which he wrote out on one of his usual joke file index cards:

SCOOP

A comedy idea for the Marx Bros. They run a newspaper—Groucho editing, Harpo a lynotyper, and Chico a reporter. Chico brings in so many scoops and Groucho rips out the front page so often they can't get one edition on the streets. Vice crusade.

Week in the Village

Greenwich Village! Artists—musicians—poets—writers—models—etc. Groucho—a starving artist. Maybe the last of the Van Dycks [sic]. Harpo—a Village violin maker and repairer. Chico—a hurdy-gurdy man with a monkey. Brings organ to Harpo to fix.

Scene in Art Museum. Harpo talking on violin!!! Harpo mimicking Groucho painting—uses water on oil—uncovers old master.

Monkey teaching Harpo tricks. Groucho uses Harpo and Chico for models. Artists display their wares on Village streets. They make their own exhibition—block party. Chico plays Hurdy-gurdy as piano.

Rapp owned (and still does own) the rights to *Deputy Seraph*, which has recently ended up on a DVD entitled *The Unknown Marx Brothers* (WinStar Home Entertainment, 1997). The film sat in Phil's garage for 21 years collecting dust, with little interest from film historians or fans alike. Only in recent years has the mini-project become infamous.

CHAPTER 12
THE 1960s CHANGES EVERYTHING

My mother told me in 1950 I would live to see $25 hamburgers and hot dogs. Well, I have—at the Peninsula Hotel in Beverly Hills and several other places.
—**Paul Rapp**

On May 20, 1959, Rapp received a letter from his attorney, Kupferman, finally announcing that the Gleason case had been marked for the trial calendar for the October term. He and Gleason's attorney, Eldridge, had gone into court that very day to discuss a rock-bottom settlement price, which Kupferman said was $10,000. Eldridge said he would give that figure to the Seaboard insurance company. Though it's unknown what the final settlement figure was (as this is the last amount mentioned in Rapp's papers), it's likely that this was the settlement which closed the case.

After the trial business of the letter was over, the New York attorney moved onto something new:

"I do not recall whether I ever spoke to you about the possibility of doing a musical comedy based on Pepe Romero's book *Mexican Jumping Bean*. If not, let me tell you the following:

"Romero writes a column in English for the English-language newspaper in Mexico, and also one in Spanish. He was a bit part actor in Hollywood many years ago, and is a painter and jack of all trades. He had an exhibition at the Hammer Galleries in New York some two years ago of his paintings, and also one in your area.

"Pepe has written a meandering outline of what the story could be about, and I think it would make an excellent musical comedy, with the opening setting in the lobby of the Del Prado Hotel in Mexico City, which is Pepe's office. E.g., he comes into his office, sits down on the couch in the lobby and asks for room service.

"The book can contribute little anecdotes, but the story will be basically the story of the columnist, an airline stewardess and a bullfighter.

"If you have any interest, I will send on to you a copy of the book and Pepe's outline, and if there is further interest, you can arrange to visit him in Mexico City and work there with one of the excellent Mexican composers.

"I think that once we get started, raising money for the production will not be difficult because Pepe has hundreds of friends throughout the United States, not only among celebrities but among tourists, many of whom he mentioned in his columns and with whom he corresponds."

The horror of *Spring in Brazil* was still probably darkly fresh in Phil's mind, even at the turn of the decade, but even so, Rapp had plenty of radio and television work to keep him occupied. As of May 1959 the Bickersons (Lew Parker and Betty Kean) were loudly snoring up radio commercials for General Motors via the D. P. Brother & Company Advertising Agency, and were receiving ample compliments from the bigwigs. At least three commercials were recorded (called simply "Train," "Seashore" and "Neighbors") and placed in shows such as *Monitor, Mitch Miller, Have Gun, Will Travel, Johnny Dollar, Suspense,* and *Gunsmoke,* from June 22 through July 26. They were one-minute ads for GM's Guardian Maintenance service. Rapp received $1,500, out of which he would pay the actors, though the sponsor would assume all production costs. The tracks were laid down at Universal Recorders in Hollywood on June 12 or 13.

The Bickersons had already done several TV appearances, including reuniting Don Ameche with Frances Langford for a New York *Ed Sullivan Show* in March of 1958. This is most likely what prompted sponsors to seek out the highly argumentative duo for a wealth of advertisements. It was an odd comedy team to have pitching products, but not only did it work, it was incredibly popular. John and Blanche were soon bickering for Top Value Stamps in July of 1958. The sixty-second spot involved John giving his wife a book of Top Value Stamps for Armistice Day, "I mean our anniversary," says John. It's what she wanted since John never gave her spending money. But he didn't do a good job licking the 1,500 stamps into the books during rush hour. At first she wanted to get John a new shirt for his collection. "*Collection*!? Blanche, I've only got one shirt. Remember—you burned up the others in the oven the day the dryer wouldn't work." Just for that insult, Blanche decided to use the stamps to buy more groceries so she could get more stamps.

The anti-lovebirds even argued over oven cleaner, in front of millions of people:

FADE IN: MAIN TITLE

EASY-OFF PRESENTS

"THE BICKERSONS"

The Announcer's VOICE is HEARD over the main title.

ANN'R (VOICE O.S.)
EASY-OFF presents "The Bickersons"—
Philip Rapp's domestic comedy creation!

DISSOLVE:
FULL SHOT
INT. BICKERSON KITCHEN DAY

It is tiny and modest without being shabby. The stove and refrigerator are not this year's model. There is a goldfish bowl on a pedestal, a cat's sandbox and scratching post on the floor, and a canary sings gaily in a cage hung strategically in the only available spot, the arched doorway leading off to the bedroom. This is calculated to give you a good knock on the head as you enter. There isn't even room for a breakfast table, and an ironing board that lets itself down from the wall serves the purpose. JOHN BICKERSON, still sleep-ridden and haggard, struggles to attach a meat grinder near the end of the ironing board.

MED SHOT AT IRONING BOARD

As John finally clamps the meat grinder on. He now feeds halved oranges into the mouth of the grinder, grinds away, and succeeds in getting a mess of pulp and skin but very little juice in the Mason jar he has cleverly placed beneath the grinder. He seems too sleepy to care.

WIDER ANGLE

As Blanche enters. From long practice she neatly ducks the swinging birdcage and makes for the refrigerator. She looks fresh and attractive with a little ribbon in her hair. She speaks to her husband over her shoulder as she removes some cream from the box.

CLOSE SHOT BLANCHE

As she reaches for the cream.

> **BLANCHE**
> Have you seen Nature Boy, John?

CLOSE SHOT JOHN

Still grinding.

> **JOHN**
> (sourly)
> Who's Nature Boy?

MED TWO SHOT JOHN AND BLANCHE

> **BLANCHE**
> The cat, silly. Did you let him out?

> **JOHN**
> No.

> **BLANCHE**
> Why not?

> **JOHN**
> He never came in.

BLANCHE
Oh, John. You promised you'd—

(sees the mess)

John Bickerson! What are you doing!

JOHN
I couldn't find the squeezer.

He drinks the debris and makes a wry face.

JOHN
(continuing)
I gotta go, Blanche. Where's my hat?

BLANCHE
(starting to clean up)
In the stove.

JOHN
Where's my lunch?

BLANCHE
In your hat. No coffee?

JOHN
(as he goes to oven)
No time.

He opens the oven door and the CAT LEAPS OUT. Recovering, he stares after the animal malevolently. He then reaches into the oven and removes his hat and what's left of his lunch. Nobody knows how Nature Boy manages to get into the stove. From a torn paper bag inside his hat John extracts a perfect skeleton of a fish. Blanche, who has witnessed all, wilts under John's look.

BLANCHE
Don't blame me, John—I didn't put him in the oven.

JOHN
Why do you have to put my hat in the oven, Blanche? Why?

BLANCHE
(wailing)
It's that greasy old stove. It smokes all the time and I just used your hat to fan it away.

JOHN
(moving closer to her)
Why don't you clean it? You don't fan a stove, Blanche—you clean it! I bought you a sixty-nine-cent jar of the best stove-cleaner in the world! Where's that jar of EASY-OFF?

BLANCHE
(pointing)
Right there on the sink. Show me how it works.

JOHN
(he hadn't figured on this)
Er—I'll show you when I come home.

BLANCHE
(gets the jar)
You say it but you won't do it. Do it now! I'll get you a rag.

JOHN
(as he takes jar)
You don't need a rag. The brush comes free with the jar.

He removes the brush and waves it thru the air simulating easy application. WIPES ON SUPER "SPREAD IT ON."

> **JOHN**
> **(continuing)**
> You just spread it on . . . let it set . . .

INSERT

CLOSE SHOT EASY-OFF JAR WITH SUPERS: "LET SET!" "WIPE CLEAN!"

> **JOHN'S VOICE (O.S.)**
> . . . and before you can say Nature Boy, you can wipe that oven clean as a whistle!

BACK TO SCENE

Blanche has put on rubber gloves and John hands her the jar. She starts to apply it to the stove as John warms to his subject.

> **JOHN**
> That's it. You don't have to scrape or smell the place up with ammonia. EASY-OFF is another scientific triumph over household drudgery! 'Bye, Drudge–I mean Blanche!

He starts to go. Blanche turns.

> **BLANCHE**
> Would it kill you to kiss me goodbye?

John turns back, gives her a swift peck on the cheek.

> **BLANCHE**
> There! Did that hurt?

> **JOHN**
> (blithely)
> Didn't feel a thing! 'Bye, Blanche.
>
> **BLANCHE**
> (with a tolerant smile)
> 'Bye, John.

And he exits, knocking his head against the birdcage, as he will do for the rest of his life. Blanche turns back to the stove as we

FADE OUT.

The Bickersons never lost their popularity, even though they didn't have a regular TV series of their own. Phil was always getting offers, as this letter from Rapp to Don Ameche on November 25, 1959 illustrates:

> **Dear Dominick,**
> **I talked to Honey [Don's wife] in New York about five minutes after you left for Pineapple Land.**
>
> **Charlie Wick called me to inform me that Perry Como had called and asked whether you and Frances would do a Bickersons spot on his program. I agreed to provide this spot, all other things being equal, and they are trying to schedule for mid January or early February.**
>
> **I presume there is considerably less than a half million dollars apiece in it for all of us, but we do have a lot of fun. Please let Marty Baum know whether we can work this out and have him call me.**
>
> **I was delighted to read in the racing form that Dom Perignon broke his maiden.**
> **All my love,**
> **Philip**

By the time Don and Frances appeared on Perry Como's show in 1960, Phil Rapp was already working hard on several other independent projects, but as usual, The Bickersons got top priority. He sent Como a sketch of the set, for his approval. Rapp would arrive in New York City three days earlier, as requested, to direct the March 15 show.

Meantime, by the end of January 1960 he had a revised script of his drama, *Man of the House*, ready for filming. And filmed it was, budgeted at a total estimated cost of approximately $30,000. The story involved young Davy Farrell (played by Teddy Rooney, son of Mickey Rooney) trying to take care of his baby brother and ailing mother, who is in bed grieving the one-year anniversary of her husband's death. Tomorrow is Christmas, and Davy wants to get his mother a medallion so she'll be happy again. Not understanding the concept of collateral, he shows the shopkeeper his late dad's Medal of Honor, hoping he'll then give Davy the medallion. The shopkeeper gently explains that the medal is much more valuable to the family than to anyone else, and they must keep it.

Rapp scored major publicity for the series when *Variety*'s Light and Airy columnist Jack Hellman gave it and Rapp's current career a large block of type. It talked of his coming *I Married a Dog*, The Bickersons, and ended on an optimistic note for *House*: "Rapp will handle the sale himself and none will deny his persuasive salesmanship." However, as Rapp himself said in the interview, "There's nothing wrong with the men who run the networks; it's their thinking on programs that needs retooling." Indeed, one wacky change the network insisted on was a laugh track, which seemed wholly inappropriate when mixed with the tender nature of the story. Whether or not the program aired on television is unknown.

I Married a Dog, however, *was* broadcast. A budget was prepared on March 7, 1960 for five days of shooting at California Studios (which Rapp was hoping to purchase) for 11.5 hours a day. The costs for story, cast, producer and staff was set at $14,325, but when "below the line" costs were added, the budget soared to $51,878.

The story: Peter Chad (Hal March) meets and marries beautiful Joyce (Marcia Henderson) after a whirlwind courtship in Las Vegas, then goes with her to her opulent Los Angeles home. He didn't realize he has married into money! But he soon learns that there's another man in her life—her poodle, Jonah, who is literally a pampered movie star. Jonah loves Joyce, but barks at Peter. He asks for a few moments alone with the dog so they can get to know each other, and proceeds to have a heart-to-heart talk with him, explaining that *he's* the master and Jonah is the dog. Peter thinks he has reached an understanding with the pooch and returns triumphantly to the living room to tell his wife. That's when Jonah comes out wet, and limping. Of course, Joyce thinks Peter hit the dog and tossed him in the tub. "One of us has to go!" says Peter. Jonah brings him his hat. When it looks like Peter's going to be ousted and Joyce leaves the room, Jonah dances for joy. When she returns, he limps again.

On August 4, 1961 *I Married a Dog* was broadcast on *Westinghouse Preview Theatre*, scoring a high TVQ (rating), but failed to make a sale to the network. "It's so different from anything now on the air that it defies classification," wrote Hellman again in *Variety*. "It's the kind of refreshing humor that sneaks up on you without batting you on the head. You're laughing all the while without breaking up."

Don Ameche had been Rapp's first choice to play Peter. During this Phil was also reviving The Bickersons for yet another new ten-minute sketch to be done for the Rexall Drug Company in April of 1960. It was a special which aired over NBC-TV and with its guests of Hermione Gingold, Johnny Mathis, The Three Stooges and others put the Bickersons, with Don and Frances again, in great company. Music was arranged and conducted by Ray Heindorf, with special music and lyrics by Earl K. Brent.

The following month NBC's New York office approved Phil's trip to England to arrange a TV special starring Peter Sellers. Transportation and living expenses were to be paid for a week. Rapp's chief function wasn't to be an agent, but to discuss the creative elements of the show with Sellers. If the trip was successful, NBC expected a detailed treatment of the show with enough information so they could prepare sales material and a budget. Sellers was said to be receptive to the whole idea, and discussions carried on into September. Unfortunately, NBC pulled out of the concept at the top of October when Sellers wanted upfront money, ruling out pay for his services until after the show was sold. NBC wanted some kind of control over Sellers, thinking the best way was by withholding money. The matter was closed as far as NBC was concerned, though they were greatly interested in it. For Rapp, it was back to his own projects.

"I remember Dad telling me that TV would eventually sink to complete mediocrity because it was impossible to find enough decent writers to handle so many channels," says Paul Rapp. "He predicted that the highest-rated program would come from watching two trains crashing head on, killing hundreds. In this reality TV world of ours, with countless stations in dire need of content, he was right on when he said that I could sell a series starring a waiter reading a menu while seated on a toilet, and it might become a highly rated show! There simply aren't enough ideas to fill the space of the broadcast spectrum. He made these remarks when TV was in its infancy, so he foresaw the future very clearly.

"Meanwhile, Mom was keeping busy in real estate during the 1940s, '50s and '60s. She bought fantastic pieces of land, mostly in the San Fernando Valley, and sold them all at a nice profit. Picture, if you will, a 90-degree curve with three houses: House 1 was built and sold to Werner Klemperer of *Hogan's Heroes*, House 2 was the main house, remodeled, and House 3 was totally new with a swimming pool, which was hopefully going to be my parents' last house. With that in mind, after we had remodeled House 2 beautifully and she had discovered the extra lots on each side of the house, we built House 3, and she sold House 2 to husband-and-wife TV writers. My son Brian was learning to swim in House 3, which was now finished in the late '60s. It was a very beautiful home with a nice den for Dad to write in.

"I was not watching any of Mom's finances when I should have been, especially in the matter of Hillcrest Country Club, which she resolved without my input. She felt that Dad's use of the club he loved was now minimal at best and that she would be happier with the money. This was after all of his main friends had passed on, including members of the famous Round Table. I had use of the club, being his son, but I felt ill at ease using it. I made several deals in my career there and that was all I thought it was good for. The staff at the club really loved Dad because he socialized with them and was head of the Food and Beverage Committee, to which he contributed his culinary skills.

"When it came time to sell House 3, she sold it to singer O. C. Smith (famous for "Little Green Apples"). Its cost to build was in the $75,000 range, the same amount for which she sold it to O. C. Smith; now it's selling for over a million, of course. These three houses consumed a huge amount of Mom's time, so Dad was at the country club a great deal to stay out of the way. And I was busy with my career and caring for Brian. In the years of 1972–74, there was a sizable recession, which ate into her real estate transactions, and she was convinced the financial markets were over for her. However, had she held on to some of these properties they would be worth many millions of dollars today. Dad kept telling her that show business would take care of us just fine. Who that knew most of her purchases would be comparable to midtown Manhattan times two!

"With regard to household money, Dad specifically had nothing to do with it except spend it. Mom paid all the bills and made all the investments. It's very hard to explain the mind of a person with Alzheimer's but the more I look back on it, the more I realize how incredibly it affects all aspects of the thought processes. Mom seemed to be worried about money from as young as I can remember. I'm sure it had something to do with her background, being one of ten children. She was very, very tight with money, but she never said no if Dad wanted some. He never had anything to do with buying real estate or stocks or any other investments outside of his TV deals. Dad absolutely was John Bickerson—he never knew where any money was or anything about it. He had his own checking account. He was never worried about money, and I never heard him talk about it in any way, shape or form. She made sure he had handmade suits and shirts and that he always drove a new Cadillac and had enough to do whatever he wanted.

"He would often complain that real estate was going to destroy him financially. The fantastic properties that she purchased were always sold prematurely because he thought real estate was a poor investment and that show business was the way to get rich, when we both know it's just the opposite. The more I think about it, he really was John Bickerson. Let me reiterate: he had no interest in money other than to spend it, and he spent it very fast, with a great deal of fun. He always picked up the tab for everybody. And, remember, he spent a sizable fortune in the horse racing world, too.

"We spent every summer in Del Mar during the early '50s, then again later in the '60s and '70s. My mother always rented a house on the beach despite the fact she owned a beautiful corner lot a couple of blocks away that she never developed. My son Brian's summers were really fantastic fun for him and he learned to surf and everything else during these summers. Mom would go the track almost every day, and Dad, depending on his commitments, would go occasionally, because he preferred to stay on the beach. There were many celebrities that came and went during the racing season, such as Betty Grable, Harry James, and famed gossip columnist Louella Parsons. J. Edgar Hoover rented a house there every summer and stayed with his later-to-be-discovered male lover, which caused a storm to many different political people in the U.S. It seemed that he had dirt on every single person on the planet that he felt necessary so that he was never in jeopardy of losing his job. I can even remember a very brief moment when he flirted with me. For most people in Hollywood he was a very despised man, but you didn't want to get on his shit list.

"I can't emphasize enough how much Dad earned in comparison to today's dollar. To drive off with a Cadillac for $1,000 back then seems absurd today. It explains a great deal of how his lifestyle was and how he was able to maintain it. I know when I started as an assistant director my salary was $250 a week, and when I finished *Avalanche* for Roger Corman, my salary was $7,500 a week as executive producer. If Dad had only left me some of those large 1937 dollar piggy banks, I would be very happy today.

"My mom's fancy clothes were made by Mansour of Hollywood on Sunset Blvd. I had to go along with Mom to a lot of her fittings when I was young and listen to this fantastic queen rave on and on about his love for one dress after another—he even designed and made hats along with everything else. Today I love women's hats, which are a long-lost accessory. Mansour would make copies of expensive gowns Mom saw in magazines, though she hated to spend money on clothes. Even in later life she would shop at more reduced places. It was amazing to see Mom winning all the golf tournaments at Hillcrest, having a nose for the best real estate and dressing as if she bought all her clothes from Wal-Mart.

"My mother, over many years, would frequently state that her job in life was to make Dad feel important and on a pedestal. She felt that women in general were a pain in the ass and didn't have any idea how to treat their husbands. She stated on many occasions that Phil was number one in the entire family and should be made to know that frequently. I know this conflicts with Mrs. Bickerson being based on her, but it really was the way it was."

Since Phil was using the place so much, *Variety*'s September 28, 1960 issue reported that Rapp and Fred Jordon were negotiating to buy California Studios, one of Hollywood's oldest studios, which had been used mainly for television productions for the past five years. Owner Phil Krasne had a $2 million price tag on the property. It wasn't to be an outright buy, but "a leasing arrangement for a long term."

"Most all of Dad's pilots were shot at California Studios, now known as Raleigh Studios," Paul states. "The studio had an interesting history. USC, my alma mater, was bequeathed the property. Fred Jordan bought the lease from Phil Krasne, who helped finance some of Dad's pilots. He ultimately sold it to Televisa, a huge Mexican firm. Fred liked to connect himself to Dad. The publicity gave the studio credibility. It has been Raleigh Studios now for many years. I know the present owners and they put a great sum of money into it. It is across the street from Paramount. Also, Roger Corman did a number of his films there, including Joel's retakes of *Battle of Blood Island* where I first met Roger. *Gunsmoke* was shot there for many, many years. I shot *Curious Female* there, which I directed, and Dad shot *Man of the House*, the Marx Bros. pilot, and *Joan of Arkansas*." *The Adventures of Superman* and Corman's *The Pit and the Pendulum* were also filmed there.

By November 7, 1960 *Variety* was reporting that Rapp was confident, saying the California Studios deal was already "locked in" for the studio already in trouble with a mortgage of $600,000 due, plus $170,000 due in back taxes, and $140,000 owed to Consolidated Laboratories. Rapp and Jordon would have to put up $350,000 out of their own pockets for the $900,000 necessary. Jordon was an economist, oilman and friend of Jack Lemmon who had financed Lemmon's Broadway play, *Face of a Hero*. The duo was to change the name of the studio, once owning the controlling stock (putting

Rapp in as chairman of the board), to Producers Studios. The ten-year leasing arrangement was to go through Clune Memorial Trust, which controlled the property, with the balance of the $900k to be paid within the five-year extended lease.

As the world changed and the last particles of radio were fading into the music-only format, the conception of comedy also seemed to be veering into new expressions, especially where television was concerned. In his autobiography, an unhappy Rapp clearly defines *The Gripes of Rapp*:

> The dusty corners of Comedy are littered with the trash of the stand-up comics who have fallen on their faces. The stand-up comic is a special breed of non-comedian who reads jokes, such as they are, to an audience who rarely pays to see or hear him. He is the illegitimate spawn of the gifted after-dinner speaker or the former vaudeville monologist who had an "act." He is indigenous to television and nightclubs, borscht circuit hotels and weddings, places to which people would go even if he wasn't there. His earnings may be microscopic or astronomical, depending on his "drawing power," which has nothing in common with talent. He depends entirely on a series of disconnected one-liners, liberally punctuated by grimaces, gestures, or stock adlibs designed to convict his listeners of the crime of denseness. As a rule, his listeners accept their sentence with great cheer and gales of laughter. These people deserve no time off for good behavior. Their encouragement, marked by handclapping and guffaws at each sally, is the fertilizer that promotes the weeds in the vast wasteland of television. The comic is like a drunk in a shooting gallery. A few stray bullets of wit occasionally hit the target, but many more would hit the intellect of the innocent bystander.
> This indictment of the stand-up comic is naturally not all-inclusive. There are the talented few who are genuinely funny in their approach to humor, but finding them is like looking for grapes in a field of thistles. In the main the stand-up comic belongs to a sub- literate group. With acclaim and financial success he usually develops a patina of intellect and an urge to

use big words and high flown phrases plus an arrogance actually heightened by his pretense at humility. Two such graduates with whom I have had intimate writing contact, Danny Kaye and Danny Thomas, are fair examples. Their ascent to the Olympus of the entertainment world, both from the most humble of beginnings, need not puzzle anybody. Kaye, in particular, brought more to his audiences than a barrage of jokes. Danny Kaye is loaded with true talent. He sings agreeably, can dance with the best of them, and is a superb mimic. He can imitate anything or anyone—even a comedian. But the imitation shows itself for what it really is—an imitation. His comedy has the spurious ring of a lead half-dollar. His motion pictures for Samuel Goldwyn, most of which I worked on, were his only real successes. They were masterpieces of camouflage and nobody found out he wasn't really a comedian at all. He was an entertainer. After he left Goldwyn's magic management he made The Inspector General at Warner's, an adaptation of the Gogol story which I wrote with the late Harry Kurnitz. The role required a certain amount of acting ability, something that Danny had never had to display before. He imitated an actor acting and for all his cunning he came across wearing the mythical Robe of the legendary Emperor. His nakedness was stark and the picture was a financial failure, though Danny was not really to blame. The choice of the original material could never have supplied the vestments to clothe his particular weakness but rather pointed it up. Curiously enough, while the public rejected the picture, the highly regarded critics had praise for it and it became a success d'estime, a tragic fact which led him to do worse and worse pictures. I quote here one review which seems to give the lie to all my maunderings, but believe me, Danny Kaye is not a funny man, nor can he act.

In the outline to Gripes, Phil wrote,

The stand-up comics and their one-liners—they might just as well be reading from a joke book. They depend a great deal on the failure of the material to get laughs so they can use prepared adlibs that indicate there is something lacking in the audience. Audiences are masochistic, perverted, and the worst possible gauge of a comedian. Audiences that are sat up to indicate the potential of pilot films by means of machines, etc. are particularly dangerous. They automatically become critics, inhibited and are given a feeling of superiority.

To prove that comics are not funny: everybody has played in *The Odd Couple* and everybody gets laughs. Same with Bix [The Bickersons].

It may have been the lack of TV success after *Topper* that turned Phil a little bitter towards the ever-changing industry. Executive producers were getting younger and were more concerned with today's headlines than yesterday's headliners.

But he did still keep his hand in with speculation scripts for *My Favorite Martian* (which Joel Rapp wrote for) and *The Man from U.N.C.L.E*, among other TV shows.

Joel said, "He was my idol. Always had a teeny bit of British in him, in his speech and dress . . . Brilliant. I think he must have memorized such diverse writings as the dictionary and *Gray's Anatomy*. He was *funny*—needless to say. A complete spendthrift, too—make a thousand, spend two . . .

"Friend: 'Phil, you want to go fishing tomorrow? Dad: 'Sure.' (Reaches for phone) 'Hello, Private Yacht rentals? I want to rent a boat tomorrow, skipper, cook, the works . . . just me and my friend.' Generous to a fault. There was nothing he wouldn't give to me and Paul and my mother and anybody else who wanted something . . . He was handsome, dashing even, albeit fairly short. Everybody, repeat *everybody*, loved him including all my friends, girlfriends, etc . . . ."

By 1960, Tab Hunter wanted to get into television, having recently been turned down for the role of Tony in the film version of West Side Story. Owning fifty percent of a new NBC series about a cartoonist in Malibu Beach, he changed the name from *Bachelor at Large* to *The Tab Hunter Show*. He formed Shunto Productions and found sponsors: Newport cigarettes, Timex watches, and later, Chrysler. The author of the pilot had been the Oscar-winning co-writer of *Pillow Talk*, Stanley Shapiro, who was then put on as writer/producer/director, pleasing Tab to no end. The trouble was, Shapiro was only around for the pilot; Hollywood called with offers of feature films. The girls on the series were gorgeous—Elizabeth Montgomery, Tuesday Weld, Suzanne Pleshette, Nita Talbot—but they couldn't take the place of compelling stories.

First Norman Tokar came in to fix up the scripts, but the countless hours of revisions didn't seem to get anywhere. As Tab stated in his autobiography, *Tab Hunter Confidential*, "When Norman burned out, a director named Phil Rapp was brought in. I can still hear him barking out his lone theory of comedy: 'Fast is funny, but faster is funnier!'"

As Phil told *Telefilm* magazine in 1961, "It looked like a hopeless situation. Six segments had been shown; 14 additional segments were in works, most of these completed. I screened several of those and they were *awful*. I thoroughly agreed with the client but the network asked me to salvage what, at the moment, was a sinking ship. They could not afford such a quick cancellation—reputation wise—so I said I would do everything possible. A fortune had already been spent. It would take another huge amount to save the original investment."

So, Rapp was given a contract to serve mainly as director of *The Tab Hunter Show*, from October 3, 1960 to April 29, 1961, with duties of executive producer, story editor, writer and supervisor on the side. The original director was fired and Rapp rewrote and/or reshot major portions of the 14 completed scripts. The revamps cost the network at an additional $550,000. But it worked. The sponsor was happy enough not only to go through with the deal, but they upped their desire for 39 episodes (up from 26), after viewing rushes of the new material. But, as Rapp later found out, the deal included repeats, not all original episodes.

Rapp's first draft contract of August 1, 1960 had him receiving, on top of his directing fees, $319 per story, $951.50 for a teleplay, and $1,210 for each story & teleplay he submitted that was used. By October he was offered an Executive Producer credit for $1,500 a week for 26 weeks, plus an option for a second season. He was also in negotiations with NBC for an 18-month guarantee of employment as producer, director and writer for the X number of shows that they or Rapp would create.

The series was set with a budget at around $50,000 per episode (from $45,000 to $57,000 usually, the most expensive being "One Blonde Too Many," at a whopping $67,495).

Phil seemed to be working mostly for the advertising people

rather than the TV network. On October 28, 1960, Jane Daly at Wade Advertising wrote to him: "I was delighted to read that you were brought in as the new producer of the *Tab Hunter Show*. When they get in trouble they really call for the pros, don't they?" Closing his response letter a week later Phil wrote, "With regards to the *Tab Hunter Show*, all I can do is hope and pray. The rectifying task is enormous." He also put a pitch in for a series he'd written for Hal March, saying that if they put in an order for that he'd "give you the biggest bargain hit in fifty years."

The senior vice-president of Lennen & Newell Inc. (another advertising agency), Nicholas E. Keesely, was quite optimistic, writing to Phil: "I have done a lot of checking around, and I find that in families where there are teenagers the response to Hunter is very wholesome, and my hunch is that the audience will build if we can come up with enough strong shows in the coming six weeks. I just want to tell you how happy we are that you are on the team and giving us the benefit of your knowledge and experience." He also complained that the opening shows relied too much on the one-joke marriage theme.

Rapp's December 1 letter to Keesely was a thoughtful reply to the long road of work ahead: "I cannot begin to tell you the enormous amount of major surgery that was necessary on the films already shot, but suffice it to say we are doing everything possible to repair them. Naturally, we are applying every ounce of energy, industry and creative ability into making these past sins acceptable, even more viewable. Unfortunately, we will not really have a new and pure product until early January.

"Nick, I have a feeling that the new stuff and the new thinking will produce a far better brand of entertainment, and I must thank you and your group for the views expressed in Woodruff's letter. Wherever possible, these ideas will be carried out. Aside from enlarging on Tab's character and giving him more vigor and vitality in his playing, I am concentrating on peopling the stories with more glamorous girls and more elaborate production. I am dead certain that while the stories themselves should be intelligent and literate, they should never be so cumbersome as to get in the way of the uninhibited fun."

In a letter to "Felix" on January 4, 1961, Rapp wrote: "With the start of the New Year I am pleased to say that six scripts are in preparation, outlines of which will soon be on your desk, and I have started a crash program to secure enough material so that careful study for quality and economy can prevail. I think Dick Kinon will prove most effective as director, and as you know I'll always be willing to take over during any emergency. I have grown to like Tab very much, and he responds by giving me his very best all the time."

Less than two weeks later Rapp wrote to Daniel Ladd of the P. Lorillard Company: "It pleases me to think that you have detected improvement in the recent efforts, and you have my word that I'll continue to break my back to supply you with a good product.

"Here's hoping you sell zillions of cigarettes."

But no matter how many cute friends Tab brought in for sex appeal, no matter how punched up the scripts could become, the series was doomed for several reasons. For some unfathomable explanation, just like *Hiram Holiday*, the network saw fit to put the series on opposite the latter half of the most popular variety show in history, *The Ed Sullivan Show*.

"Another mistake," Phil told *Telefilm* magazine at the time, "is the fact that *The Tab Hunter Show* followed *National Velvet*. The latter has strong, wholesome, family appeal, particularly for younger kids, whereas *The Tab Hunter Show* was made adult and sexy, to attract the gay young sophisticates, and beatniks, to sell them cigarettes.

"There was such a jam-up of upper-level interference that it was like a crack-up on a freeway which draws so much attention from watchers that the ambulance cannot get through, to reach the wreck."

Though Phil was able to bring costs in to $50,000 less than the original budget per episode, it was over. Too much was stacked against it. "Well, at least I gave it a nice funeral," Rapp later said.

Plus, just months before the series premiere, Tab was wrongfully accused of severely beating his dog by jealous neighbors, a story embraced fully by the press to the point that Tab had to go to court (a month after the pilot aired). The hate mail that stacked up against the "dog hater" was incredible, much sent directly to the sponsors.

On September 4, 1963 Rapp had signed a three-year contract with the William Morris Agency to be his sole representative, which kept the author working on a lot of solo/indie projects he hoped WMA would help with placing as TV series. One such project, *Monsieur Cognac*, didn't sell to television, but did go to Universal. They changed the name to *Wild and Wonderful* (1964), with Tony Curtis and Christine Kaufman in the starring roles. Phil had signed up as "director or producer" at the rate of $1,750 per week, for a minimum period of 20 weeks. He and Richard M. Powell received $10,000 for writing *Monsieur Cognac*, each owning a third of the rights. It was a revamped, expanded version of *I Married a Dog*.

One project that was all Rapp, which he filmed himself, was *Mimi*, starring husband-and-wife comedy team Mimi Hines (most famous for replacing Barbra Streisand in *Funny Girl* on Broadway) and Phil Ford.

Shooting began for Four Star Television on November 1, 1963, from 9 a.m. until 6:40 p.m., with an hour lunch commencing at 12:42 on the dot. For five days (which included four days of rehearsals) Mimi Hines was the first to arrive at 7 a.m. for make-up, with husband Phil following at 8. She was also the very last to leave at 6:40. Filming stopped on November 6.

The budget/cost report had been compiled on October 31, 1963 for four days of shooting at $115,742, with $19,176 going to cast, $8,611 to producer, and $8,290 to story. Publicity was strangely only budgeted for $100, but this was only an estimate, hoping to keep costs down enough for approval of the project to live past a pilot. There would obviously be an original score for the piece, as music was estimated at $5,500 for a composer.

The story puts Mimi and Phil in The Garden of Eden, "The world's most luxurious health resort and spa," where Mimi constant wool-gathers that she wants to *be* somebody—opera singer, ballet star, anything. Mr. Osaka, a Japanese jockey who is also a compulsive eater, has come to Eden to be fed nothing but kelp juice to get his weight down for the great International Sweepstakes race tomorrow. He's insured for $100,000 (the Sweepstakes prize) with Eden that he'll lose the necessary six pounds by the morning. But when Mimi and Phil give the little man the wrong, sumptuous meal, they have to get *twelve* pounds off him by morning, or else Mr. Peavy, the manager, will have their hides. In the gym they go, nearly killing poor Mr. Osaka with the whirlpool bath and exercise horse, and after a rigorous night, the pounds come off. But the commotion has left Osaka so dazed that Mimi ends up taking his place at the weigh-in at the racetrack. It doesn't matter: Osaka's horse is scratched anyway because it got into the feed room the night before and ate itself sick. Mimi gets a raise for helping with Osaka, and Peavy promotes Phil to chief dietician. Though she says she's content with being a big fish in a small pond, it doesn't stop her from sneaking away for a ballet audition with the group of ballerinas staying at Eden.

The exterior Garden of Eden scenes were to be the first to be shot at the Sportsman's Lodge Hotel, at 12825 Ventura Blvd., then Mimi's number/main titles, and the end scene in which Mimi gets into the audition. Interiors were to be filmed in Stage 17, 10 and 23 at California Studios.

Variety's November 14, 1964 "Light and Airy" column by Jack Hellman reported that *Mimi* was wrapped up and awaited inspection by sponsor General Foods, who ended up putting $100,000 into the production. Rapp was already planning other plots so it could be quickly sold as a network series. "It'll be 90% physical comedy," he told *Variety*, "and what's left, for dialog. Mimi is the greatest clown since Fanny Brice, an amazing talent who should carve a permanent niche in television. She's a bouncy, sexy chipmunk, a grown-up Baby Snooks." *Variety* called Rapp one of TV's two greatest salesman—the other being Bill Bacher. "Wind him up and yes men will pop up all over the place." That's how he sold Four Star and Tom McDermott on *Mimi*. Unfortunately, it still failed to sell to the network as a series.

Whatever job he immersed himself in, the Bickersons would never leave him alone, and vice versa. Exchanges had been steadily increasing to have Don and Frances perform their squabbling skit again on *The Perry Como Show*. In a letter to Como, Rapp asked, "I have one small favor to ask of you, Perry—would you please play Dr. Hersey for me? It's a lot of fun, and would add to the overall entertainment value."

But Phil kept hoping for the sale of a stand-alone Bix series. On February 2, 1961, Phil wrote to Les Goldman at Quartet Films:

I hereby give you the right to help create and develop a cartoon series with the tentative title, 'The Three Worlds of

John Bickerson,' and use of all the characters including John and Blanche Bickerson, which I created and own lock, stock and barrel. From our many meetings and work sessions, I am convinced that you and your colleagues are men of honor and I trust you regard me in the same light. That being the case, we will consider ourselves together for better or worse in this new venture, and at the earliest convenient moment attorneys can draw up terms defining the short strokes. It is, of course, understood that my scripts and characters will be tied up for a reasonable length of time in order to procure a sale and/or recoup any investment monies that may have been expended.

Briefly, the general setup of *The Three Worlds of John Bickerson* will follow this pattern.

1. It will be divided into three separable segments for future sales as a whole or in part.

2. The bedroom domestic scene between John and Blanche would be one of the segments.

3. His comic snoring would act as a bridge. Then, into his dream world. Here he always fancies himself as Merlin in the Arthurian legend. But because he is John Bickerson he is a bumbling magician, and as in real life rarely accomplishes anything. Blanche's counterpart will be the crow (read "Merlin") and other characters in Camelot will be found in John's everyday world.

4. The third segment is a musical one, with rather advanced graphic design. This is cleverly worked in by virtue of the fact that John always had a second job, or avocation. His main job, as always, is that of a bowling ball salesman, but he is also a bass fiddle player. He plays at weddings, dances, TV shows, the opera, anywhere he can get the extra job. He naturally hates the bull fiddle and also music, the conductor represents his nagging wife, and other characters that appear in the show he is playing are viewed thru his eyes as his bêtes-noir. For instance, when playing the bass fiddle during a performance

of *Carmen*, he pictures himself on the stage as Escamillo, Carmen as Blanche, Dr. Hersey as the Sergeant, and the bull as Nature Boy, the cat. (John Bickerson hates this cat more than anything in the world. The men at Quartet Films have made the most astonishing feline ever seen. He towers over Bickerson and makes his life miserable.)

Of course, there will be various other scenes during the life of the series. At breakfast. In the office. In the hospital. On a train. At Dr. Hersey's, or any other suitable place. But on the whole, the three segments will remain, i.e., the bedroom scene, the launching into the dream world of Merlin, and the musical sequence.

I want you to propose that NBC take a financial position, and that they further agree to finance at least thirteen scripts and story boards. If they don't want to take a position in the expenditures already made, and the rest of the financing for a suitable demonstration, that's okay—but the script plan must be carried out. It's the most sensible approach to designing a complete series ever made with a minimal investment.

Stepping away from the Bix for a moment, Rapp also submitted the followed proposal to Screen Gems Television in 1968:

The series concerns the life of a judge. The trials and tribulations, both comic and emotional. Most judges, despite their charismatic and regal appearance, are ordinary men. They are often far less gifted than the legal batteries they face, and sometimes more ordinary than the defendant they must judge. But our Judge Chambers is no ordinary man. In fact, Judge Chambers is a woman. Hopefully, she will be portrayed by Lauren Bacall, or somebody equally prestigious, and with her range of delivery and looks.

Her background? Brilliant law student, married a bounder before graduation, and abandoned just before she bore his child. No widow, she. Left almost penniless but buoyed by her great love for her child, she worked her way thru the final term, passed her bar exam with highest honors, hung out her shingle, and soon made a bundle by displaying in court a combination of sex, legal brilliance and forensic skill. Her subsequent judgeship was well-earned and her credentials impeccable.

Her beautiful daughter is now nineteen and might be classified as a border-line delinquent. Not really. She is just one of the "now" people. A protestor, terribly vocal, intelligent with a bunch of friends to match.

Presiding in court, Judge Chambers dispenses justice with wisdom, compassion, and an unerring eye for the quasi-legal skullduggery employed by the more eloquent attorneys. These shysters she puts down with firmness tempered with gentle, chiding wit.

Her Worship is worshipped by her bailiff, a man who has spent most of his adult life (about fifty years) in and around the Hall of Justice. He is a colorful character, a former hustler and bail bondsman with a petty criminal record, now completely adjusted to society and law. He also has a great depth of understanding for the plight of the offender, and has been known to confer with the judge regarding decisions. I don't know his name.

While in her judicial robes she is exceedingly attractive and feminine, away from the bench a remarkable transformation takes place in Judge Chambers. She dresses like a high fashion model, is always exquisitely coiffed, vivacious and youthful-looking, and I'll lay eight to five she'd confound the panel of *What's My Line?*, blindfolded or otherwise.

Her penthouse apartment on the East River is enormous and a decorator's dream. It's the casual hangout for her many friends, none of whom are in the legal profession. They are a varied group of many colors—from the theatre, art world, journalists, top representatives of the sports arena, male and female—and just plain people. Her rebel daughter rarely mingles with this group and only then to disagree and start a hassle. Judge Chambers has a live-in cook and housekeeper, a widow (I guess you just gotta have a widow in a series this year) with three children who also live in the apartment. The kids are no better than they should be and the Judge tolerates their childish activities with a resignation born of understanding. So much for her household.

Her closest friend and constant squire is Red McDonald, ace sports writer and announcer for all athletic events. The Judge never misses any contest and possesses unbelievable knowledge of all the rules. She can quote batting averages, boxing and football statistics and is the only woman ever to serve as a scoring judge in a recent World's Series.

Persistent a suitor as Red is, and far from unattractive (Vin Scully?) he will never, never coax the Judge into marriage.

It seems to be a series that could break virgin ground, combining humor, action, character and emotional problems all set in motion by a central catalyst—a woman of grace, beauty and talent. Of course, the inarguable attraction of the courtroom and its procedures needs no elaboration. I don't have a title for it, but for the critics who want to knock it, I submit these free of charge.
INCOMPETENT, IRRELEVENT AND NO MATERIAL OBJECTION!
DISORDER IN THE COURT

Unfortunately, the idea didn't get very far with a representative of Screen Gems Television, who wrote, "I am sorry to have to tell you that this just simply doesn't tweak me. For one thing, I fear it would turn out to be a conglomerate of program types—a little bit of situation comedy, a dash of suspense melodrama in the courtroom, a little bit of 'Mother Knows Best,' plus a romance. Additionally, the fact that her beau operates in a totally different field from hers would seem to offer some story difficulty in bringing the two worlds together."

Unlike their father, Joel and Paul Rapp were finding the 1960s highly lucrative, however. Paul had a successful, significant career as Roger Corman's right-hand man in some of his classic, low-budget films, beginning with 1957's *Battle of Blood Island*. He was Associate Producer and uncredited writer on *The Girls on the Beach* (1965, for Roger's brother Gene), and Unit Production Manager/Second Unit Director on *Wasp Woman* (1958), *Little Shop of Horrors* (1960), *The Pit & the Pendulum* (1961), *The Raven* (1963), *Terror* (1963), and functioned in various producing roles through the early 1980s. His most prestigious film may have been Martin Scorsese's early feature, *Mean Streets* (1973), which helped established the careers of Robert De Niro and Harvey Keitel. Paul's complete credits can be found at imdb.com.

Paul states: "My brother Joel first met up with Roger Corman, who graduated from Beverly High. Joel made a deal with him to go shoot a film in Puerto Rico. About that time I was the youngest member of the Directors Guild, as an assistant director in 1957. When Joel returned from the location, he needed to shoot some additional scenes so I worked as the assistant director for about a week on the stage. One day Roger came to the set and asked me how we were doing. I told him we were about a half a day behind. He took my script and looked at it for a couple of minutes. Then he tore out a couple of pages and said, 'Now you are back on schedule!' That was my first contact with Roger.

"Shortly after that I worked on a film that Roger was directing and my relationship was firmly established into the future. As far as the Corman film I most liked working on, I would have to say *The Wild Angeles* or *The Trip* because my contribution was a lot in each [see imdb.com]. The best part of working with Roger was that he gave me so much freedom to use my creative talents in all of the films I did. He gave me total freedom and authority to let me run the whole production.

"My first film for Roger was *Ski Troop Attack* in 1960. He also hired me to be a stunt person, the wardrobe person, the assistant prop person, and I had a small acting part. We drove to the location in Deadwood, South Dakota—which is where Wild Bill was shot to death, and is near Mt. Rushmore—in my Volkswagen Beetle because he was able to save money on plane tickets, I was able to buy blank bullets for the rifles."

Oldest son Joel Rapp was a successful writer for TV in the 1960s. He tells of his serendipitous fall into television in his autobiography, *Radio, TV, Mother Earth & Me*:

"Lots of young, aspiring writers have asked me over the years, 'How did you break into the business?' Having a father who was a Hollywood writer-director certainly didn't hurt, but my show-biz breakthrough was a combination of talent, luck, hard-work, and luck.

"I graduated from USC in June of 1955, and by August I was working on a Hollywood soundstage as a second-assistant director. (The show was called *Crossroads* and if you remember it, you really should get a life.) The job is as menial as it sounds, consisting of making out the daily call sheet, herding actors to and from their dressing rooms, hiring the extras, and generally trying to help the first assistant-director as much as you can. But I was thrilled to have the gig, in spite of the fact we worked six days a week, 12 to 14 hours a day. The money, for 1955, was great—a gross check of $208 a week found its way into my bank account, and best of all I was a part of the sacred and beloved business I had come to love.

"There is nowhere to go from being a second-assistant except to becoming a first-assistant or a production manager, and writing was what I wanted to do. So in my spare time (hah!) I slaved at my typewriter, knocking out short stories and spec scripts of all types and genres. I did pretty well with the short stories—several sales to second-tier men's magazines such as *Gentleman, Dude, Chic,* and the like. The scripts, however, languished in my drawer and all my father's influence couldn't land me a writing job.

"The luck struck in late 1956 at a party given by a friend of mine. There was a young agent at the bash—his name was Bill Belasco, and he was related in some way to a very prominent New York theatrical family—and he took a liking to me right off the bat. He was frank to admit to me he was gay, which in those days really took a lot of courage, but it wasn't my body he was after, it was my mind. He knew of my father, of course, and after a half-hour conversation about my dreams of following in Dad's footsteps, he beckoned me to follow him into the bedroom. I balked—I thought I'd made it clear that I wasn't of that persuasion. No, no, he assured me. He was going to make a call and get me a job writing a script.

"Into the bedroom we went, and a moment later Bill was on the phone with a close friend of his, a man named Jon Epstein, who was in charge of hiring writers at a studio called 'Ziv Productions.' Ziv was a syndicating outfit that churned out half-hour shows such as *Sea Hunt, Science Fiction Theater, Flipper* and the like. Bill gushed to his friend that he'd met a hot new talent—me—and asked Jon if he would give me a job. Bill guaranteed Jon he wouldn't be sorry. A few moments passed, and Bill, grinning ear to ear, passed me the phone. I introduced myself to Jon, and before I knew it he was telling me to come to his office Monday morning—he was going to assign me to write an episode of *Highway Patrol!* The pay was scale—$700—but I couldn't have been more thrilled if it had been a million! My writing career had begun, and I was determined not to blow the opportunity.

"Thank God they loved the script I wrote for *Highway Patrol* (with only the slightest help from Papa) and put me under contract forthwith. In the next two years I wrote at least a hundred shows for that outfit, and the good news was that even though the pay remained at 700 a pop, six reruns were virtually guaranteed and in those days that meant an additional 150% of minimum. As much as I enjoyed my days at Ziv, however, I yearned for bigger and better things—comedy shows, that's what I wanted—but Bill deemed I wasn't ready yet. He did, however, have a step-up in mind—that step being to leave Ziv and put myself onto the freelance market where scale had now risen to 1100 bucks!

"I found myself working steadily on shows like *Lassie, Peter Gunn, Brothers Brannigan, M-Squad* (where I wrote several episodes with a young up-and-coming talent named Robert Altman), and *Whirlybirds*—half-hour shows that were well thought of in their day. But I still craved a crack at comedy, which I was sure would come along sooner or later.

"Around that time—1958—Bill Belasco died an untimely death (is there such a thing as a 'timely death'?) in an automobile accident, and an agent at William Morris, Shelly Wile, romanced me with the promise of comedy-writing jobs. I signed with William Morris, and before the ink was dry Shelly came through.

"'I've got a gig for you,' he said. 'A writer named Danny Simon has an assignment to write six episodes of a show called *Pete & Gladys*. He's getting Three Grand a script and he wants a young partner to bounce stuff off of—to mentor, if you will. He's willing to pay a Grand a script, and I think you should jump at it.'

"And jump at it I did. Danny Simon was Neil Simon's brother, and a really top-notch comedy guy. He had been part of the staff of the Sid Caesar show in New York, working alongside Mel Brooks, Howie Morris, Sheldon Keller, and, of course, his brother Neil. I was a bit nervous about going to work with him—okay, I was a lot nervous. I mean, I was just a 24-year-old wet-behind-the-ears kid and he was a famous writer. But I proved up to the task, and by the third script we did together I was pulling my weight. And then I got another call from Shelly.

"'They're starting a new show at Four-Star called *Peter Loves Mary*,' he said, 'and they're putting together a writing staff of four people—two teams. They've got one team from New York signed already—Mel Tolkin and Mel Diamond, and a third New Yorker, a playwright named Sam Locke who needs to find a partner.' Shelly went on to tell me that the show was firm for 39 episodes, was to star Peter Lind Hayes and his wife, Mary Healy, and was being produced by a man named Billy Friedberg, whose last assignment had been as producer of Phil Silvers' TV classic, *You'll Never Get Rich*, better known as *Sgt. Bilko*. The three writers already aboard were going to make a thousand dollars a week, and Shelly had offered me up for 500. 'But don't worry,' he said. 'It's a one-year guarantee, and if you can cut the mustard they'll bump you up to a G after the first 13 weeks.' I told Danny about the chance, and he was very supportive. 'I hate to see you go,' he said, 'but if it doesn't work out, I'd love to have you back with me.'

"So off I went with Shelly to meet with Billy Friedberg. We sat in Billy's office for about 15 minutes, bantering and chatting about the show and the world in general, and finally Billy looked at Shelly and nodded. 'If he's okay with Sam, he's okay with me,' he said. My heart was racing. 'Where might I find Sam?' I asked, and Billy directed me to an office just down the hall. 'I'll be right back,' I said, and scurried down the hall to Sam's office. I opened the door and there, behind his typewriter, sat a little curly-haired guy about twenty years my senior pounding away on a script. 'Are you Sam Locke?' I asked. 'Yep,' he said. 'Well, I'm Joel Rapp, your new partner,' I said, and darted back to Billy's office where I grinned broadly. 'It's okay with Sam,' I said, and we shook hands on the deal.

"And thus began an eleven-year partnership that was more like a marriage. A strong, happy marriage. I got my raise to a thousand a week after only six weeks on the job, and Sam Locke & Joel Rapp became one of the most respected writing teams in the business. Together we wrote at least a couple of hundred TV shows and a handful of B-movies under the pseudonym David Malcolm, a combination of our middle names. Sam had an extraordinary wit and a fabulous sense of script construction, and best of all he could recall in an instant the plot of any past movie or play ever produced, a vitally important asset in the world of TV sitcoms. I think I learned more about writing from Sam than anyone with the possible exception of my father, and although we broke up as a team in 1968 when I decided to go off on my own and try for bigger things, he remained my dearest friend until the day he died."

Joel and Phil never wrote anything together, however, apart from the Bickersons play, *Match Please, Darling.*

Though The Bickersons had been around for more than twenty years now, it had somehow escaped its day on the legitimate stage. The time was ripe for rectifying this. Though Phil was plenty busy writing a "first and final draft screenplay" tentatively called *Room for Scandal* for Dale Robertson under Robertson's company, Juggernaut, Inc., for the sum of $20,000, in installments, he and son Joel both made time to put together a proper and original Bix play, *Match Please, Darling* (a line in the play), which Phil would direct.

Of course Don Ameche and Frances Langford were Phil's top choices to star in the play. As Frances herself admitted in 1967, "I wouldn't think of doing the Bickersons unless Phil was around to direct it, even if it's one of our old routines. It's the timing and everything he puts into it that makes us so real and funny." But the timing was not right for either star who had to respectfully decline.

In August of 1967, a Dramatists Guild contract was signed between Joel and Philip Rapp, since the initial production was to be performed locally.

In a funny promo piece written for the newspapers, Phil wrote of his *MPD* collaboration with Joel:

I am typing this manuscript on a Remington noiseless (Quiet-Riter) portable machine that is exactly thirty-one years old. [He typed with two fingers all his life.] **I have never been able to use another machine, though I have tried many times. No dice. My two gifted sons tried to foist an electric on me, but I soon discovered that electrik typewriters are for typists and not for writers. The nerve-shattering buzzing while you wait for the next line to formulate is too much. It won't let you think in peace. Now, this antique that I use can be just as frustrating. In fact, I take a solemn oath that it has a mind of its own. I swear to God it will accept only the words that fit the situation, and jam in one way or another when the unfinished line is wrong. I**

can begin feverishly to write a line that I'm sure is hilarious and before I can confide it to paper, on many occasions, things begin to happen. At the touch of one letter all the keys fly up together in resistance. Or the platen will run away. (For the benefit of non-typists the platen is the roller.) Also, witness the misspelling of the word "electric" in the first part of this piece. My typewriter rejected it out of pure hatred for its electric cousin. There it goes again!

Joel, my first born, and a fantastic comedy writer with a mile-long list of credits, collaborated on a play with me called *Match, please, Darling*. (Apparently my machine has warned me again.) I lost over thirty thousand dollars of my own money on the production and it was proclaimed by all the trades as an enormous hit. The correst tiel (see what happens?) the correct title is "Match, please, Darling." My typewriter gave me fair warning. In the second act the protagonist is caught in an impossible situation. He is perfectly innocent of any marital indiscretion but a pregnant Bunny from the Blanche Club is found assuring him of fathering her unborn child.

See how the frigging typewriter balked at the word "pregnant?" I swear it was not deliberate–the bloody machine is even prudish. Okay, machine, how about "enceinte?" You were reluctant, but accepted it. "Family way?" Wow! It damn near typed itself! The Bunny is in full regalia, or some of her is in it, the man is in pajamas, his small apartment bed is rumpled, and they face each other as the door flies open to disclose the man's wife. There is a deafening silence as the wife waits for some explanation of tableau. None of the actors have moved a muscle. When I was writing the aforementioned scene on this machine I called on Joel for help in the solution of it. What to say and who's to say it? This is going to be a curtain line—words guaranteed to fracture the audience and shake the walls of the theater. Joel put on his thinking face and I looked heavenward hoping for an inspiration. Nothing. A fretful ten minutes passed as I paced up and down. Joel was already eating corned beef sandwiches—he had a theory about eating when you run into a roadblock on a script—and I lit one cigarette after another. Suddenly it came to me and I flew to the typewriter and attacked it viciously. Halfway thru the line, the keys jammed, the carriage flew off its moorings and the ribbon snapped.

"What happened?" said Joel. "Was the line that funny that it could make a typewriter explode?"

"Don't be a comedian," I snarled. "Fix that poltergeist-infested machine so I can record the biggest blackout in history!"

Joel stared at the paper still locked in the dangling platen. "A package of—a package of what, dad?"

"Wings."

"Wings??" Joel roared with laughter.

"I told you it was funny! What else could the poor schmo say in a situation like that? To a Bunny. 'A Package of Wings, please.' Makes it all look innocent, he thinks."

"Wings?"

"Yeah, Wings—what's wrong?"

Joel gently pointed out that Wings cigarettes had been off the marked for over fifteen years. "The line is great, but you'd better change your brand. Make it Marlboros."

Of course he was right. Joel got the machine fixed, it accepted that microscopic change with good grace, and we got hundreds of cartons of Marlboros for free during the life of the play. Not quite thirty thousand dollars worth, though.

Joel told of the play's origin in his autobiography,

One of the most rewarding, not to mention educational, experiences of my life was writing a play with my father. It was called *Match Please, Darling*, and it ran for almost five months at the Coronet Theater on La Cienega Boulevard, here in Los Angeles.

It was 1967, and it came about this way:

I had driven up to my father's palatial Beverly Hills manse fully prepared for the conversation I knew to be inevitable; to wit, borrowing money. I winced as my father's words spilled out. "Son," he said, "do you suppose you might lend me a few dollars till next Wednesday?"

"What about the twenty you still owe me, Dad?" I asked.

"I can't pay you this week," he said sheepishly.

"That's what you told me *last* week!" was my response.

"Well," he bellowed, "I kept my word, didn't I?"

But seriously . . . . . I have already discussed my father's world-class profligacy, but he'd reached a stage in his life where he wasn't interested in working anymore and he and Mom were living off her shrewd stock and real-estate investments. I could tell he was bored with his life of golfing and losing at gin every day after lunching with his pals at the legendary Hillcrest round table, so I thought it would be a good thing for him psychologically to get his hand back in and write something. With that in mind, I put forth a proposition.

"Pop," I said, "I've got this idea for a play which is about a man and wife, an interfering couple upstairs, a Playboy Bunny, and a lawyer who's a degenerate gambler, and I think you and I could have fun writing it together. We'd be the first father and son playwriting team since—well, since forever, and I really think it could be a very funny piece."

He was frowning with some degree of interest, but he was far from convinced, so I applied what turned out to be the *coup de grace*—"And best of all, we can make the husband and wife John and Blanche Bickerson and incorporate many of their famous routines!"

That sold him. The next day we began blocking out the play.

I was alive with anticipation, excited by the prospect of working with a genuine master, my comedy-writing idol, if truth be known. I soon learned, however, that collaborating with one's father would not be all peaches and cream. I arrived at this conclusion the first time I suggested one of my jokes was funnier than one of his.

His eyes narrowed. "What did you say?"

"I said, I think my joke in this spot is better than yours."

"You really think so?" he asked quietly. I nodded. "All right, son." Then, suddenly, "Go to your room!"

"But Dad—"

"I said go to your room."

I sighed resignedly. "I lost my head, Pop. Your joke is better than mine, no doubt about it."

"That's a good boy," he beamed, and our first crisis was over.

And so it went. His jokes were always better than mine, either under the threat of bed without dinner or two weeks without my allowance or other things equally terrifying to a 33-year-old man with a wife and two children.

Working with Dad was truly amazing. I thought I'd mastered the art of comedy construction, especially with Sam Locke mentoring me on a daily basis—but I learned during the course of the next few weeks that I still had a long way to go. It was incredible learning experience to see what lines got laughs and which ones didn't. I was amazed at some of the surprises and Dad spent a lot of time with me explaining why certain things worked and others didn't. Unlike TV, where we were guaranteed mirth by the use of canned laughter, the theater was a whole new ball game, and it taught me more about comedy than I'd learned in my whole prior career.

My father directed the play himself and it got excellent reviews. Actually our entire family got into the act: My brother Paul manned the ticket booth, my mother sold sodas and muffins during the intermissions, and at some point during the run I stepped into the role of Harvey, the gambling lawyer, a part I had tailored for myself from the start.

Audiences roared at the play on a nightly basis—there were literally more laughs in *Match* than in a nearby production of *The Odd Couple*, a fact I can vouch for because I went to their show and clocked the laughs myself. During our five-month run we came very close several times to our goal of mounting a Broadway production, but it never came to pass and since we were only breaking even every week, we decided to close the show.

Although not an actor by profession, I had a knack for the craft and was really enjoying myself playing Harvey until one day during a brush-up rehearsal. I read a line in a way I thought was extremely funny, and suddenly the director bellowed, "No, no, you idiot, that's all wrong! It'll never get a laugh that way!"

"But, sir . . ." I began to protest.

"Listen, kid," said the director menacingly, "either you read the line my way or else!"

My shoulders sagged and I nodded. "Yes, Dad. Anything you say." I was damned if I was going to suffer through another night without my milk and cookies.

The original Bickersons play was a hoot of a farce which captured the flavor of the swingin' '60s, and was not unlike the pace and humor of the works of Neil Simon. Most of *Match Please, Darling*'s dialogue was new, not just a straight rehash of old Bix scripts, yet there was a lot of weaving in some of the best *old* lines for new characters:

HARVEY: How can a divorce lawyer like a married couple that spends twenty-four hours a day kissing and smooching? How can anybody stand that tactless loud-mouth and that greasy gigolo?

TEDDY: (Distastefully) Yeah . . . And now I have to go up there and lay out the paper plates and clean his tennis shoes. Mr. Jacobson, why does that man wear tennis shoes with a tuxedo??

HARVEY: He thinks he's Howard Hughes.

TEDDY: Yeah. Well, see you later, Mr. J.

HARVEY: Hey, wait a minute, Teddy. What anniversary did you say this is?

TEDDY: I told you, the Bickersons'. Their eleventh.

HARVEY: No, I mean what's the eleventh? . . . I gotta get them a present. Is that wood, tin, what?

TEDDY: Steel.

HARVEY: Good. I'll run down to Macy's—

TEDDY: (Joining with Harvey for this) —and steal something.

HARVEY: Really, Teddy. You don't want me to get 'em a cheap gift, do you?

TEDDY: No, you mustn't get 'em a cheap gift.

HARVEY: Lemme have ten dollars.

TEDDY: Get them a cheap gift.

HARVEY:	I'm good for it.
TEDDY:	Mr. Jacobson, what about the twenty dollars you already owe me?
HARVEY:	I can't pay you this week, Teddy.
TEDDY:	That's what you said last week.
HARVEY:	Well, I kept my word, didn't I?

On September 29, 1967, in Barney Glazer's gag-filled Theatre column in the *Vegas Visitor*, the reviews were great overall. Though he admitted "some of the lines date back before Achilles was a heel," he was quick to add "it's the most pleasurable evening I've spent since I dreamed that Richard Burton left Liz Taylor on my doorstep and ran off with Eddie Fisher." He thought Joey Forman's face was "priceless" as John Bickerson.

It will forever be unfortunate that Phil's precious Bix never found their way to Broadway. He had caught stage fever, briefly, during this time. One of his many '60s projects that fell through: in November of 1968 Rapp wanted to adapt *The Short Reign of Pippin IV* by John Steinbeck as a play. But the William Morris Agency informed him that it would cost $2,500 for a one-year option, plus a 2% royalty, and nothing further seemed to happen with it. What once was a lucrative business was becoming a chore that produced more misses than hits.

It was nearly time to sit back and let the kids handle things.

CHAPTER 13
AT THE END OF THE DAY

"In the 1940s Mom was buying fabulous properties in the Valley," states Paul. "Unfortunately, she sold these *incredible* properties, like the corner of Ventura and Sepulveda. A giant skyscraper went up there later! She had the right idea, but Dad drove her crazy that he was going into bankruptcy, even though she owned the most prime pieces.

"She later started complaining about the taxes on the property, and the fact she was in a highly rated fire zone, and various other complaints that she always made before selling the properties. It was the 1970s, when she was playing less golf and Dad's club friends were all passing away. She had put a lot of money into the houses and Dad continued to spend as always. Just as she had done with all of the prior real estate buys she had made, she insisted on selling instead of holding on for the future. At this point she had decided to sell the beautiful house I had helped build and wanted to move to a smaller home in the Beverly Hills flats. She was becoming increasingly concerned about having enough money for the rest of their lives and seemed to be selling everything. She was able to negotiate Dad's membership at Hillcrest, which he'd joined in 1947, with the condition that Dad retain all his rights at the club. The Board of Directors all loved him so much it was an easy pitch. The membership at that time was worth about $100,000 (it now is in the millions).

"Finally Dad's weekly golf partner, Abe Lastfogel passed away. Abe was the retired CEO of the William Morris agency and was (and still is) considered one of the most important people in the history of Hollywood. He lived out his last years in the penthouse of the Beverly Wilshire Hotel across from the William Morris agency. Having Abe Lastfogel represent you was reserved for the great and greater. Mom's dementia condition was progressing and Dad had outlived all of his friends. I used the club sparingly for a little golf, but this was the end of an era of one of the greatest groups of showbiz comedy legends ever assembled—The Hillcrest Round Table.

"It was amazing to me how he was so strong to take it in stride. But Dad knew something was wrong with Mom and he would never want to upset her. She kept saying she had to have money and was squeezing every penny to make sure there was money in the bank. Her brain was really playing tricks with her.

"I realized Dad was not getting the pension that was due him, so I began to cull his files to plead his case to the pension board and in so doing I uncovered all of his life's work which ultimately became the basis for this book."

Still, projects continued to come to Phil, especially where the Bickersons was concerned, and he was continuing to receive BMI Music royalties for the constantly played old Bickersons albums that refused to grow dusty. As late as 1970 he was also receiving BMI queries into the rights of several songs he wrote during his vaudeville days.

The love/hate relationship he had with modern humor meant Phil just couldn't leave TV alone—always writing scripts and submitting them through his agent and personal contacts. Occasionally it paid off. On June 15, 1971, Phil was offered a contract by cartoon giant Filmation for his "proposed script and concept" for a series called *Merlin*, which Filmation quickly renamed *Alley Oop*. He received $1,750 option money with the promise of a further $1,500 should they wish to extend the option beyond December 31, 1972. Phil was to receive $2,500 per script submitted to them, and a $1,000 royalty for each script produced but not written by him. This would be in addition to twenty percent of the net profits the nighttime series would generate.

As of December 14, 1971 he had an "estimating script" ready, which told the wacky tale of the inept Merlin who helped no one with his insane half-spells since they never seemed to hit the mark. In this "origin" story, Merlin tries to help King Arthur with a love potion, so Guinevere will love the first man she sees—who is, of course, by mistake, Merlin himself. And when the King is threatened with war from Chow Mein, the Emperor of Cathay (later named China), all the magician is able to do is transport Arthur and his Knights to a

Chinese restaurant in downtown Hollywood.

A strange notion for a kid's animated series indeed, and one which failed to progress past initial contracts.

Still ever one to keep pitching, the following October he soon had Skirball Productions in Century City interested in something else. SP offered Phil $12,500 plus 2.5% of the producer's profit for all rights to his story, *A Grave Undertaking*. After the deal fell through, he offered them a screenplay called *A Wolfe in Sheik's Clothing*. *Sheik* soon became a project that owner Jack H. Skirball thought would be a great vehicle for Peter Sellers. Rapp rewrote it yet again into *The Making of Robert*, for the princely sum of $100,000.

The *Robert* plot follows Edouard Arnaud, head of the perfume dept. of Tivoli Dept. Store in Paris, who has quite a reputation as a ladies' man. He's attractive and all his rich customers are mad for him, including his secretary Camille. It has its down side: the Russian Ambassador Gen. Golovin bursts into Tivoli to accuse Arnaud of having an affair with his luscious wife, Marina. Arnaud smoothly gets out of it, used to the bellowing of husbands, even though he's caught in Marina's embrace in the ambassador's car afterwards. But his 17-year-old son Robert is nothing like the old man or Arnaud's sex-crazed brother Philandre (who runs a vet clinic), who prefers working with animals to paying attention to his ravishing, neglected finacée, Marie. The farce begins when Robert overhears his mother calling Philandre about their dog, Casanova who is constantly in heat, getting every bitch in the neighborhood pregnant. After a brief bit of gossip about his father from Marie, Robert assumes the talk of infidelity and scandal is about Arnaud, and is determined to keep their happy home together. After Robert is sent to military school in punishment for altering the grades on his report card (they were already good, but Robert was promised a car if his grades showed improvement), he begins pleading with Arnaud's customers to leave Arnaud. When they want to know why they should give him up, Robert promises his own beefy hunk of flesh in return, which the hot married ladies eagerly accept. He meets them at night, Monday through Sunday, at Philandre's place of business, but the sex comedy comes to a racing and racy conclusion when all the ladies and husbands show up on one particular night, assuming that Arnaud (there to stop his son from eloping with poor, ignored

Marie) is the true Casanova of the family. When Arnaud escapes to collect his fried wits outside, a bus containing the whole chorus from the Folies Bergère arrive. They excitedly say, "He's got the technique . . . He brought joy to all of us!" Before they can explain how wonderful Robert was in curing their mascot, Arnaud faints dead away. The final scene comes in the honeymoon suite where the exhausted Robert is ordering two dozen oysters. He and Marie are now married, but poor Marie is still out of luck.

The 1970s brought a lot of work and false starts, but there was nothing Phil liked better than the thrill of the game. In 1970 all looked good for a Bickersons cartoon series to happen with KFI Films, Inc. A short, limited-animation demo was produced using one of the original Don/Frances tapes, but the series failed to get the go-ahead. In February of 1974 Rapp was contracted to write *The Caper*, "a one-half hour television show starring or featuring Dora Hall" for $1,500, within a year's time. Two years later, he was offered a book publishing contract for *With Love and Curses*, most likely his autobiography, with an advance on a ten percent royalty.

Even though Phil was still at the top of his game mentally, too many deals weren't panning out. Finally, Rapp had to face facts. Times had changed and there was new blood making the decisions these days. He had a few tough decisions to make himself:
(Written on Hillcrest Country Club stationery)
April 5, 1976

Dear Bud:
This is a painful letter for me to write. It has become common knowledge at the club that I am no longer in a financial position to maintain my membership.

I have been pressed by well-meaning member-friends to make a request for relief of my obligations (dues and assessments) and be allowed the facilities of my home away from home, so that I may continue to mingle with those I dearly love and respect. A quarter of a century is a long time, and while I am grateful for those many happy years as a regular member, I must face reality because of the inclemencies of fortune.

To go on would only be creating a soap opera, but a personal meeting with you and the board, or anybody you designate, would make the picture clear.

I will be available at your convenience any time, any place.
Most sincerely,
Philip Rapp

The following month Hillcrest granted Phil status as an ex-member so that he could sell his membership in the club and not worry about dues any longer, though he was still granted use of the club. He was requested to return his membership certificate so that "we can begin the process of the sale of said membership." After thoughtful consideration, Phil declined. He couldn't bear to sell his stake in the club. It was very difficult, but he requested to be reinstated as a member without dues. The Board met, and agreed. Phil was also forced to repeat the difficulty the following year.

"I can tell you," says Joel, "I had a *good* case of writer's block at one time which I know was brought on by seeing Dad not working, or not being able to get a job, or whatever. Was he jealous or resentful of me? I don't think so . . . he never expressed any negativity about my writing career, and was, in the early years, very supportive and helpful. And of course we wrote the play together which was in no way a competitive collaboration . . . later on he seemed to lose interest in what I was doing, especially after we opened Mother Earth [plant store]. He was beginning his slide into a deep depression by then and I'm sure that would account for his disinterest."

Still Phil Rapp kept writing. At some point, he busied his thoughts with writing a humorous cookbook, a feat that would showcase both his skills as comedy writer and Cordon Bleu chef. His notes ran as follows:

HOW TO COOK WITHOUT FOOD

Cooking in the nude
Sex in cookery

Samuel Johnson in Boswell's Life April 15, 1778 said: "Women cannot make a good book of cookery."

There is a French proverb, loosely translated—"Hunger is the first course of a good dinner."

The Talmud says—"Up to the age of forty, eating is beneficial, after forty, drinking."

ALL ABOUT COOKING
ALL ABOUT FISH
ALL ABOUT MEAT
ALL ABOUT FOWL
ALL ABOUT SAUCE
ALL ABOUT SOUP
ALL ABOUT HORS D'OEUVRES
ETC.

Twenty small volumes encased in a bookcase shaped like a stove.

Phil had always been an exemplary cook. More than that, according to Paul: "Dad always had all these different types of barbeques. On Sundays he would invite a dozen friends out to the ranch. Ribs and chicken and Chinese food made from vegies from the garden. He'd fire up those pig garbage cans and put in about 50 ears of corn. We had an acre of corn near the stables in the back. He had these big wooden Chinese bowls. Great big giant forks, funny, silly things.

"In the 1950s or '60s he had an idea for a cooking show which he thought would be a great combination of comedy and sponsorship by a gas company. And I remember he had a famous recipe for Deviled Bones that he gave to the world-famous Chasen's restaurant in Beverly Hills. His food was just incredible."

Even though by this point Philip Rapp had given up the quest for pitching new projects, he was still bringing in money from his old screen credits. A statement for the period ending March 31, 1975, sent by the Writers Guild of America West, came with a check for $57.34, "50% of 8%-" of the gross of *The Inspector General*'s $1,433.50 broadcast sales.

From 1974 to 1977 Rapp was also receiving very meager royalties from CBS Records for *The Bickersons* and *The Bickersons Fight Back* albums for which he received a mere fifteen cents per unit sold.

One 1975 royalty statement showed Rapp netting $189.75. But the Bickersons was still selling and was and *is still* a viable name. Shows were still sizzling on the air, and bootleggers were profiting from the gray area of copyright law that still haunts old-time radio shows today.

Metacom was a company producing old-time radio cassettes for fans which thought OTR was fair game and in the public domain. But in 1978 Paul Rapp, now having power of attorney for his dad's estate, had informed the FBI that Philip Rapp was the creator and owner of the Bickersons. Metacom claimed that no federal copyright protection existed for sound recordings made prior to February 15, 1972, that being the date that the Federal Copyright Act was amended for permitting the copyrighting of sound recordings. What they were disturbed about was that some of the shows they were distributing had come from records made after that date, with Rapp functioning as producer and thereby owning part/all of the property. Metacom wanted a copy of Rapp's agreement with CBS to resolve the matter, after which they could discuss their licensing (or discontinuing) the product.

The Rapps' attorney, Gordon Levoy, wrote to Metacom's attorney, George H. Frisch, asserting that they were correct about the 1972 copyright law, but reminded them of the "literally hundreds of legal decisions affording protection and substantial recovery. There are also many different approaches which have been successfully asserted and accepted by the courts: Protection under state common law copyright which has existed since 1834. Basic rights by virtue of plagiarism. The principle of unfair competition." Levoy also reminded them that the name "Bickersons," though not copyrighted, had a secondary meaning which needed to be authorized. "To anyone in the active portion of the entertainment industry, and to the general viewing and listening audiences, the title 'Bickersons' is firmly entrenched and specifically identified with the name of Phil Rapp and his works."

Metacom's Director of Marketing James I. McCann wrote on September 22, 1978 to explain that if the Rapps could furnish proof of their rights, Metacom would like to discuss a non-exclusive use of their shows. They preferred to pay on pressing rather than on sales, paying a minimum royalty over a five-year period. Levoy's office was concerned about proving rights, but the Rapp files contained more than enough author and rights proof to secure a long-term Metacom contract that renewed yearly.

Meantime, a July 28, 1980 contract was signed between Phil and Radio Renaissance to produce a new Bickersons radio pilot show based upon the old scripts and characters, to be produced in Canada and globally distributed. Phil received $1,500 (Canadian dollars) for exclusive option to the Bickersons name in Canada for 180 days and world radio broadcast rights to all Bickersons material. The sum of $250 (Canadian) would be paid for each and every sketch produced in preparation for the coming series, plus 10% of the net receipts. The series was most likely not produced.

Lack of a steady income produced some tough choices in the later years. "Dad said the ranch was too much upkeep," Paul states. "If Mom had waited two years . . . overnight that area went from a sleepy little nothing to a huge development, the entire Valley. But she felt that they'd never get enough water in that area. Plus, the racing stable was taking up too much time and money. I pass by it occasionally now. It's been divided into apartments and single resident homes. The wall is still up, the entrance to the ranch.

"After she sold the Hillside house she bought a small house in the Beverly Hills Flats. I was, at this point, growing very confused with her actions. Everything was topsy-turvy in my life and I was not paying enough attention to everything. I had directed the *Happy Days* episode with Fonzie jumping the shark cage (2nd unit action) [which gave rise to the expression "jumping the shark"]. I was also trying to develop the *Beverly Hills Cop* idea; Dad had interviewed chief of detectives of Beverly Hills police, Lynn Franklin, at my house. Over a number of tape-recorded sessions he then wrote the treatment, "Beverly Hills is my Beat" which I gave to Ed Milkas, one of the senior producers of *Happy Days* who passed it on to Eddie Murphy's people. The rest is history. It still steams me up when I think of the *Beverly Hills Cop* series.

"By this time Mom was growing more and more disoriented which consumed me a lot. I would frequently have to go over to her place (five minutes away) to pick her up off the floor. My son Brian was very helpful during this period.

"It was at this time that I secured a copyright on the Bickersons.

My best friend and family lawyer, Leonard Maizlish, passed away in the mid-eighties, which left me without the most important person in my life. Everything was very chaotic for me and I was struggling to keep it together. In 1987 I started Legal Video Services with Brian's help. It became a very important source of money." LVS still films depositions for court cases, "Providing professional quality video for: computer graphics, satellite/telephonic depositions, settlement documentaries, product liability." Their clients include the Coudert Brothers, Kinsella Weitzman, Paul Hastings, Sullivan & Cromwell, and a host of other law firms, plus some high profile entertainment-related cases, such as Michael Jackson.

Paul had his hands full with the Rapp legacy, especially the Bickersons, which everyone seemed to want. On April 23, 1981 Paul gave Ross LaManna permission to submit a proposal to Hanna-Barbera to produce an animated or live-action Bickersons series, and in November, United Airlines had programmed a Bickersons album into their in-flight entertainment "because we feel it is an excellent piece of humor that cuts across all age groups." Over four million passengers had an opportunity to hear the comedy in the two months it was broadcast.

Also that November Paul received a query from Wyaduck Productions, Inc. wishing to license a few minutes of the *Deputy Seraph* footage for an upcoming PBS documentary called *The Marx Brothers in a Nutshell*. They were to pay Phil $275 per half-minute of footage used, making a total of $1,100. The 105-minute film would be distributed by Universal films after the airing, though they did not use the footage.

A year later Paul gave the green light to Vince Viverito and Ruth Landis who had written a play that dealt with the off-mike relationship of the characters who play John and Blanche Bickerson on-mike. An attorney sent an agreement for the writers to sign but talks were still in the works about what specific Bickersons material would be used. The playwrights also hoped to keep film rights open, just in case. They wanted to use some material from *The Bickersons Rematch*. The play had been optioned by a "major Chicago commercial theatrical producer" who first wanted confirmation of rights to the Bickersons. The Apollo Theater Center was interested.

John Joslyn of the Westgate Group was likewise very keen to do a Bickersons skit for TV as late as March 1983: "A new treatment has been written utilizing the same era. Actresses being considered are Dyan Cannon and Cher. If the network show does not come to fruition then we will approach the cable networks.

"Philip, I'm convinced that 'the Bickersons' will see air again or perhaps a run on Broadway. Your property is as fresh today as it was when it was written."

Two years later, Joslyn reported that Showtime was very interested in the property, as a half-hour format for the husband-and-wife comedy team of Jerry Stiller and Anne Meara. One script was "in hand" and another story had been begun, but not by Rapp. A creative meeting was called for all involved on Friday, October 18, but again, it was not to be.

Later, serious discussions were beginning with Twentieth Television (Fox) to produce a pilot of *The Bickersons*. The purchase price offered was $10,000, with a one-year option for $2,500, and 10% of the net profits. Paul Rapp submitted a counter-offer of a $25,000 purchase price, $10,000 option and the same ten percent. A consultant fee for Paul would net him $5,000 per episode, but when a compromise could not be met, especially over absolute rights to the name BICKERSONS, the deal fell through.

Significantly, *Married with Children* began soon after . . .

The Bickersons refused to die on the radio, however. Tapes were still circulating among old-time radio fans and were receiving constant play at several major comedy radio stations (as in New York City, where *The Bickersons Rematch* was the #1 most requested comedy album). All of this only perpetuated the love-hate relationship between Metacom and the Rapp family. On April 14, 1983 a letter arrived from Metacom president James I. McCann who wanted exclusive rights to the Bickersons, and immediate air play rights as well, otherwise they didn't want to discuss a catalog deal further. They were desperate to have tapes that would be ready for a Christmastime release.

Five years later Metacom operated under the theory that all radio programs were in public domain so they weren't receptive to licensing requests. But after three lawsuits with estates of radio actors and authors, they paid $250,000 in back royalties and set up licensing agreements. Royalties paid out to licensors in 1982 alone was in the six figures. During the fiscal year ending September 30, 1983, Metacom had manufactured over two million old radio shows. This was 25 times bigger than their only licensed competitor, Nostalgia Lane.

The Bickersons had been dropped because Metacom couldn't secure a license. Now they were eagerly anxious for Paul Rapp to say yes, knowing that Rapp's take could equal $5,000 to $10,000 in royalties the first year, perhaps more. It would cost $10,000 that year just preparing the artwork and the packaging.

Metacom was jealous and forceful of their rights, as big businesses are who invest a lot of money in product. In 1987 cease and decease letters were sent to infringing sellers, such as Jonathan Sonneborn, president of Premier Electronic Laboratories, Inc., for making and selling Bickersons tapes.

Paul Rapp likewise caught a bootlegger that year. As he wrote to a business associate, "I have had a chance to peruse the Xerox copy of a record album entitled *The Return of the Bickersons!* and listen to the tapes. First let me say that I have never heard of Radiola and I can assure you they will wish they never heard from me. That aside I will make some points. They are clearly guilty of a number of serious crimes. Copyright violation, unfair competition, false advertising, forgery, and libel, to name a few. Such blatant piracy is shocking. Since Metacom has the license to sell The Bickersons as contracted by me it is obvious that you must move swiftly to cause them to cease and desist. Before I take any action I would like a report from you as to what and how you are going to proceed. Metacom is all too familiar with how I deal with people who steal my father's property. I have records of payment for royalties dating back to 1960 to the very present and since these thieves claim to have been marketing the property since 1970 to the present I shall not take the matter lightly. As you know I have been acquiring a number of the old radio shows to add to your catalogue of present material that you now have. I would like to impress upon you that I am currently talking with networks to put The Bickersons on TV and as you well know the option for same is held by MGM. It is no small joke to see the remarks—which are false—regarding The Bickersons and television."

Frank G. Peppiatt, co-creator/producer/writer of *Hee Haw* and many music specials for Frank Sinatra, Judy Garland, etc., started out on the *right* foot when he wrote to Paul on April 28, 1986:

"My name is Frank Peppiatt and my associate is Lester Gottlieb. We would like to develop your property The Bickersons for a half-hour situation comedy. We would up-date Blanche and John and make them grandparents in the '80s. They would have visible children and grandchildren and would bicker about contemporary things like women's lib (something that Blanche doesn't quite understand but defends to the death, John's death, not hers), drugs in America, Ronald Reagan, international politics and economics, etc., etc.

"The Bickersons will mirror the confusion of the older generation and give them a comedy voice to trickle down and sometimes avalanche down to the middle-aged yuppies and teenagers. Blanche and John will champion a group that has been standing idly by while the world, in their view, has been plunged into the hands of the OPEC knaves, the Mafia monsters and Washington wise-guys. Blanche and John will never agree on corrective measures but, believe me, they will certainly let the world know that something is amiss. They will join groups and societies that hope to correct some of the world's ills. They won't, however, join the same groups. Their separate societies will have the same goals but far different methods of obtaining them. Just like the Bickersons, who want the same results. Peace, jobs, less poverty, civil rights for everyone, a stable dollar and no in-laws staying over more than one night but are diametrically opposed to one another's reasons for wanting them."

It was another fine idea for Phil's legacy that never quite panned out.

The Bickersons holds a charm—stronger than mere nostalgia—that makes people remember them. They define a *kind* of relationship (to quote John Bickerson: "Marriage isn't a word, it's a sentence!"), and still permeate the media today. Watch *The Proposal* (2009) and you'll hear Sandra Bullock compare their characters to the Bickersons; they were even mentioned in the film *M*A*S*H*.

Poor husband John, Nature Boy and the ever strident Blanche will forever live on in this world and the next, though their beloved creator passed on to that great bourbon repository in the sky. Mariam Rapp died on May 25 1993. Phil followed just a few years later, on January 23, 1996.

"Mom was a real beauty in her day," Joel recalls; ". . . very loving, fun-loving, smart as a whip about investments and such. And a tigress when it came to defending Dad or her kids. He and my mother were the real-life Bickersons, but they were married over sixty years and after she died, he just gave up living . . ."

"She had to be the best horserace handicapper of all time," says Paul. "She had this strange tool that looked like a slide rule that was incredible at showing you who should win a particular race. She was still using it into her seventies. Tragically, she contracted Alzheimer's disease in her eighties and it ravaged her so bad that thankfully she died in her sleep at 85. Had she not had that awful illness I believe she would have made it to 100 easily.

"Dad had moved in after the night of my mother's passing and lived with me. One morning I came into Dad's room and he was sitting on the edge of the bed. I asked how he was and he told me he had a very bad dream and said he was afraid of dying. Looking back I should have taken much more time and compassion but I lacked the knowledge that I now know. I dismissed his thought by explaining that we all have to die and maybe he would outlive me. I lacked the knowledge of how to treat someone concerned about death and dismissed it too lightly. I talked a little about the end of life and when I asked about cremation he said definitely, with quite a sense of humor, he didn't want anyone trampling all over him and that seemed to close the subject. I left his room feeling very disturbed and to this day I cannot help but look back a the opportunity I should have taken to discuss death and comfort him more.

"Soon after that he had several small strokes which lasted for a few minutes each. I decided it was time to call his doctor and after a couple of days when he took more time to respond to me than usual, I called Dr. Fred Kahn. I had a 24 hour nurse, Estelle Ross, and she was at his bedside when Dr Kahn arrived. He began examining Dad as he slept, who briefly awoke with open eyes and grabbed the doctors hands with an emotion of deep thanks to be seeing him. He then seemed to close his eyes. The doctor concluded his exam. I will never forget what he said to me when I asked him his thoughts. He raised his voice with sadness and anger. Dr Kahn said, 'The man is trying to die.' There was considerable emotion in his statement and he asked Estelle if she had felt a large lump in his left side. She responded yes and asked him what it was. He said he didn't know and didn't want to know.

"I knew the end was going to be coming soon. Dad hated hospitals and it was not necessary to put him in one. Dad had always said people go to hospitals to die and he never wanted to go. Christmas had just passed and I bought him some new pajamas which I had tailored to fit him properly and he really was like a kid with a new toy. He looked at the pajamas as a uniform and he was so proud to show them off. At the same Christmas I purposely gave him a single slipper, so he could complain about his missing slipper like John Bickerson.

"It was about one in the morning, when I was awakened by my dog Shaka, who was making a strange howling sound. I went downstairs and was met by Dad's nurse, Estelle Ross. We went into Dad's bedroom and Shaka was next to Dad's bed. Shaka immediately came to me as Estelle checked Dad. She told me he had passed away. I thought immediately—John Bickerson is finally going to get the sleep he has always craved."

Paul Rapp signed an authorization for scattering Phil's ashes five miles off the Newport Beach coastline in Orange County.

"When Dad died," says Joel, "he was honored with a half-page obituary in the *New York Times* and a similar remembrance in the *Los Angeles Times*. But the most touching tribute came a couple of days after he died as I was driving down Wilshire Boulevard, listening to the radio. A wonderful program on National Public Radio called *All Things Considered* was on, and suddenly I realized they had just started a story about somebody who we had just lost who had contributed so much to the humor history of our country. In an instant I knew it was Dad they were talking about, and I pulled over to the curb to listen. They played snippets of the Bickersons and snippets of Snooks, and at the end of a simply beautiful tribute, they signed off with a song that goes, 'We'll meet again, don't know where, don't know when . . .' That was the first time since he'd passed away that I cried."

Goodnight, John.

Goodnight, Blanche.

PHOTO GALLERY
SECTION THREE

In Colorado, Paul directing stunt with Rock Hudson on Roger Corman's film *Avalanche* in 1978.

In Arkansas Roger Corman and Paul discuss production of *Boxcar Bertha*, Martin Scorsese's directorial debut in 1970.

Paul Rapp on the set of *Boxcar Bertha*, 1972.

Phil.

Phil doing his Bickerson best, September 1969. Grandson Brian in foreground aboard Paul's yacht.

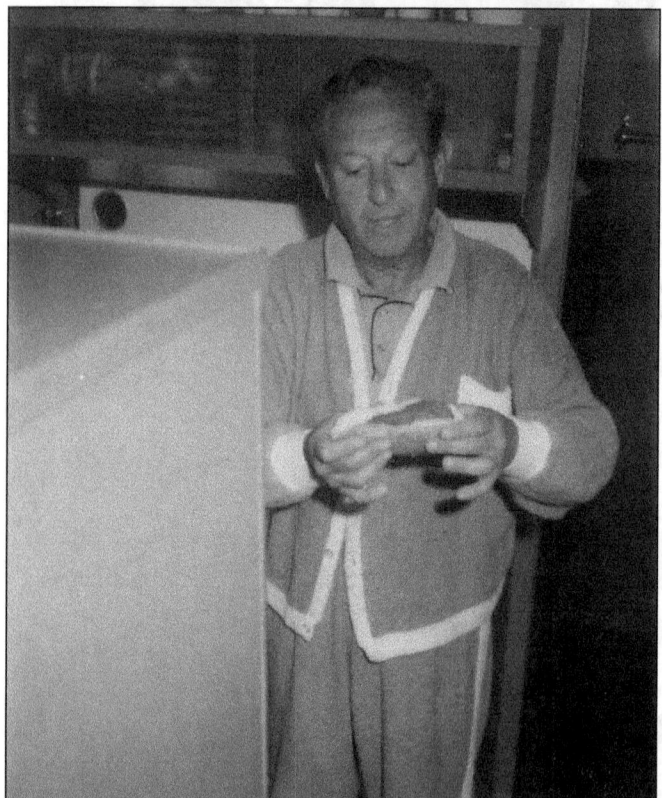

Phil rolls his own late-night hot dog.

Mariam Rapp & Frances Langford, October 1966.

Mariam Rapp, October 1966.

Paul: "Dad decided to take up painting in his seventies. One of his first oils was the Indian. The ship was an oil he threw together in one afternoon. The bird is a watercolor. He really seemed to enjoy doing paintings in his seventies and eighties."

Paul with Brian who was playing Bruce Dern's son in the film, *The St. Valentine's Day Massacre* (1967).

Paul and Brian, a tad later in life.

```
ABBOTT LABORATORIES
PREAM
ONE 60-SECOND ET RADIO COMMERCIAL
"RED CABBAGE"
#6-60
```

SOUND: (CLATTER OF DISHES)

JOHN: ~~(SNORING SOUNDS)~~ (SNORES LIGHTLY)

BLANCHE: John Bickerson, wake up!

JOHN: Uhuh ... uhuh ... Whatsamatter, Blanche?

BLANCHE: How can you sleep at the breakfast table? I've been talking for two minutes & you never heard a word.

JOHN: ~~It's my only defense against your cooking.~~ Oh, eat your breakfast. Said!

BLANCHE: ~~What's wrong with my cooking?~~ No sir! Nobody is gonna make JOHN: Mm. BLANCHE: What sort of

JOHN: ~~Look at these! Whoever heard of~~ purple pancakes? an affliction

BLANCHE: Those aren't pancakes, John. That's a red cabbage stuffed omelet, with curried tapioca, is it well an aphid in it a dive

JOHN: ~~For breakfast?~~ I wouldn't touch it! give up!

BLANCHE: Well, you don't like the normal things people eat for breakfast ...

JOHN: I like normal breakfasts, Blanche. You just don't know how to make 'em that way!

BLANCHE: Oh John, I try so hard to make everything nice. I even fixed your coffee a different way this morning.

JOHN: ~~Didn't burn it, huh?~~ that's for sure!

BLANCHE: I put Pream in it, John. Pream tastes better than cream in your coffee.

JOHN: Maybe it'll drown out the taste altogether.

BLANCHE: You never appreciate anything I do! I used new Pream especially for you. Now you better taste it, John Bickerson! Go ahead. Taste it!

A rewritten page from a Bickersons radio commercial in the 1970s.

This is John Bickerson.

Brian Rapp and Grandma Mariam. Joel's portrait hangs in the background.

Paul: "My grandson Jamie and I at Sycamore Canyon Beach, ten miles north of Malibu. Jamie is about two years old in this picture, circa 2000 or 2001."

A few of Phil's golf trophies.

The good life in Aspen with wife Wora, stepson Nick, and Brian circa 2004.

Phil's legacy from left to right, great-grandsons Oliver and Jamie and son Paul.

Wora & Paul, guests of the Prime Minister of Thailand, Wora's homeland.

River rafting in Thailand, Paul & Wora in foreground.

*This is to Certify
that the Cremated Remains of*

Philip Rapp

have been respectfully delivered into the sea

off the   Newport Beach   *Coastline*

Approximate Latitude 33°32:70N *Longitude* 117°54:50W

on this day of   February 13th   *year of*   1996

according to the laws of this State

Captain

APPENDIX 1

1. RAPP'S TYPEWRITTEN LIST OF SNOOKS/MORGAN SKETCHES FROM *MHCT*
(ALL BITS WRITTEN BY RAPP)

MAXWELL HOUSE COFFEE TIME
1941 – SPOTS

DATE	BABY SNOOKS	FRANK MORGAN
JANUARY 2, 1941	SNOOKS KEEPS DADDY HOME	MORGAN RETURN—WHALE SPOT
JANUARY 9, 1941	ART MUSEUM	INDIA SPOT
JANUARY 16, 1941	STAMP COLLECTION	FLYING TO SUN VALLEY—SHINING
JANUARY 23, 1941	OVERNITE IN A BARN	CHEMISTRY SPOT
JANUARY 30, 1941	DADDY ON THE JURY	SURGEON
FEBRUARY 6, 1941	BOTANICAL GARDENS	HIGHLAND FAMILY–GOLF
FEBRUARY 13, 1941	INCOME TAX	ORIENTAL MANHUNT

APPENDIX 1

DATE	BABY SNOOKS	FRANK MORGAN
FEBRUARY 20, 1941	ON THE YACHT	FALCON SPOT
FEBRUARY 27, 1941	AT SANTA ANITA	ELEPHANTS' GRAVEYARD
MARCH 6, 1941	CARD TRICKS	MORGAN MURDER CASE
MARCH 13, 1941	PSYCHO-ANALYSIS	DIAMOND SPOT
MARCH 20, 1941	PICTURE TAKING	PHRENOLOGY SPOT
MARCH 27, 1941	BUYING SHOES	ANTHROPOLOGY SPOT
APRIL 3, 1941	ZOOLOGICAL GARDENS	ARCHITECT SPOT
APRIL 10, 1941	FISHING TRIP	COMPOSER SPOT
APRIL 17, 1941	OPENING GAME—BASEBALL	RETURN FROM MEXICO
APRIL 24, 1941	DADDY COOKS SUPPER	PSYCHO-ANALYSIS SPOT
MAY 1, 1941	A GOLF GAME	SECRET INVENTION—BISCULAR
MAY 8, 1941	HORSEBACK RIDING	FACING CAR PILOT
MAY 15, 1941	AT THE BEACH	DENTIST
MAY 22, 1941	HOMEWORK	CAMERAMEN
MAY 29, 1941	AUCTION SALE	HORTICULTURIST
JUNE 5, 1941	SETTING-UP EXERCISES	ART COLLECTION

DATE	BABY SNOOKS	FRANK MORGAN
June 12, 1941	Guinea Pigs	Seaman
June 19, 1941	Father's Day	Monte Carlo
June 26, 1941	Daddy paints a picture	Fire Chief
July 3, 1941	Plane trip	Motion pictures
July 10, 1941	Snooks goes to camp	Discoverer

July 17, 1941–August 28, 1941—Show Off Air

September 4, 1941	Allan Jones (No Snooks)	Snooks runs away
September 11, 1941	Corinne Mura (Singer)	Bureau of Investigation (Joseph Dunn)
September 18, 1941	Corinna Mura	Astrology (Blanca Holmen)
September 25, 1941	Corinna Mura	Prison warden (Clyde Plummer)
October 2, 1941	Blood hounds after Snooks	Baseball spot
October 9, 1941	Snooks returns	Football (Mike Frankovitch)
October 16, 1941	Beauty shop	Magician (Dante)
October 23, 1941	Duck-hunting	Swords man (Fred Caocas)

DATE	BABY SNOOKS	FRANK MORGAN
OCTOBER 30, 1941	HALLOWEEN	ARCHER (LARRY HUGHES)
NOVEMBER 6, 1941	BUYING DEFENSE STAMPS	GOLF (BETTY HICKS NOWELL)
NOVEMBER 13, 1941	MARKETING	DOCTOR
NOVEMBER 20, 1941	THANKSGIVING DINNER	MOUNTED POLICE (BRUCE CARRUTHERS)
NOVEMBER 27, 1941	THE OPERA	MODEL (KEY ALDRIDGE) (PURITAN)
DECEMBER 4, 1941	VISITING SANTA	FISH & GAME DIV. (CAPT. OBER)
DECEMBER 11, 1941	VISITING AN OCULIST	MOUNTAIN CLIMBER (PAUL PETZOLDT)
DECEMBER 18, 1941	AIR RAID WARDEN	KING OF HOBOS (DUSTY NELSON)
DECEMBER 25, 1941	TOYS COME TO . LIFE	EGYPTIAN SCARAB (ANTIQUES)

1942

DATE	BABY SNOOKS	FRANK MORGAN
JANUARY 1, 1942	DADDY'S HANGOVER	POLO SPOT (SNOWY BAKER)
JANUARY 8, 1942	VICTORY GARDEN	DEEPSEA DIVING (GEO. M. CHASE)
JANUARY 15, 1942	RED IS HOUSE GUEST	PHYSICAL CULTURE (TERRY HUNT)

DATE	BABY SNOOKS	FRANK MORGAN
January 22, 1942	Restaurant spot	Ballet dancer (Tilly Looch)
January 29, 1942	Report card forgery	Radio invention spot
February 5, 1942	Knitting spot	Druggist (Jack Schwab)
February 12, 1942	Red & Snooks erect tent	Stewardess (Edna Mae Jones)
February 19, 1942	Insurance spot	Don, the Beachcomber (guest)
February 26, 1942	Synthetic rubber (drawn)	"Whom the Gods Would Destroy"
March 5, 1942	Examination preparation	Income tax spot
March 12, 1942	Income tax spot	Sailor spot
March 19, 1942	Measles (false alarm)	Animal husbandry
March 26, 1942	First aid exam	Feather bureau (Harry Douglas)
April 2, 1942	April Fool spot	Dr. H. H. Chang (guest) (different)
April 9, 1942	Daddy's birthday	Tennis spot (Bill Tilden)

Appendix 1

DATE	BABY SNOOKS	FRANK MORGAN
April 16, 1942	Liniment spot	Nurse spot
April 23, 1942	Fishing tackle	Trapeze spot–Circus
April 30, 1942	Fishing tackle (cont.)	Electrical inventor
May 7, 1942	Red & Snooks (tackle)	Forestry spot–Botany
May 14, 1942	Wedding spot (Snooks ill)	U. Soo. (Dr. Giannini)
May 21, 1942	Sugar invention	Lumber camp spot
May 28, 1942	Psycho-analysis spot	Poet spot
June 4, 1942	Wedding anniversary	Alienist spot (Dr. Gordon)
June 11, 1942	Twins are born	Groucho Marx (no Morgan)
June 18, 1942	Bathing the twins	Amnesia spot
June 25, 1942	Botanical Garden spot	Pat O'Malley (no Morgan)
July 2, 1942	Christening the twins	Reginald Gardiner (no Morgan)
July 9, 1942	Preparation for camp	Jimmy Durante (no Morgan)

DATE	BABY SNOOKS	FRANK MORGAN
July 16, 1942	Snooks goes to camp	Frank Fay (no Morgan)
July 23, 1942	"New York Tale" (Hallinger)	Amnesia disappears (Morgan return)
July 30, 1942	"Last Request" (Hallinger)	Alaska spot (Ann Southern)
August 6, 1942	"All's Well"	Mechanical women
August 13, 1942	"Warden's Orders"	Frank Buck (guest)
August 20, 1942	"It's Fun To Be Fooled"	Concert vocalist
August 27, 1942	"Episode of a Train"	Psychologist spot
September 3, 1942 (Stettinius)	Return from camp	Commando spot
September 10, 1942	Stolen duck	Delinquent girls
September 17, 1942	Turkish bath	Ice-skating (Betty Atkinson)
September 24, 1942	Movie spot	Coal Mining spot
October 1, 1942	Insomnia spot	Newspaper editor (Manchester Boddy)
October 8, 1942	Boat christening	Gasoline substitute
October 15, 1942	Fuel conservation	Indian chief spot

APPENDIX 1

DATE	BABY SNOOKS	FRANK MORGAN
October 22, 1942	Boss invited to dinner	Radium discovery
October 29, 1942	Office spot—Boss comes home to play cards	Taxidermy (Walter Brandler)
November 5, 1942	Halloween spot	Psychiatry spot (Dr. Gordon)
November 12, 1942	Junior Red Cross	Duck hunting (Harry Fleischman)
November 19, 1942	Tonsil spot	Conscience spot
November 26, 1942	Thanksgiving spot	Football spot (Frank Bull)
December 3, 1942	Synthetic gasoline	Willson farewell—Gen. Morgan
December 10, 1942	Duck-hunting	Intro—Frank Tours (British ancestor)
December 17, 1942	Christians program (school)	Atlantic cable spot
December 24, 1942	Toys come to life	Egyptian scarab
December 31, 1942	Skiing spot	Test pilot (LaVerne Brown)

1943—SPOTS

DATE	BABY SNOOKS	FRANK MORGAN
January 7, 1943	Synthetic dairy products	CWI spot

DATE	BABY SNOOKS	FRANK MORGAN
January 14, 1943	School medal	Glass blower
January 21, 1943	Blood bank	Hockey (Jonny Polich)
January 28, 1943	Visit to Observatory	Casablanca
February 4, 1943	V-Mail	Conte disappears
February 11, 1943	Snooks keeps house	Conte returns (Interior Decorator)
February 18, 1943	Leather invention	Paleontology – Bones
February 25, 1943	Rationing	Pioneers
March 4, 1943	Beauty parlor	Female wrestler (Clara Mortensen)
March 11, 1943	Uncle Bushrod's visit	Income tax
March 18, 1943	Public library	Hydroponics— Botony
March 25, 1943	Daddy's sore back	Ballet (Maria Gambaralli)
April 1, 1943	April Fool's Day	Telepathy (Dr. Heger)
April 8, 1943	Easter outfit	Cast wants to do dramatics

Appendix 1

DATE	BABY SNOOKS	FRANK MORGAN
April 15, 1943	Snooks sore throat	Cast wants to do dramatics (cont.)
April 22, 1943	Uncle Bushrod's place	Architect
April 29, 1943	2nd War Loan—Threatre lobby	Circus barker (Paris Peggy)
May 6, 1943	Snooks swallows dime	Gardener
May 13, 1943	Faucet leaks	Regarding dogs
May 20, 1943	Point rationing	Deep sea fishing
May 27, 1943	Fat salvage	Lawyer
June 3, 1943	Snooks learns to ride	Railroad engineer
June 10, 1943	Killing the chicken	Canary Island
June 17, 1943	Morgan's Farm (cont.)	Commander Morgan

OFF AIR FOR SUMMER, 1943
(Blind date replaced for eight weeks from New York.)

September 2, 1943	Making a bed	War correspondent
September 9, 1943	Third War Loan	Palmistry
September 16, 1943	School starts	Bullfighter in Mexico

DATE	BABY SNOOKS	FRANK MORGAN
September 23, 1943	Hiring a sitter	Endocrinologist (Bunny Waters & Dorothy Ford)
September 30, 1943	Renting a house	Inventor (Albert Burns)
October 7, 1943	Daddy has a séance.	Steamship line (Morgan sings "Sonny Boy")
October 14, 1943	Interview at school	Cowboy (Jeanne Godshall)
October 21, 1943	Brentwood is tied up with serial wire.	Chef (Chef Milani)
October 28, 1943	Paper conservation	Musician (Wingy Manone)
November 4, 1943	Mudge court case	Private detective (Marjorie Henderson)
November 11, 1943	Mudge fight	March Field (Doris Merrick)
November 18, 1943	Burglar in the house	Stunt man (Billy Jones)
November 25, 1943	Turn into turkeys	Raising the Normandie
December 2, 1943	Ice box light	Stolen turkeys (Hill Gargan)

DATE	BABY SNOOKS	FRANK MORGAN
December 9, 1943	Wrong restaurant	Volcanoes (Leo Marks)
December 16, 1943	Salesman (Eddie Marr)	Psychiatrist (Dr. Wright)
December 23, 1943	Hunting an Xmas tree	Claims kin to Santa Claus
December 30, 1943	Zoo (with Morgan)	"Thousands Cheer" (Marilyn Maxwell)

1944

DATE	BABY SNOOKS	FRANK MORGAN
January 6, 1944	New Year's Resolution	Superman
January 13, 1944	Papering the house	British Intelligence
January 20, 1944	School play	March of Time
January 27, 1944	Talent Scout	Penicillin
February 3, 1944	At The Station	Voodooism (Sharon Douglas)
February 10, 1944 (Warner's)	On the Train for Hollywood	Genealogy (Dorris Merrick)
February 17, 1944	Arrival in Hollywood	Mynah bird spot
February 24, 1944	Screen test	Fighter Eddie Marcus

DATE	BABY SNOOKS	FRANK MORGAN
March 2, 1944	Share-the-Ride	Truth Drug
March 9, 1944	Hitch-biking	Lady Jockey
March 16, 1944	Uncle Norman Byron	Mairzy Doats Opera (Mostyn Thomas)
March 23, 1944	Looking for Gold	Agriculturalist
March 30, 1944 (Brice ill)	Barber Shop spot	Reincarnation
April 6, 1944 (Brice ill)	Burns & Allen	School for Brides (Roscoe Karns)
April 13, 1944	Arriving home	Pre-fabricated houses
April 20, 1944	Rehearsing speech	Morgan's Memoirs
April 27, 1944	Firing the Maid	Hypnosis spot
May 4, 1944	Relaxation spot	Dehydration
May 11, 1944	Snooks' marriage	Coffee spot MGM
May 18, 1944	Piano lesson	Electric Eye
May 25, 1944	Fishing spot	Vitamin spot
June 1, 1944	Snooks insomnia	RDX spot
June 8, 1944	Rodeo spot	Architect spot

MORGAN MATERIAL—DECEMBER 16, 1937 TO JUNE 30, 1938

DATE	TITLE	PROGRAM #
DECEMBER 16, 1937	PAUL REVERE	7
DECEMBER 23, 1937	BROKER SKETCH	8
DECEMBER 30, 1937	SERVICE (TICKET AGENCY—KAUFFMAN-DONNELLY)	9
JANUARY 6, 1938	TELEPHONE SKETCH MORGAN'S TRIP TO ENGLAND	10
JANUARY 13, 1938	MORGAN'S BOOK ON HORSE RACING	11
JANUARY 20, 1938	MORGAN'S ACCIDENT	12
JANUARY 27, 1938	MORGAN'S NEW MAIL-ORDER HOUSE	13
FEBRUARY 3, 1938	MORGAN, HUNTING FOR HIS HOUSE	14
FEBRUARY 10, 1938	MORGAN'S TRIP TO EUROPE	15
FEBRUARY 17, 1938	MORGAN, THE OLYMPIC CHAMPION	16
FEBRUARY 24, 1938	MORGAN, THE DETECTIVE	17
MARCH 3, 1938	MORGAN, THE HORSE EXPERT	18

DATE	TITLE	PROGRAM #
MARCH 10, 1938	MORGAN, THE PHYSICAL SPECIMEN	19
MARCH 17, 1938	MORGAN, THE WRESTLER	20
MARCH 24, 1938	F. C. C. SPOT / SANTA ANITA SPOT	21
MARCH 31, 1938	MORGAN'S FLEA, Tchaikovsky	22
APRIL 7, 1938	MORGAN, THE MUSICIAN	23
APRIL 14, 1938	MORGAN MEN'S STYLE LEADER	24
APRIL 21, 1938	MORGAN, THE GOURMET	25
APRIL 28, 1938	FRENCH SPOT	26
MAY 5, 1938	FRANK MORGAN'S ESCORT SERVICE	27
MAY 12, 1938	ESCORT SERVICE	28
MAY 19, 1938	MORGAN OPERA SPOT	29
MAY 26, 1938	MORGAN, THE SONG WRITER	30
JUNE 2, 1938	MORGAN, THE SPANISH SCOTCHMAN	31
JUNE 9, 1938	DOG ROUTINE	32

Appendix 1

DATE	TITLE	PROGRAM #
JUNE 16, 1938	TICKETS TO EUROPE	33
JUNE 23, 1938	MORGAN, THE TENNIS CHAMPION	34
JUNE 30, 1938	MORGAN, AS "ABDUL"	35
SEPTEMBER 1, 1938	MORGAN, THE DOCTOR	36
SEPTEMBER, 8, 1938	MORGAN, THE GENERAL	37
SEPTEMBER 15, 1938	MORGAN, THE LAWYER	38
SEPTEMBER 22, 1938	MORGAN, THE FIGHTER (MORGAN FOR SENATOR –SONG)	39
SEPTEMBER 29, 1938	MORGAN CAMERAMAN SPOT	40
OCTOBER 6, 1938	MORGAN, THE COMMISSIONER	41
OCTOBER 13, 1938	MORGAN, THE DANCER	42
OCTOBER 20, 1938	MORGAN, THE AMBASSADOR	43
OCTOBER 27, 1938	MORGAN, THE NEWSPAPERMAN	44
NOVEMBER 3, 1938	MORGAN, THE VIOLINIST	45
NOVEMBER 10, 1938	MORGAN, THE ANIMAL TRAINER	46

DATE	TITLE	PROGRAM #
NOVEMBER 17, 1938	MORGAN AND THE BURGLARS	47
NOVEMBER 24, 1938	MORGAN, THE MINER	48
DECEMBER 1, 1938	MORGAN, THE CHEMIST	49
DECEMBER 8, 1938	MORGAN, THE MAGICIAN	50
DECEMBER 15, 1938	MORGAN SUED FOR MAGIC	51
DECEMBER 22, 1938	MORGAN, THE SWISS MOUNTAIN CLIMBER	52
DECEMBER 29, 1938	MORGAN, THE FOOTBALL PLAYER	53
JANUARY 5, 1939	MORGAN, PROFESSOR OF PHONETICS	54
JANUARY 12, 1939	MORGAN AT MONTE CARLO	55
JANUARY 19, 1939	MORGAN, THE G-MAN	56
JANUARY 26, 1939	MORGAN, TRAVELER AND HUNTER	57
FEBRUARY 2, 1939	MORGAN, THE IMPRESARIO	58
FEBRUARY 9, 1939	MORGAN, THE PEARL DIVER	59

DATE	TITLE	PROGRAM #
FEBRUARY 16, 1939	MORGAN'S EXPEDITION UP THE NILE	60
FEBRUARY 23, 1939	MORGAN DIGGING FOR JADE	61
MARCH 2, 1939	MORGAN OF THE MOUNTED	62
MARCH 9, 1939	MORGAN'S TWENTY-FIFTH ANNIVERSARY	63
MARCH 16, 1939	MORGAN, THE PARISIAN PAINTER	64
MARCH 23, 1939	MORGAN, THE FARMER (TREE SURGEON)	65
MARCH 30, 1939	MORGAN, THE AVIATOR	66
APRIL 6, 1939	MORGAN, THE INSPECTOR (SCOTLAND YARD)	67
APRIL 13, 1939	MORGAN, THE SCOTCHMAN	68
APRIL 20, 1939	MORGAN, THE CHEMIST	69
APRIL 27, 1939	MORGAN, THE NAVIGATOR	70
MAY 4, 1939	MORGAN, THE HORSE TRAINER	71
MAY 11, 1939	MORGAN, THE REPORTER	72

DATE	TITLE	PROGRAM #
MAY 18, 1939	MORGAN, THE SPY	73
MAY 25, 1939	MORGAN, THE SPY (CONTINUED)	74
JUNE 1, 1939	MORGAN, IN FRONT OF THE FIRING SQUAD	75
JUNE 8, 1939	THE FIRING SQUAD FIRES	76
JUNE 15, 1939	MORGAN AT THE N.Y. WORLD'S FAIR	77
JUNE 22, 1939	MORGAN, THE ELEPHANT HUNTER (IVORY)	78
JUNE 29, 1939		79

2. The Jocks Talk (complete text)

It was a wonderful experience and I wouldn't have missed it for the world. I'm back home now waiting for my brother, Johnny, to show up with his wire recorder so I can play the spools and listen to the world-shattering inside stuff I picked up in the jockeys' room at Jamaica Race Track. He should be here any minute.

Three months ago nobody offered me much encouragement. Eddie Arcaro, the greatest jock that ever lived for my money, was frankly skeptical. He said it couldn't be done.

We were sitting around at Romanoff's chewing the fat. With the prices that Mike charges for his steaks a man's a fool if he doesn't chew the fat and eat the bone, too. The Santa Anita meeting was over and Arcaro was going down to Florida for some golf and fishing and it was a sort of a farewell party. Ameche was there and Jack Sullivan and Mike Romanoff and Dave Chasen (it was Monday night and Dave's joint was closed) and a half a dozen others, all licking their wounds from a disastrous season at the track. I listened, enthralled, as these great raconteurs, each of them wise in the ways of the turf, told stories about the bangtails. At the same time I felt a little inadequate because I couldn't contribute. It didn't really make sense for I was the only one in that crowd who owned a racehorse, as a hobby, you understand.

Of course, owning racehorses doesn't make a man an oracle on handicapping and turf history any more than buying a hundred shares of Saltpeter Aviation makes one an authority on instrument flying. I got into the Sport of Kings purely by accident.

About seven years earlier an improvident friend of mine put the bite on me for a sum of money I could ill afford. I have never suffered from banker's heart, but my sketchy ken of business plus my thorough knowledge of this character's character made me ask for security. I should have suspected from his willingness to put up collateral that I was in a fair way of being rogered. The security turned out to be an oat burner by the name of Orphan Cribber, a nine-year-old maiden gelding. I felt rather sheepish about accepting the horse because it was the man's only means of transportation. It goes without saying that I never saw my friend or my money again and I was left holding the nag. So I became an owner and have been ever since.

It was because of this fact that Paul Warwick, the advertising man, approached me with his idea.

Paul Warwick, as you may know, is head of a large advertising agency, Warwick and Legler, and a more energetic man never breathed. Ideas shoot from his fertile brain like corn popping in a pan. Corn also pops from his brain, but it seems to pay off in the advertising business.

Briefly, this is what he had in mind. I was to interview the jockeys in their natural habitat, i.e., the jockeys' room, and write an intimate piece that would disclose facts and facets of the little men that had never before been revealed. Not an exposé or a whitewash job, but a piece about jockeys practically by jockeys. Make them talk, said Paul, and I'll guarantee the public will gobble it up.

He had it all figured out. He would contact the Jockey's Guild, get the necessary permission and make sure that a large percentage of the proceeds, if any, would go to that worthy organization. An okay from the State Racing Commission would give me open sesame to the jocks' room at four or five major tracks. At that time I didn't realize that it was easier to steal the bullion from Fort Knox than for an outsider to get into the jocks' room.

At first I demurred, reminding Paul that while I was an owner my knowledge of racing was limited to paying feed bills. In fact, I almost never visit the track even to see my own horses lose.

Warwick didn't consider this any drawback. On the contrary he pointed out that the virgin approach to the story would be infinitely better than the blasé reporting of a hardened aficionado. While I was mulling this over he was already on the phone getting the blessings of the Jockey's Guild and the New York and California State Racing Commissions.

Well, here I was in Romanoff's telling the boys about it and Eddie Arcaro was shaking his head, skeptically.

"It's a wonderful idea," said the Champ, "and a wonderful title, *The Jocks Talk*, but I know jocks and they won't."

"Won't what?"

"Talk."

I pondered that for a moment. Once at Hollywood Park, as I was waiting in line at the two dollar window I caught a snatch of a conversation that had the same effect on me. A harried-looking horseplayer had collared a tout-like gentleman who was chewing on a cigar twice his size and he was pleading for information. This is exactly what I heard, so help me Calumet.

"I'm hooked, Barney. Gimme a horse. I lose seven straight."

"Leave me look at the card."

A pause. Then:

"This one backs up . . . This is nothin'. . . . He's only out for the air... They aren't trying with this one—I'm sorry, Max, there aren't a horse in the race can win it."

It took a minute and a half for this to penetrate. When I turned to look at the maker of this profound remark he'd already disappeared. I was so shaken that I made a mistake and bought number four instead of number five as I had originally intended, and number four won and paid sixty-seven forty for two. At the time it seemed to prove something, but I can't for the life of me think what it was.

I must confess I left Romanoff's with an uneasy feeling, and climbed into my car with mixed emotions. I was proceeding down Santa Monica Boulevard, at a moderate rate of speed, when I suddenly saw careening towards me a huge car obviously out of control. By an amazing piece of quick thinking I managed to meet him head-on. Fortunately, nobody was injured, but I couldn't help feeling that this was a sort of an omen.

That night in bed I tossed fitfully, worried about Arcaro's words of warning. Finally, unable to sleep at all, I got out of bed, slipped into my mukluks and padded quietly into the den, my dog, Phar Lap, at my heels. He couldn't sleep either.

It has long been my custom to fight insomnia with books, a wonderful form of relaxation. Scanning the bookshelves, my hand automatically went for a heavy tome labeled *Interior Decorating* by John Jameson, the well-known Irish interior decorator. The bottle, so artfully nestling in the hollowed-out pages, was empty. It looked as though I was going to have to read, after all.

Swallowing my disappointment, a poor substitute for the Jameson's, I reached for my well-thumbed copy of Immanuel Kant's *Critique of Pure Reason*, and opened it to the fifth categorical imperative. I laid the book on the rug in front of the fireplace, beckoned to Phar Lap, who dutifully left off, lapping his cannikin of beer. With one bound he landed on the book and was soon fast asleep. I offer this as evidence that heavy literature is a soporific, and also an excellent means of keeping dog hairs off the rug.

The night wore on and I began to be beset by grave doubts that I could fulfill the assignment. Why should the Jocks talk? And if they would talk, what would they say? More important, who would care what the Jocks said if they talked? What was I getting into? It wasn't until the sun came up that I had answered these questions to my own satisfaction. With this feeling of confidence I reached for the phone and sent a telegram to Paul Warwick telling him to get himself another boy.

Looking back, I can understand my bookmaker's mystification on receiving this wire, and also Warwick's surprise when Western Union delivered him instructions to place ten dollars across the board on a horse in the Fifth at Pimlico.

April 22nd, 5:15 a.m. Golden Gate Fields, Albany, Calif. Armed with my credentials and a notebook, I entered the racecourse through the clubhouse gate and made for the min track. Already the place was alive with horses, jockeys, exercise boys, clockers, grooms—an unforgettable sight to a novice early riser like myself. Breasting a sharp breeze coming from the bay, I headed towards the rail, my loosely-knit balbriggan no match for the penetrating wind. I began to regret not having worn something under it.

Shivering, I clutched the rail and watched. Horses. More horses. Hundreds of them. Galloping, breezing, driving. Whoops from the exercise boys as they thundered into the stretch. The smart resounding crack of the whip against flank. This is the racetrack, I thought. A shrewd observation considering I was still groggy with sleep and martinis.

But I had a job to do and this was part of it. To be able to get the jocks to talk I had cagily figured I would need an understanding of their language. Where better to get it than at the racetrack itself? I moved closer to a group of men at the rail, alert, ready to record any gleanings I might pick up. One man held a stopwatch, eyes glued intently on a thoroughbred approaching the finish line.

I had never seen a watch like that before. It was like miniature cyclotron and incorporated a second hand, split second hand, calendar, compass, wind-velocity indicator, seismograph, tire gauge, bottle-opener, nail clipper and three sizes of screw drivers. Fascinated by this formidable contraption, I asked the clocker whether the watch was any good for timing horses. "Good?" he snorted. "Yesterday with this watch I caught a horse working a minute in 59 seconds flat!"

I turned my attention back to the horses with a dim suspicion that this wiseacre was pulling my leg, as they say in racing circles.

The sights, the sounds, the smells of the track began to do something to me. These were the simple things that make one feel great to be alive. And as I weaved away from the rail I fervently wished that I was.

Now to the stables, I thought squeamishly, the real backstage of racing. This part of every racetrack is very carefully policed, and the strictest rules pertaining to strangers are enforced.

It is at this point that I wish to express my heartfelt thanks to Bert Thompson, Western Manager for the Jockey's Guild, for having thoughtfully provided me with the necessary credentials. Otherwise, I feel dead certain that nothing short of disguising myself as a horse would have gotten me past the wide-awake guard at the gate. As it is I was hated several times by suspicious Pinkerton men, Security police, and other obstacles in my path, as I picked my way carefully through the barn area.

Rows upon rows of box stalls with their equine tenants greeted my bloodshot eyes. Hot walkers plodding along with their charges, beating a circular path during the cooling out process. Hundreds of healthy animals, sleek and glossy, all shapes and sizes, devouring tons of feed. Greedy youngsters rattling their pails. Lively fillies rolling in the sand. It was a nostalgic reminder of those not-so-pleasant Sunday afternoons at Pismo Beach.

In a well-barricaded stall at the very end of Barn 31 stood a massive ebony stallion, muscles rippling under his fine coat, nostrils distended as he pawed incessantly at the kickboards. He had the eye of a rogue and a man with less courage would have thought twice before venturing to pet such a forbidding animal. Recklessly I reached forward and stroked him on the muzzle. I've since wondered what would have happened if he hadn't been wearing one.

A glance at my watch told me I had been at the track for over two hours without meeting a single jockey. Again I was assailed by the qualms that the jocks wouldn't talk, particularly if I didn't get to meet them. I remembered that Bert Thompson had told me that a good place to begin would be in the track cafeteria. Everybody gathers at the cafeteria after the morning workouts.

The huge, spotless establishment was thronged with race-trackers. Snatches of conversation could be distinguished over the hubbub. In order not to arouse suspicion, I surreptitiously concealed my notebook in a large bowl of haggis (the jockey's staple diet, I later discovered), and my ball-point pen fairly flew as I recorded for posterity the quaint phrases and patois of the jockeys themselves. The following is a faithful transcription of my notes:

"I'm on top by four when he grabs himself at the eighth pole."

"I'm all dried out and I still can't do not better 'n' nine."

". . . . . hung in the last two jumps."

"Mac makes all his bug-boys work ace-deuce."

"She's a lock if she don't get cut down."

The rest of my notes are slightly illegible and confined mostly to abbreviations, none of which I am able to translate at the moment.

Well, it began to look like Arcaro was wrong after all. The jocks were certainly talking. Talking so fast I could hardly get anything down. The only trouble was I didn't know what they were talking about. But that was a minor detail, something to be ironed out when I got with them in the sacred confines of the jockeys' room. I was beginning to look forward with eager anticipation to this next step.

Still making notes at a feverish clip, I became aware of a diminishing of the conversation. Sentences were left hanging in mid-air. As if on cue, a sudden pall of silence enveloped the cafeteria. The only sound was the scratching of my pen. Vaguely sensing something had gone wrong I looked up to discover all eyes were on me. The expressions were definitely hostile. It was obvious that they had pegged me for an outlander and clammed up forthwith. I simply had to dispel this impression and get them off-guard again.

With one swift motion I fashioned my Racing Form into a fair replica of a jockey's cap, looped my necktie around the back of my chair, which I had now straddled for maximum effect, and scooted down the aisle all the while slapping at my flank much in the manner of a race rider. This simple, but clever ruse had the desired result. The tension was relieved and conversation immediately resumed.

Scuttling towards the steam counter I managed to pick up these random phrases:

"Who let that jerk in here?"

"Hey, whatsa matter Fatty—you blowing your cork?"

"Get the net, somebody."

Convinced by their good-natured raillery that I had already been accepted as one of them, I dismounted from my chair and cantered unobtrusively out of the cafeteria. This stratagem deceived everybody except the cashier who pursued me and forced me to pay my check.

It now occurred to me that the best plan would be to engage a jockey in conversation in surroundings that would be most conducive to uninhibited responses. Where would I find such a place? Dimly I recalled in my earlier conversations with the very helpful Thompson that most of the riders spend a little time each morning in the Steam Box. Weight is the arch-enemy of the jockey and he must submit to this enervating form of torture to relieve himself of excess poundage. My spirits rose as I headed for the Sweat Room, the one place that must certainly be the solution to my problem.

Approaching cautiously from the rear of the small building I peered into one of the windows. I could see nothing. The shades were modestly drawn, fair proof that decorum is the watchword amongst the jockeys. This is a character facet rarely touched upon even by the most discerning of sports writers.

There was no reason for me to be stealthy about my movements, I remembered, so fingering my badge and a letter from the State Racing Commission, I boldly circled the place and started for the entrance. At last I was going to beard the jockey in his lair. He would have to talk. What else could he do in his weakened condition, hemmed in by the prison-like individual steam cabinet? If he made a run for it the chances are he would catch a severe cold, or at best be arrested for indecent exposure. You see, Mr. Arcaro hadn't counted on my ingenuity when he made his arbitrary statement. And while I'm on the subject of the pessimistic Arcaro, if you've ever taken a good look at his classic features you'll understand why he will never have to resort to the steam-box if he gets too heavy. All he has to do is have his nose bobbed.

As I rounded the corner and reached for the door knob, the door opened and a small figure stepped out. Through the open door I could see the place was entirely empty. I felt a keen shock of disappointment but soon recovered and turned to the little man with a winning smile.

"Have a good sweat?" I asked humorously. He stared at me as though I had two heads and maintained a sullen silence.

But I was not to be thwarted. Placing my towering five feet five inches in front of him so as to block any escape, I offered him a cigarette. I didn't take a practiced eye to see I was face to face with a jockey. I couldn't lose him now.

"How about a weed?" was my next gambit. The easy use of track vernacular was calculated to break down his reserve. He took the bait! Extending a huge, ham-like hand, the distinctive feature of the seasoned reinsman, he accepted a cigarette from the pack. I did the same.

As he took the first puff of his Helmar, I studied his features. Lean, tanned face, sharp penetrating eyes, tight little mouth and a freckled snub nose. I judged his height to be slightly under five feet, his weight in the vicinity of a hundred pounds. He was balanced lightly on the balls of his feet, body slumped forward slightly almost like in a racing crouch. Fearful lest I was becoming too obvious in my scrutiny I turned my back on him and pointing towards the track, murmured something unintelligible.

Quick as a flash he voiced his disagreement, and immediately informed me that while it was heavy now, the strip would dry out before the first race and that Lucky Regards, who was carrying a feather, was a mortal cinch to romp.

How about that, Mr. Arcaro! I hadn't even asked him a question and already he was volunteering information. Soon we were jabbering like old pals, reminiscing about racecourses all over the country, famous horses and other famous jockeys. He was a veritable mine of interesting data.

Once he got started, nothing could stop him. The fact that I was scribbling furiously on my notepad made no impression on him whatsoever. What I was getting was no idle track gossip, this was the real McCoy, straight from the jockey's mouth. You will no doubt be as amazed as I was to learn, for instance, that all apprentice riders are forced to ride beetles for two years until they become full-fledged jockeys. That is why they are called bug boys. That Johnny

Longden, the Chinese jockey, who owns half of the city of Arcadia and most of the state of Oregon, never carries lead in his saddle. He wears a money belt stuffed with annuities to bring his weight up to scale. Are you surprised to hear that Gordon Glisson, the Portugese Pepperpot, is really close to fifty years old and the father of Jockey Lester Balaski? That Jackie Westrope's perfect seat astride a horse is due to the fact that he spreads airplane cement on his riding pants?

These and other choice tidbits he volunteered without any pressure on my part. When I asked him a few particulars about himself he confided that his name was Jones, that he weighed 102 pounds, that he didn't intend to become a trainer when he retired from his present profession. Probing a little further, I discovered he had never been on a horse in his life. Startled, I asked him what he was doing in the Jockeys' Sweat Room and he told me he was a delivery boy for the Grimos Towel and Sheet Service in Oakland.

Crushed by this new turn of events I stumbled blindly to a telephone and begged Bert Thompson to hasten to the track to assist me in my next move. Time was growing short, the jockeys would soon be filing into the jocks' room to fulfill their day's engagements and I was once again beginning to feel mine was a hopeless task.

An hour later Thompson arrived, all smiles and optimism, and bearing a reticule containing fresh linen, a fifth of cough medicine and two legal pads. Fortified by a generous dose of the medicine, I accompanied him to the board of Stewards.

Putting on my best company manners I shook hands with James C. McGill, presiding Steward, Chester C. Jones of the California Horse Racing Board, and Mr. R. E. Leighninger, a dour gentleman with a surprising sense of humor. As Thompson explained my mission the three officials regarded me somewhat dubiously and echoed Arcaro's sentiments. All of them had been interviewing jockeys for almost a quarter of a century and had never been able to make them talk. It seemed that a jockey's vocabulary, at least when confronted by the stewards, was limited to "I coulda swore I was in the clear." This testimony, or any form of it, usually nets them a five-day suspension anyway.

It was then that I was blessed with a miraculous idea. It was simplicity itself. All I had to do was procure a recording machine, one of those with the wire spools that run for an hour straight, place the contraption in some little used corner of the jocks' room and hide the sensitive microphone so that none of the riders would know that their words were being preserved. To further disarm them I would openly place another wire recorder into the office of the clerk of the scales, George D. Murphy, and interview them individually on the off chance that they might say something.

Even if I was unsuccessful in the interviews, I would still have enough material on the wild spool. Imagine the authentic remarks of the jockeys as they are getting into their silks! Their enlightening comments as they leave to receive their riding instructions, their emotional outbursts as they return to the jocks' room to discard one set of silks and hurry into another! I could barely contain my excitement as I proposed this plan to the Stewards.

My triumphant smile melted into profound despair as I looked at their stony faces. Mr. McGill coldly informed me that such practice was without precedent, unethical, and detrimental to the best interests of racing. Both Messrs. Leighninger and Jones concurred and added a few biting remarks of their own. I had an uncanny feeling I was about to be ruled off for life. If Bert Thompson hadn't come to my rescue this piece would never have been written. Now you know who's to blame.

Bert, or Silver Tongue, as he is known at the Jockeys Guild, used all of the oratory for which he is famous. Fifteen minutes of convincing reasons why I should be allowed to proceed with a wire recorder finally evoked from all three gentlemen a flat refusal.

I like to think it was my dejected countenance that caused them to relent. At any rate, they finally agreed to contact the chairman of the horse-racing board in Sacramento and get his opinion. Twenty minutes later I got the green light.

It was almost eleven o'clock when men showed up the wire recorders. Since the extent of my mechanical ability was limited to operating a bottle opener or removing a cork I was forced to engage him to monitor the complicated apparatus. He was a tall rangy fellow with a spring in his step, apples in his cheeks and a banana in his pocket. While he went about the business of setting up the machines in the jockeys' room I sat cross-legged on a carton of General Electric batteries munching contentedly on his banana. It never occurred to me to inquire what possible connection there was between a case of batteries and a jockey's room. I finally came to the conclusion that they were there in the event of a power failure.

At the moment, except for a ruddy-faced little man who was prying the heels off of a pair of riding boots, the place was empty. I assumed instantly that this was the track cobbler, already hard at work. Both assumptions were wrong. I was soon to discover that the industrious little man was a jockey's valet and he was in the act of recovering yesterday's mutual tickets which he had prudently placed in the heels for safe-keeping.

So Jockeys had valets. Well, that was something. This particular one belonged to Ralph Neves, ace West Coast rider. (On consulting my notes I find a reference to "Neves Jeeves." I vaguely recall having tried this witty phrase on my wire recorder man and being rewarded with a friendly snarl.)

This would be a good time, I think, to clear up a common misconception regarding the function of a jockey's valet. Contrary to popular belief, this racetrack retainer is not the counterpart of the gentleman's gentleman who dishes up the cold bottle and the hot bird, draws the drapes and takes the evening off. A jockey's valet may serve two or three of the boys, polishing their boots and tack, and is supplied by the racetrack. When a jockey is wealthy enough, he hires his own personal valet. And if you want to know how wealthy some jockeys get, Eddie Aroaro has a valet who has a valet.

Satisfying the valet's natural curiosity about our stealthy activities, I warned him to keep mum and set about inspecting the place. At the door stood a Pinkerton operative and a uniformed track policeman. The room itself was large, and I noted the absence of lockers. Unlike most jockeys' rooms, which I have since been privileged to examine, this one had little niches set in the walls, each recess containing a small bench, and overhead a series of hooks. On the hooks hung the silks the jockeys were to wear, arranged one on top of the other in the proper order.

The office of the clerk of the scales was no more than a glassed-in cubicle set against the rear wall, and directly in front of this office were the scales. All weighing out was done there. Or maybe it was weighing-in. I never quite got that straight. I do know, however, that jockeys have to be weighed before the race and after the race.

Apparently, this is a precautionary measure taken by the racing authorities in order to maintain a state of good health in the jockey. The service is gratis, but the officials render it with a dogged insistence, even going so far as to suspend a jockey for allowing his weight to diminish more than a microscopic amount during the running of a race. Obviously, the ruling is to allow the offender a few days rest to regain his former good health.

Some jockeys, even after winning a race, have felt the wrath of the stewards, despite the fact that their weight never fluctuated an ounce. Why should they blame the boy if his saddle lost three or four pounds? Personally, I find this whole weight business very confusing and a little silly. After all, they're jockeys, not models. An extra pound more or less might give them a dumpy appearance but I can't see how it affects their riding ability.

I glanced down the length of the jockeys' room and saw my recording engineer tangled in a row of overhead steam pipes. Alarmed, I rushed to his assistance but he assured me that he was all right and that he was merely concealing the microphone as per my instructions.

It was completely hidden from sight and not a chance on earth that it would pick up any of the jockey's conversation. In fact, he had so skillfully concealed the microphone that it took him fifteen minutes to locate it.

Soon we found a likely spot for it, camouflaged it with old scratch sheets and everything was in readiness. A glance at my watch told me I still had a thirty minute wait before the jockeys would make their appearance. I suggested to my assistant that he go out and grab himself a cup of coffee while I sketched out some questions for the interviews. He asked me if he had enough time to do that before the show started. I blinked.

"Show? What show? There isn't any show here."

He pointed to the racing silks. "Then what's all them costumes doing here?"

It was inconceivable that this man, even allowing for his doltish appearance, should not know that he was at a racetrack. I venture to say that there are many people who have never visited a track but I feel quite certain they would be able to distinguish one from, say, a drive-in theatre. I report the profundity of the man's ignorance to prove a point I shall make later.

I enlightened him with a complete sketch of the racing picture in general, feeling rather patronizing in my superior knowledge. I told him everything I knew before and everything I had learned up until now. The fellow was intensely interested. So interested that I was forced to snatch the little keychain device he was peeping through to see what was interesting him . . . . She was no Jane Russell, but she had her points.

After he had left to get his coffee, still having fifteen minutes to waste, I wandered into the clerk's office and perused a chart on the wall which, much to my delight, contained the articles and rules of racing as laid down by the Jockey Club. I shall print some of them herewith, mainly those that are pertinent to the jockeys, and try to give a fuller interpretation of each one so that the layman can understand them.

THE RULES OF RACING
(AS ABRIDGED AND INTERPRETED BY THE AUTHOR)

You will notice I deliberately omit Rules 1 to 132 inclusive, on the grounds that they tend to confuse the reader rather than educate him. But starting with rule 133 we find that:

> "Every jockey must be weighed for a specified horse not less than thirty minutes before the time fixed for the race, and the number of the horse shall be exhibited officially as soon as possible."

Now at a casual glance this rule would seem to be self-explanatory and rather useless, but upon closer examination the true purpose of the rule is revealed. Regard the words "EVERY JOCKEY MUST BE WEIGHED FOR A SPECIFIED HORSE." The rest of the rule is just so much padding.

Here's the catch. *Every jockey must be weighed for a specified horse.* Using inverse reasoning we see that the true meaning is—every specified horse must get a jockey who has been weighed. This is to prevent horses, whether specified or unspecified, from running in a race without the burden of a jockey. Although this practice is not common, it is, on the other hand, not rare. A glance at your Daily Racing Form, or favorite handicapper, will bear this out. How many times have you seen an entry described as follows:

HORSE	WT	COMMENT
FALLING CLUTCH (NO BOY)	98	**Carrying a feather.**

There you have the horse Falling Clutch carrying a feather but no boy on his back. This feather business may tickle an owner but is looked upon with extreme disfavor by the Jockey Club. Hence Rule 133.

Rule 145c is quite interesting because of its abstruse ramifications. I give it to you in its entirety:

> "A horse in the hands of the Starter SHALL RECEIVE NO FURTHER CARE FROM ANYONE AT THE STARTING POST, except the assistant starters, provided that if any accident happens to a jockey or his equipment, the Starter may permit any jockey or jockeys to dismount and the horses to be cared for during the delay; OTHERWISE NO JOCKEY SHALL DISMOUNT."

The Capitals are mine. Even with my skimpy knowledge of racing I'd always known that some jockeys were of little or no help to a horse, either at the gate or during the race, but I was certainly surprised to find out that the Jockey Club had made it compulsory.

And what about the portion of the rule that forbids a jockey to dismount without permission? I wonder how many of those original rule-makers ever rode a thoroughbred. Not to dismount, indeed! Any jockey will tell you that such orders from headquarters are often countermanded by orders from hindquarters.

Rule 152. (Printed in part)

> ". . . . . A jockey riding a horse with which his owner has not declared to win must on no account stop such horse except in favor of the stable companion on whose behalf declaration to win has been made."

Now let us assume that the jockey in question, who is not supposed to win the race, is coasting ten lengths in front of his field at the head of the stretch. Being a conscientious jockey, he consults his rule book (which all riders carry in a leathern taffeta attached to the cantle. This last bit of parenthetical information I cannot positively vouch for since it came to me third handed from a palimpsest, which is purported to repose in the London Museum) and take immediate action. To begin with, locating one's stable companion in a band of charging thoroughbreds is no easy matter. He may then follow any one of these courses to comply with the aforementioned ruling.

He may transmit a code message via a portable sending set and inquire the immediate whereabouts of his stable companion, provided said stable companion is equipped with a receiver.

Lap the field and approach the horses from the rear, which gives him a better vantage point for close scrutiny.

Fall from his horse without stopping him, light out across the infield and enlist at the nearest Naval Recruiting Station.

I must agree that all these methods sound a little drastic and are rarely employed except in cases of extreme emergency. I know of no other way, however, of successfully carrying out Rule 152.

Rule 153a.

> "When clear, a horse may be taken to any part of the course provided that crossing or weaving in front of contenders may constitute interference or intimidation for which the offender may be disciplined."

The only inference I can draw from this rule is that a horse may earn the privilege to visit any part of the course, including the cocktail lounge, but must behave like a gentleman at all times, and refrain from weaving under his load.

Rule 155.

> "If a horse leaves the course he must turn back and run the course from the point at which he left it."

Ignoring the presumptuous wording of this rule, and eschewing the valid reasons that a horse may be either undesirous or unable to return to the course at the point at which he left it, this regulation has a deep significance. A horse with superior intelligence would soon discover that a shortcut across the infield would cut his racing time in half, conserve his energy, and give him a decided advantage over the rest of his field.

Rule 161.

> "If a jockey does not present himself to weigh in; or, if he be more than one pound short of his weight; or, if he be guilty of any fraudulent practice with respect to weight or weighing; or, except as provided in Rule 159, if he dismounts before reaching the scales, or dismounts without permission; or, if he touches (except accidentally) before weighing in any person or thing other than his own equipment, his horse may be disqualified and he himself may be fined or suspended."

This has been discussed before elsewhere in the report and it is merely an elaboration on the Jockey Club's almost fetish-like desire to protect the health and well-being of the jockey. Without question, the admonition to the jockey not to touch anything or person outside of his own apparently sterilized equipment shows the Jockey Club's awareness of the danger of contagion.

Rule 216 d.

> "If any person shall have in his possession in or

> about the racetrack or shall use appliances electrical or mechanical, other than the ordinary equipment, for the purpose of affecting the speed or the racing condition of a horse . . . . (he) may be fined, ruled off, or otherwise punished at the discretion of . . . (the) . . . Stewards."

This rule was way at the top of the chart and I had to stand on the carton of batteries to read it. Unable to understand the import of the measure I refrain from making any further comment. I never did manage to get the rest of the rules because right about then the jockeys began making their appearance.

My heart commenced to pound wildly for I realized that I now stood upon the threshold of success or failure. Would my plan work? Would the jocks talk? They entered the jocks room singly, in twos and threes, babbling away a mile a minute. Such gaiety! Such good-natured badinage! There they were talking and revealing their innermost thoughts. Re-hashing the running of yesterday's races. Speculating about the horses they were to ride today.

Using a copy of *Montee's Jockey Guide*, which I had picked up for a trifle at an old bookstall on Figueroa Street, I was able to identify most of the boys from the rather faded photographs contained in the booklet.

I recognized Silvio Coucci, "Snapper" Garrison, the famous come-from-behinder, Don Meade, Fred Teral, Isaac Murphy, Tod Sloane and the promising youngster, Winnie O'Connor. Curiosity prompted me to look for the date on the Guide, and as I did so I marveled at the stamina of these boys who had been riding since 1901. I must say they looked their age, however.

Of course, I was too excited to remember any of the things they were saying and I prayed that they wouldn't spot the microphone that had been so cleverly planted. I looked over at the recording machine to make sure everything was ship-shape and got the jolt of my life. That Tony Lumpkin of an engineer had forgotten to turn it on! He was out getting coffee or playing with the yo-yo while history was being made and not recorded!

It was while I was cursing myself for ever letting the dolt leave my sight that he returned. He was licking at a Gargantuan mass of cotton candy and carrying a kewpie doll under his left arm. I couldn't imagine where he'd been. Not stopping to question him I hissed that the recorder was not running. With amazing unconcern, and the dexterity born of years of experience, he flipped on the switch, and the spool of wire began to spin. Fortunately, the jockeys had all gone into the Clerk of the Scales office, so this went unnoticed.

As soon as they came out and retired to their little niches to change into their riding clothes, all the while yelling to each other and exchanging pleasantries, I casually sauntered amongst them and introduced myself.

It turned out I had been mistaken about their identities but that was of little consequence. It was just as important, I concluded, to meet such boys as Ralph Neves, Nick Combest, Jack Westrope, Sevio Cardiali, Walter Litzenberg, Lester Balaski, Melvin Lewis, Charlie Ralls, the Zufelt brothers, Willie Shoemaker, Gordon Glisson, Johnny Longden and a host of others.

If I had any fears about getting the jockeys into the clerk's office to be interviewed they were soon calmed. They actually haggled over who would go first. The only way that could be settled was by drawing cards. Each one drew a card from the deck and turned it face up on the rubbing table. Ralph Neves chortled with glee as he displayed a king. Two other boys registered dismay as they showed a nine and a four respectively. But they were all relieved when Charley Ralls drew a two of spades and was forced to accompany me to the wire recorder.

He mumbled something about not being able to shuffle the horses and faced me truculently. As you will see from the following transcribed interview, faithful to the last comma, I managed to penetrate his armor and coax at least a few words out of him. I am not prepared to defend the quality of the material that was produced, I merely submit it as proof that the jocks *do* talk.

Q: How long have you been riding, Charlie?

A: Well . . . lemme see. Since 1921. How many years is that (Oh, this was a cagey one. I had hardly begun my interview and already he was asking ME question. I fenced brilliantly).

Q: I'm sorry, Charlie. I can't add that well.

A: I can't, neither. (This is going to be a hard man to shave.)

Q: Let's call it a long time, Charlie, huh? Now I'd like to ask you something about yourstyle of riding. Do you have any special style?

A: No, I wouldn't say that, no. What do you mean by special style? (He's trying to trap me, I thought. But I rose to the occasion.)

Q: Well, style. For instance—uh—some jockeys—uh—there are certain ways—

A: If you mean like ridin' side-saddle, I give that up when I was seven. (This sally evoked a hearty guffaw from the rest of the jockeys.)

Q: (COLDLY) That's not what I mean at all. What's this business they mean by riding with an acey-deucey?

A: You mean ace-deuce?

Q: That's right. Do you ride that way?

A: Yare.

Q: What does that mean?

A: Well, it means riding with one stirrup longer than the other. Uneven-like.

Q: Why do you ride that way?

A: Well, the reason I ride ace-deuce is it seems I get a better purchase on the horse around the turn.

Q: Which stirrup is shorter?

A: The right stirrup.

Q: And do you really get a better purchase or do you just imagine it?

A: Well, it's possible that I just imagine it but I think I do. Because a horse does bank as he moves around the turn the same as an automobile.

Q: How do you hold your reins, Charlie?

A: I ride with a long hold. I'm a natural long hold rider. I take him up pretty short when I'm coming out of the gate, but I'm a long-hold rider when I got my cross.

Q: Your cross? What does that mean? (He demonstrated how a jockey takes his cross by using my suspenders. After he got off my back we went on with the interview.)

A: You see, you have to get your cross after the start before the first turn. You have to do that to get your horse under control.

Q: I see. Now what about whipping? Can you whip with both hands?

A: Not at the same time, no.

Q: Well, I should have said whip with either hand.

A: I knew what you meant, I was just kiddin'. Yes, I can whip with both hands. I'm more or less ambidextrous, but not wholly so. I prefer to whip with my right hand.

Q: That's curious. Most jockeys prefer to use a whip.

A: Okay, we're even now.

Q: Tell me something about judging pace.

A: Well, that comes under the heading of many years of experience of rating horses. Now when you first start out to be a race rider, a trainer will tell you to go, say, a half in fifty-two or a half in fifty-two. If you go a half in fifty-two, you know you must go an eighty in thirteen. After a while you get to know just about how fast you're goin', and if you're aimin' to do a half in 50 you shouldn't miss by over a fifth.

Q: That's a kind of a gift, isn't it?

A: No, I wouldn't say that, no. You just naturally know how to get to do it the same as you know how to pick up your knife and eat your mashed potatoes.

Q: Every time you go out to ride in a race you get your riding instructions from the trainer, don't you? What do they usually tell you?

A: Well, they're mostly all different. A lot of times you go out to ride for a man and he'll say, "There he is; you ride him and I'll root for him." Of course, I used to ride for one fellow and he said, "There he is, Charlie. Go out there and louse it up like you always do."

Q: Are you supposed to report to the stewards anything that would come under the heading of queer instructions?

A: Well, naturally, you get a queer instruction—if the man tells you to put the brakes on, you're not supposed to do it.

Q: You mean that if you're on a horse that's a frontrunner and your instructions are to stay behind the field?

A: That's what I mean. I try to ride to a man's instructions as near as I can, but sometimes there's no way I can possibly do it. I once had an owner tell me to lay about fourth until I hit the head of the stretch, then for me to come away, take to the front and open up a big lead. Well, when I finished next to last the owner asked me why I didn't come away like he told me. I said, "Mister, I could come away but I didn't wanna leave the horse." You see, you can't always do what they tell you.

Q: I see what you mean.

A: Sometimes there's a lot of horses in the race that gets the same instructions that you do. And maybe everybody is told to lay third and then you got a helluva race where nobody comes in first.

Q: Well, Charlie, confidentially, did you ever get any queer instructions?

A: Not that I know of. (Loud laughter from the other jockeys.)

Q: Oh, you can talk to me. This isn't going to be printed or anything like that.

A: Oh, I don't pay much attention to them instructions, anyway. A lot of times the officials ask you why wasn't you on the leader right up there? Some horse moved up there, why didn't you move with him? You're at the five-eighths pole, you got five-eighths of a mile to go. What's the use of knockin' him out? You're gonna get beat anyway, so what's the use of ridin' him wrong?

Q: Did a horse ever run away with you?

A: Not that I know of. I've had 'em gallop a little fast with me, but I don't never remember one of them runnin' off.

Q: Are you ever nervous at the start of a race?

A: No, but I've ridden a lot of races with a cramp in my stomach.

Q: What was the cramp from?

A: Well, you can't tell. Probably from gas on your stomach, or maybe from reducin'.

Q: Did you have the cramp before you got on the horse?

A: No, probably maybe at the gate or somethin', and the gas pocket would hold right there until after the race. But you had to go right on and ride. You gotta keep goin'. You can't raise up to get the cramp out.

Q: Why not?

A: Well, somebody might think you was pullin' the horse.

Q: Did you ever have any humorous experience during the running of a race?

A: Well, nothin' that would make me laugh right out. I used to ride with a fella called Rigney Yergan, he was quite a card. They used to call him Cnewtobacker Yergan.

Q: What did he do?

A: He always had a big Climax plug in his jaw—if he'd ever get on the lead, well, and see one coming, he'd spit in a horse's eye, or a jockey's eye, and well, the whole business. I was always careful to ride on the lee side of him when the wind was blowin'.

Q: Have you got any superstitions?

A: I haven't got a superstition in the world, knock wood.

Q: Charlie, I see that Mr. Hayes wants you to get going here. We'll be done in one minute. Have you had any serious spills?

A: I've had quite a few spills.

Q: Real bad ones?

A: Well, one spill was the first year I rode. I fell and broke four ribs, my collar bone and my arm. That laid me up for a few months. Then I had a lot of minor spills, I broke my foot at one time.

Q: Who was responsible for this real bad one?

A: Well, it's hard to tell, I got caught in a speed jam. And the last one that I fell with was at Bay Meadows and I lost a kidney over that deal.

Q: Well, thanks a lot, Charlie. You're riding in the first, aren't you?

A: Yes, I am.

Q: Go out there and win it.

We were forced to conclude the interview at this point to allow Ralls to ride his first mount of the day, a maiden two-year-old filly called Campus Chatter.

The jocks' room at Golden Gate adjoins the saddling paddock which is right on the finish line, in full view of all the spectators. I can't recall any other track with a similar arrangement, most of the jocks' rooms being some distance from the track itself. There were about fifteen riders without mounts in the first race and they all went to the rail to watch. I went along with them and it was an education to listen to their comments as the actual race was run.

Talk about your back-seat driving. These boys could give your wife cards and spades and still do more quarterbacking from the comparative safety of the rail. I say comparative safety, because I fell or was pushed off of it at least twice during the race. It was incredible that such excitement could prevail amongst a crew of veteran race riders such as these. They acted like shrieking, hysterical high school girls rooting for the senior volley ball team.

I, of course, maintained an almost catatonic calm, betraying no clue to my true emotions beyond unraveling my underwear and gouging great chunks out of the rail with my fingernails.

To make a perfect story, and this is gospel, Campus Chatter won going away at something like fifteen to one. I don't suppose Ralls would care to admit it, but the few words of advice I gave him before the race on how to handle his filly must have counted for something. It was with a sense of power and accomplishment that I returned to the jocks' room to work on my next victim.

This was a lad named Richard Smith, a fair-haired, blue-eyed little ball of fire who was riding a forty-to-one shot in the third. As I started to question him I could hear from outside the cubicle the shouts and banter of the jockeys who had taken part in the first race, and I reveled in the thought that my concealed recorder was picking it all up.

I bade young Smith not to be nervous, and instructed him to project his voice directly into the microphone without getting too close. Apparently there was some misunderstanding about what I wanted of him, because before I could stop him he had sung two choruses of "The Hutsut Song," and was already working furiously on a harmonica which he produced from his moleskins. There is no way of translating this interlude to paper, and it would be too cumbersome, not to say expensive, to provide a duplicate of the spool and a Webster-Chicago wire recorder with every copy of this piece. Therefore I advisedly omit the interview with Jockey Richard Smith. It did serve some purpose, however, because now we know that the jocks not only talk, they sing and dance, too. (Which reminds me, where the hell is my brother Johnny with that recorder of his? It's been two hours since he left for my place which is exactly a block and a half from his.)

Well, the third race was coming up at Golden Gate and all I had so far was the Ralls interview and the Smith Concerto. My giddy recording engineer who had been missing for some time suddenly put in an appearance.

He was lapping a jelly apple and twirling a beribboned cane, and bits of popcorn dotted the airplane beanie which now replaced the more sedate helmet liner he had worn earlier. This man must have found a carnival somewhere, I conjectured, and I stared at him in wonder. Without offering any explanation he put a fresh spool on the machine in the clerk's office, checked the other machine in the jocks' room and disappeared again.

There was still a little time before the third race and I now had Jockey Melvin Lewis at the microphone. Mel is rather a tall boy, had been riding about eighteen years, and was known as a long-shot rider. Here's the transcript:

Q: Mel, you were in the room while I was interviewing Charlie Ralls, weren't you?

A: Yes, sir.

Q: You understand the purpose of this recording?

A: It's for a picture or something, aren't it?

Q: Well, maybe later on. Right now we're trying to get enough material for some magazine articles and possibly a book. You're riding in this next race, is that right?

A: That's right. I'm on Geo. McManus—that's the number ten horse. You can see the tote board from here.

Q: We'll have to hurry, Mel. They're bringing the horses into the saddling paddock.

A: Right now he's forty-five to one.

Q: Yes. Well, I just heard one of the jockeys talking about ace-deuce, and I wondered—

A: He's up to fifty now.

Q: Uh-huh. Well, I wondered whether there was any truth—

A: That goat can run when he's fresh.

Q: Who?

A: The Number Ten horse. I'm riding him. He's fifty to one. **(PAUSE)**

Q: Er—you think he has a chance?

A: He's fresh. **(PAUSE)**

Q: The Number Ten horse, huh? Fifty to one.

A: He shouldn't oughta be no better 'n even money. **(PAUSE)**

Q: Hmmmm . . . . Well, let's get back to this ace-deuce business—You think a man ought to make a bet on this Geo. McManus?

A: Look, I am not sayin' nothin' about bettin'. All I know is the Number Ten horse is gonna win from here to there . . . . Hey, where you goin'?

There were a few other remarks on the spool which I have deleted, but they were all relatively unimportant. I had to get to the Mutual windows in a hurry . . . . Geo. McManus—the Number Ten horse.

I was on my way out of the saddling paddock when one of the Stewards, I believe it was Mr. McGill, beckoned to me. It was right then that I found out it was even harder to get out of this area during the racing day than it was to get into it. It was an iron clad rule that nobody could leave the jockeys' quarters in order to make a bet.

I pretended to be a little indignant that Mr. McGill should suspect me of entertaining such a thought, but the fact that I kept addressing him as Mr. McManus and had my two dollars clutched in my fist weakened my position to end.

He corrected me gently regarding his name and gazed pointedly at the money in my hand. With a convincing laugh that I was sure wouldn't have deceived a two-year-old I explained that I was just taking the money out to purchase another spool of wire for the recording machine. Mr. McGill indicated that my assistant could go for the wire but that I had to remain.

By this time the horses where almost at the post. The odds on George McManus had dropped to forty-five to one, but I was still willing to take a chance with my two dollars. I handed my recording man the money, and in loud clear tones told him to go out and pick up another spool of wire. In tones as loud and clear he started to inform me that he had eight fresh spools in his pocket. I cut him off before the stewards had a chance to hear him, and whispered frenziedly for him to take the two dollars and bet it all on Number Ten to win.

You might have thought I had asked him to decipher the hieroglyphics on the Rosetta Stone from the look he gave me. I repeated out of the side of my mouth, pressing the money into his paw, "Buy me a two-dollar ticket on the Number Ten Horse to win." Suddenly, a look of almost human understanding crossed his Neanderthal face. It was with great relief that I watched him turn and bound out of the paddock on his pogo stick.

Well, there's no need to drag this out. Just like Mel Lewis said, the Number Ten horse George McManus won from here to there. He won by the length of the grandstand. The prices went up on the tote board and my heart skipped a beat. My two dollars was no worth $92.50. Paul Warwick was right! You see, it pays to make the jockeys talk!

I waited anxiously for my assistant to return with the loot. In due time he returned and his next words made me wish I was dead.

"I couldn't find the two-dollar window," he said. I was staggered. I should have known better than to send this bungling idiot on such an important errand. Ninety-two dollars and fifty cents! All that money would have been mine if only he had made the bet. Well, it was no use crying over spilled milk. I held out my hand and angrily demanded my two dollars back. He thumbed through four twenties and a ten-dollar bill and handed me the two singles, meanwhile blowing the smoke from his fifty-cent cigar in my face.

Sometimes I wonder—no, he was too dumb for that!

I was too upset to get any more individual interviews from the jockeys but it didn't really matter because I had the other machine still going with the wild spool. At the end of the racing day, after all the boys had departed we disconnected the recorder and I took the plane back to Los Angeles with the precious reels in my briefcase.

Brother Johnny was on his toes that night, and he was waiting for me with his wire recorder. (God knows where he is tonight!) Shoving aside the other reels, I had him place the wild one on the machine. I held my breath in anticipation as it started to roll. Who knew what startling tidbits I might have picked up from the unsuspecting jockeys?

I leaped a foot in the air as I heard the first voice. It was that of my stupid assistant. The words were as clear as a bell.

"This is it, right here, fellows," he said. "See, the mike is under them scratch sheets. And thanks for that tip on Geo. McManus."

My whole body tensed. He had not only rooked me, but he had tipped the jocks off.

Well, the jocks talked, all right—but they didn't say anything I could print.

Well, that's all water under the bridge. The stuff I got on this new reel from Jamaica racetrack is different. That much I know. I just wish Johnny would get over here with his wire recorder. I'm getting more nervous by the minute.

3. Phil Rapp's Testimony in the Rapp vs. Gleason Case

"Exaimnation before trial of Philip Rapp" before a Notary Public of NY at Suite 8L-M, Waldorf-Astoria Hotel, NYC, on Jan. 9, 1956. Theodore Kupferman for plaintiff (Rapp). Carleton Eldridge, Jr. for defendents (CBS & Jackie Gleason).

CBS attorneys listened to June 5, 1951 & July 17, 1951 Bickersons recordings, as well as some videos (*Star Time*) from Nov. 1950. Paul: Johnny would write Lew Parker's Chef Armando skits.

Rapp worked out of home at 601 N. Palm Dr. since 1949. Prior to that, since 1937, at 620 N. Oakhurst Dr.

Then Eddie Cantor for *Chase & Sanborn Coffee*. Teamed with "the late David Freedman, noted writer" and wrote *Eddie Cantor Program, George Grivot Program, Block & Sully Program, Fanny Brice Program* (for another sponsor then), *The Plymouth Program, The Ex-Lax Program* (starring Lulu McConnell, and Lou Holtz, monologist, for Chesterfield—Lew had male stooge Benny Baker) between 1933 and late 1935. During this time David and he wrote *Ziegfeld Follies of 1933* and *Life Begins at 8:40*, two shows ran three years. Then he went alone with Cantor show, David and he went separate ways.

"Satire was very popular in those days, and the skits themselves were mainly satirical skits. Everything that was parodied had to be cleared through the networks so we could only use public domain stuff."

"I think the first credit ever given to a writer was given to me on an Eddie Cantor show in 1936."

"The Plymouth show was a milder type of show. I can't even recall the star of it because it was based on a fictitious character called 'Elmer Everett Yess.'"

Stayed with Cantor until about 1938, wrote *Texaco Show* and *Pebeco* (toothpaste) *Show* for him. Contract with Cantor, not sponsor. Left to take a rest. "I thought my health was not too good at that period." About Cantor's show: "Sketches were done, usually a monologue. People would appear from nowhere and do little odd jokes, you know. It didn't have very much form." Had Deanna Durbin and Bobby Breen on the program; "we were always on the search for some discovery."

"In 1938, I was approached by the William Morris office to come in and take over the writing of the Fanny Brice material on the MGM show broadcast from Hollywood, then known as the *Good News Show*. Fanny Brice was doing Baby Snooks, and it was apparent that she had run out of the material that I had written for her in earlier years and she wanted me to resume writing further scripts." Did this for six to eight weeks, was then asked to write whole show and direct. He agreed. Wrote and directed *Maxwell House Coffeetime* from 1938 to 1943. "It starred Frank Morgan, Fanny Brice, various MGM stars from Robert Taylor through to Clark Gable. Carole Lombard. In fact, every star on their roster." At some point it was reduced from hour to half-hour and MGM stepped out. Robert Young was host, then John Conte. Meantime, he wrote a play called *Open House* which premiered at the Lobero Theatre in Santa Barbara. Had a short run "and we closed it after its session at the Lobero."

"At Goldwyn Studios, I did quite a good deal of doctoring on scripts for Mr. Goldwyn for which I received no screen credit."

Next was *Spring in Brazil*, for six months, writing and direction of the book. Then came back to California to take over the direction of Frank Morgan's *The Fabulous Dr. Tweedy Show*, not written by Rapp. Less than 20 weeks. Then went back to Goldwyn studios to do *The Bishop's Wife*. Wrote screenplay with Lawrence Watkin, but it wasn't used. Goldwyn called in Robert Sherwood to do another adaptation.

Next, *Drene* show in 1946. "The program which featured Don Ameche and Pinky Lee was ailing and the William Morris office sent for me to see if I couldn't bring some new life into it." Wrote and directed it. "When I came in, two new elements were added by the William Morris office. One was Danny Thomas, and the other was Frances Langford. I was asked to provide a format for the show." Half-hour. "I divided it into two separate sections. I provided Danny Thomas with some characteristics and comic dialogue that was executed by Ameche and Thomas and Carmen Dragon, and I devoted the second part of the program to a new character sketch I had created called 'The Honeymoon Is Over' starring Don Ameche and Frances Langford." This was before Dec. 1946. He did this for 19 or 22 weeks. "Early in the series, it was felt by Danny Thomas and his representatives that he was not coming off as well as he might have been because of the success of the vignette called 'The Honeymoon Is Over,' which sort of eclipsed his comedy, so it was suggested that extra writers be brought in to help fortify and bolster the Danny Thomas segment of the show. I quite willingly stepped aside and devoted all of my efforts to the writing and directing of 'The Honeymoon Is Over.'"

Then in 1947, *Old Gold* sponsored by Lorillard, Rapp was director and writer of entire program for CBS. 39 weeks. Again, the show was in two sections. "One consisting of Frank Morgan and the character I had created for him who engaged in comic dialogue with Frances Langford, Don Ameche, Marvin Miller, and as a rule, a special guest. And the second part of the program consisted of Frances Langford and Don Ameche, plus incidental characters, in my sketch 'The Honeymoon Is Over.' I depicted Morgan as a lusty, earthy, socialistic character with a vast fund of superficial knowledge, who was inclined a great deal towards romanticism or big fibs, if you will, who invariably got himself into some kind of box when he was up against the real article." MCA, Music Corp. of America was his rep then. Contract was with Leonard & Mitchell.

At end of *Old Gold*, Rapp made a deal to present "The Honeymoon Is Over" featuring Don Ameche and Marsha Hunt as John and Blanche on *Charlie McCarthy Show* for Chase & Sanborn Coffee. This show began around Oct. 3, 1948. Was with it 13 weeks. NBC.

After this did Rapp *Inspector General* for Warner in 1949. Also was signed to write and direct Danny Kaye in "Stop, You're Killing Me" but it wasn't made since Warners and DK "terminated their deal." Also worked on *A Song Is Born* for DK and Goldwyn. "I wrote that in collaboration with Harry Tugent and this picture, which was directed by Howard Hawks, bears no screenplay credits of any kind for the simple reason that Hawks had tampered so much with the script in the process of shooting that both Tugend and I felt it was no longer our picture, and it would be detrimental to our best interests to appear as screenwriters on this particular picture."

"That is when I accepted an offer to come to New York to write, direct, and produced portions of a television program known as *Star Time*, which was telecast over the DuMont network." October of 1949 or '50. Brought Lew Parker and Frances Langford with him. Benny Goodman and orchestra and dancer Katherine Lee were on show already. Sponsored by Grand Union Stores "and a multiple sort of sponsorship including Duff's Cake Mix, McCormack's Vanilla and Roily's Doliles, and various other shelf products of Grand Union Stores." Did it about seven months. Rep. was William Morris agency, having changed from MCA. Bickersons segment took 15 to 19 minutes of the hour format. 39 weeks, though Rapp came in after it had been going for a few weeks.

After *Star Time*, did *Ain't Misbehavin'* script for Columbia about "a not-too-well educated chorus girl who marries into high society and by her frankness and warmth convinces the husband's mother and the society people that it wasn't such a bad marriage after all."

After Philip Morris' Bickersons radio show ended at CBS in Aug. 28, 1951, he took a brief vacation and resumed by doing several guest programs: Ed Wynn on NBC, and two shots on Ed Sullivan (March 9 and 23, 1952). "Subsequent to the Philip Morris series I wrote a screenplay for Wald-Krasna which was titled *The USO Story*. This picture was subsequently shelved after the dissolution of the Wald-Krasna Company."

Continued Examination Before Trial of Philip Rapp taken before a Notary Public of State of NY, at the Hotel Netherland, NYC, Feb. 18, 1956 at 2pm. Borak Reporting Service. Civil Action File No. 89.

Theodore Kupferman for Rapp, Carleton Eldridge for defendants.

For ABC Frank Samuels contacted Rapp in the first six months of 1950 about Bix. Discussed it at William Morris Agency on Canyon Dr. in Beverly Hills. Bob Braun also present. Two or three meetings within two weeks. George Gruskin, another Rapp rep., was at one of these. Samuels, a former VP with ABC was authorized by Rapp to make a deal for Bix at ABC. But no offer came back.

"Mr. Chris Witting, an executive of DuMont Television Network, came to the Coast to discuss terms of purchase of the Bickersons for the DuMont Network with my representative, Mr. Abe Lastfogel, president of William Morris.

"I think the ear alone will tell you that the title *The Honeymooners* is similar to 'The Honeymoon Is Over.' Both titles imply the nature of the vehicle, one outright and the other in sarcastic or satiric fashion.

"The characters themselves, partners in marriage, are seemingly not too happy in their married life, engaging in a comic battle of the sexes constantly. Usually in the Bickersons, the male partner of the team is in a uniform (pajamas) and the male half of *The Honeymooners* team is in a uniform, also (a conductor's uniform). One of the most successful Bickersons sketches ever performed in radio and in television concerned the activities of John Bickerson as a conductor of a streetcar.

"In both cases the married partners are involved in numerous arguments over petty money difficulties, relative difficulties, or rather, relation difficulties, and the common and ordinary vicissitudes of having to live in rather squalid surroundings.

"The nature of the male partner is similar in a great deal of respects—I should say the nature of the male partner in the Bickersons is similar in a great deal of respects to the male partner in *The Honeymooners* in that both men seem singularly ill-equipped to handle even the smallest problem with any degree of sense, such as fixing household utensils, or carrying out any simple domestic problem.

"The brother-in-law, Barney, and sister, Clara, in the Bickersons have their counterpart in the characters of the sewer worker and his wife in *The Honeymooners*.

"Both vehicles, in *The Honeymooners* and 'The Honeymoon is Over,' are characterized by a certain violent comic quality which usually increases in tempo and diminishes toward the end of each individual sketch. Even more important than these specific comparisons which I am making is the effect of the similarity between the two vehicles upon the ear and the eye of the listener and viewer."

Rapp saw *The Honeymooners* "toward the end of the DuMont version." Saw them shortly after he read a review of the Gleason Show in *Newsweek*.

"Until the advent of 'The Honeymoon Is Over' featuring the Bickersons, the usual type of husband-and-wife program presented married partners in a rather sweet, gentle, domestic form of comedy involving difficulties, possibly with their children, regular comic teenage difficulties, or minor problems that seldom resulted in the violent type of comedy as presented by the Bickersons. Ozzie and Harriet, Ethel and Albert, Phil Harris and Alice Faye, is of the same generic type as the usual sweet and gentle marital comedy as presented." (When Rapp is asked for differences of Bix to other husband and wife shows, there's a long discussion between lawyers that it would take all day; and since Gleason's lawyer objected to being questioned on these lines, Rapp shouldn't have to either; or they both should.)

Finally, Rapp reads a "newspaper article by Mr. John Crosby, who is considered the dean of American radio and television critics. This is in 1947," defining violent marital comedy. "Mr. Crosby says,

'The air lanes are aquiver with the cooings of contented husbands and wives (Ozzie and Harriet, Phil and Alice, Ethel and Albert, to mention only a few) but there is one young couple who couldn't have been more thoroughly mismated and who make no bones about it. They are John and Blanche Bickerson, who are heard at the tail end of the *Old Gold Show*, KNX, 6:00 p.m. Fridays, and who are a sort of contemporary Jiggs and Maggie. On second thought, I withdraw the reference. Jiggs and Maggie aren't in the same league with the Bickersons.'"

Q: Have you had occasion to come across any programs wherein husband-and-wife characters were presented in an unfavorable comic light, other than in the Bickersons?

A: Yes. On one occasion a program was presented. I believe over the ABC Network, called *Two Sleepy People*, which was removed from the air because of its infringement upon the Bickersons, and once again not too far back NBC removed another copy of the Bickersons from television.

"The Bickersons is character comedy where no invented situation is necessary but just the incident of the moment occurring within the realm of the facets of the characters exposed provides either comedy or tragedy."

The Christmas episode of *Honeymooners* resembles Bickersons Christmas spot, in which husband sells a cherished possession to get a gift for wife, who also did same thing. It's also O. Henry's "Gift of the Magi," and Aristophanes did it too.

Bickersons lived on Clump Street.

Gleason did a take off on Bickersons on *Calvacade of Stars*, in which Lew Parker played the husband and Gleason played the wife. Franklin-Bruck was the ad agency, and M. J. Kleinfeld was President, from which Rapp heard about this burlesque. Exact same set and furnishings were used. Rapp reported it to WMA to do something about it.

After being told about *Honeymooners*, Rapp watched a *Cavalcade of Stars* program (which came on the West coast sporadically), of which *Honeymooners* was part.

"I think that since the development of *The Honeymooners* there has been a transposition of characters. The extravagances, the illogicalities, the petty conniving, has been transferred from the female in 'The Honeymoon Is Over' to the male in *The Honeymooners*. It is a deep psychological study which is best illustrated by the fact that when he did a take-off on the Bickersons, he played the wife."

Meeting with Guy Della Cioppa, "I found him a crashing bore with very little sense." He found the Bickersons had too much "contentiousness to it. Obviously, it meant argumentative, and he thought that the best way to make the Bickersons a star vehicle was to make it sweet and gentle like all the other married couples. At which point he lost me completely. I was transported mentally. Physically, I sat there." Purpose of the meeting was to discuss putting Bickersons back on radio. This was about three to five years after meeting with Mr. Paley.

(EXAMINATION ENDS AT 5:45 P.M.)
It continues the next day:

"I first met [Jackie Gleason] at the Dumont Theatre or, rather, the Ambassador Theatre, where we telecasted the Bickersons during rehearsals. He was introduced to me by Lew Parker who is a very good friend of his. I met him on various other occasions in restaurants and other places in New York City." This would be the third or fourth program of *Star Time*, fall of 1950. Never conversed with Gleason really, just an exchange of pleasantries.

"I was originally approached by Niles Trammell, then the president, I think, or chairman of the board of NBC and we had lunch at the St. Regis during the course of which he proposed a deal whereby NBC would be able to keep 'The Bickersons' on their network and engage me in some employee capacity to write and direct it and also conceive new and other ideas for various other presentations and programs." Around 1951. First negotiation with NBC for Bix. "Mr. Trammell suggested that the Bickersons was such a good property that he would like to see it permanently on NBC." Radio. Then met with Mr. Trammell's West coast rep, Mr. Strotz, a week later in NBC's Hollywood studios office. Small licensing fee, but made up by a generous employee contract. $200,000 for licensing as a radio show. Then he spoke of retaining Rapp for $100,000 "for many years in the capacity of an inventor." Also talk of him sharing in the profits of programs he developed for NBC, if and when sold to sponsors. Nothing developed, nothing concrete.

First discussed Bix with CBS, "I think it was in 1949, in the late spring or early summer that I received a call from one of MCA's representatives, Sonny Weerblin, in New York, telling me that Mr. Paley of the Columbia Broadcasting System was interested in making a purchase of the Bickersons. They informed me that Mr. Paley was coming to the Coast and arranged a meeting at the offices of MCA in Beverly Hills." Met in May or June of 1949. Mr. Paley, Mickey Rockford, Taft Schreiber and Sonny Weerblin present, perhaps Herbert Rosenthal. MCA was Rapp's rep.

"[The receptionist] told me that the gentlemen involved in this particular meeting were cleaning up some other matter which was terribly urgent and asked me if I would wait five or ten minutes. I then told the receptionist that I didn't have five or ten minutes to spare, and I had made a point in the telephone conversation with Sonny Weerblin to make it precisely at 12 o'clock because I had a horse running in one of the early races at Hollywood Park. It was one of my new horses and I was determined to see him run his first race for me and I wouldn't let any meeting in the world interfere with a horse race.

"She went in and conveyed this message to one of the MCA officials and Mickey Rockford then came out of the office and begged me to wait a few more minutes since a million dollars was involved and that the winning of a purse for $3,000 or $4,000 and the cashing of a small bet certainly did not compare with such a deal.

"I said I would wait a few minutes more. I did. I waited about eight or nine minutes and then my impatience grew so that I left the building and returned to my home to pick up my wife to go to the races." But at home, an annoyed Mr. Rockford called to demand he return to MCA. Mrs. Rapp calmed Phil, suggesting the money and prestige was worth it, and if the meeting was short, they'd still have time to see the horse run. (She takes care of all the finances.) He returned. Mr. Paley wanted Bix as an hour or half hour show, but "I had a feeling that the nature of the Bickersons made it almost mandatory that it be preserved in small vignette fashion and that elaboration of it or expanding it might possibly result in a lot of padding." But Paley was all for the half-hour format. "Just look at *My Friend Irma*," he said. Rapp didn't care for the show, suggesting its high rating was "because it was a coat-tail show following the biggest rated show on the air then, *Lux Theatre*. Mr. Paley bridled at this. I found out very rapidly that he was rather responsible for its success on the air and that he had fostered and nursed this particular piece of network property.

"The meeting rapidly declined after this exchange, although I did agree that I would try to concoct and fashion a half-hour radio program based on the short version of the Bickersons.

"I looked at my watch after that. I think Mr. Paley noticed my impatience to leave, and I made my farewells and went to the race course." The meeting took about 40 minutes. The general advice from the other MCA components of the room was, "Listen to what Mr. Paley says and develop it into a half hour. It will prove very lucrative."

"After coming home from the races, I felt remorseful that I had been so brusque and possibly rude to Mr. Paley in the office, so I called Mickey Rockford and asked where I could reach Mr. Paley to sort of apologize and smooth things over. I was unable to reach him during the balance of his stay in Hollywood, which I think was very brief. However, I went to work as fast as I could to make amends by actually creating a half-hour Bickersons program." Four weeks after the meeting it was done in the summer of 1949 for Frances and

Don. It was sent to the East coast MCA offices, but Paley didn't want to hear it, said Rapp's agent Sonny Weerblin. "Rather childish attitude, I thought, and I sought to make amends, but I could never get through to Mr. Paley." But it was played for Hubbell Robinson. The audition show wasn't purchased.

"[Mickey Rockford] told me that CBS was in the process of purchasing various properties that could be played not only by the original performers who created the roles but by anybody and they could be used with a certain degree of permanence, and the Bickersons had been very strongly considered as one of these properties and that its intrinsic value was easily a million dollars plus an employee contract." But after the making of the record [CBS album], nothing was discussed or done. The above quote is a conversation heard by Mickey in the hall prior to the meeting.

(EXAMINATION ENDS AT 5:30PM, AFTER A SMALL ARGUMENT ON WHEN TO FINISH THE DEPOSITION.)

APPENDIX 2

Rapp's outline for his autobiography, just as he wrote it

open with J. Walter Thompson days. John Reber Colwell et al. Georgie Price

augmented income by acting jobs. twenty-five bucks. Radio Pyro program

George Burns friars press room.

Price ragal reproductions chase and sanborn tea twice weekly

Prince of parody. sixty-five dollars. sam moore carroll colwell Faulkner abbott spencer jwt.

Own program. sun night following cantor.

Bea lillie audition. Standard brands.

Pleurisy attack check with Mariam Jackson heights

sent to Washington by JWT to meet freedman, work on cantor show and Canada dry audition. amalgam

david lost cantor and I gained brice. open for business.

friars frolic 1932 wrote for bert lahr and price

get pictures of burns jessel holtz etc. kaye. Thomas

wrote vaudeville acts for long forgotten teams. wrote act for wife and self – disaster. myrtle in Brooklyn. agent said give it up and stick to writing for other people.

rainy day when wife left on bus for Chicago — used agents card and went into hippodrome. Princess wah-let-ka told my fortune from stage.

with freedman captured everything in radio. block and sully george

gvot eddie cantor fanny brice lou holtz little king cartoons and follies of 33 and life begins at 840 ex-lax and Plymouth.

fanny without her plates – forced to do snooks. at that time she was doing mrs cohen and historical sketches in dialect. chimes from a jesters bells Robert juberdetta. started with uncle wound up with low sorin or teddy bergman as father don't remember which. Alan reed. later hanley safford.

freedman's fathers death. israel the yankee on forward. had to go to Pittsburgh. stole idea from humor mag. freedman traced it to "the two dogs" by Robert burns. saved a lawsuit.

do whole chapter on freedman and those days. title blond eggs blond cigars and carminzyme. no sleep relief playing penny game at coney island – waiting taxi. trip to Atlanta, jessel and cantor. no cigars.

title "change it to kissing" prodigious eater drank millions of bottle of Perrier water smoked cigars incessantly. joke fols. Johnny.

sydenham hospital. the break. the lawsuit freedman's death.

hollywood. i quit cantor. subsequent wires. johnny's line.

tommy riggs and betty lou. shaw and lee and jack oakie. moore and broderick joe brown many others. finally good news program.

pictures with danny kays and others.

spring in brazil with berle.

ed wynn.

soldiers in greasepaint with benny et al. quote wire from abe.

old gold. Philip morris. three of a kind.

into tv. popsicle program for fanny.

NY DuMont network startime. belafonte fifty a week.

tv films. ben blue. topper. wally cox. joan davis. ford and hines.

blue like wynn truly a funny man but could not handle dialogue. moved like chaplin.

cox articulate, literate and athletic. could handle any stunt. tell story of lion in stateroom — afraid of handler mel koontz.

underwater story magnetic mines on hull of ship. tireless worker knew lines to perfection needed very little direction but questioned almost everything. learned to fence with the skill of A MASTER.

adlibbed a ballet specter of rose.

created the bickersons in 1946. gleason. quote Crosby about Ameche and Langford.

relate incident at bev hills hotel for drene when I told them about a married couple in bed. their reactions. abe et al.

george gruskin.

mann holine — tom mcknight at services.

marx bros. shot the last picture they ever made together. tell story of chico. harpo the practical joker. groucho on morgan spot never changed a word.

use as many names as possible in connection with ad agencies, films, etc.

tab hunter show.

ray bolger.

bob hope at Stratford theater in chi.

how I turned down martin and lewis. Dean martin probably the funniest man alive. lewis intolerable.

ORGANIZE BY CHAPTER TITLE.
USE AS MANY NAMES (NON COMIC) AS POSSIBLE

STARBUSTER...THE LIBEL BIBLE.

NIL NISI BONUM

ON BRICE . . . HEADING . . . FUNNY GIRL? HORSESHIT!

This one will start with Brice, Lombard, Morgan doing rehearsal. Recount story of Follies of 33, round bed and Willie Howard.

Brice . . . Undinist and petomane. Belched to shame Wallace Beery.

Make stats of Variety story on quitting . . . Key to the city of SF.

Print letters from Hobler. Tell story of Holiner.

Why she married Rose. Like taking dope cure. Big gangster–smaller one. Home on Faring Rd.

Do a whole chapter on Danny Kaye. Went to see him at the Mastbaum Theatre in Phila. Sent by Goldwyn. Subsequent pictures at studio. Wonder Man. Mitty. Song is Born story. Tugend.

Close friendship—Hartman et al. The ranch. Chinese cooking.

Kaye was the quickest study in the world. Had to ride a horse in Mitty. Learned in ten minutes. Valdez Moody–mistaken for rudeness–shyness. Crew didn't like him.

England. Fabulous success. Pictures were designed to be a Kaye tour de force. No acting required. He could imitate anything. Vast interest in surgery. Watched operations. I'm sure he could have performed one successfully. Interest in flying.

this is not a funny book. it is a philippic. it is all true to the best of my recollection and like the cook who adds bran to his hamburger to make it go further I shall employ the use of a few stretchers.

the standup comics and their one-liners. they might just as well be reading from a joke book. depend a great deal on the failure of the material to get laughs so they can use prepared adlibs that indicate there is something lacking in the audience. audiences are masochistic, perverted, and the worst possible gauge of A COMedian. audiences that are sat up to indicate the potential of pilot films by means of machines etc. are particularly dangerous. they automatically become critics, inhibited and are given a feeling of superiority.

do a chapter on the selection of series for TV. quote from hiram holliday rating test.

edgar bergen. the truth is that Charlie was the live one and bergen managed to submerge his personality in the dummy. so much so that Bergen actually moved his lips more than the dummy. his technique was execrable but his characarizations were pure. this was the result of his radio days.

audiences are also sadistic—hence the pie in the face and the success of cartoon comedy which is based on violence of the worst kind.

clowns are the unfunniest of all comedians. actually they scare the hell out of kids and I have never yet seen an adult laugh at them unless it was to pacify the child.

chimpznzees are funny—actually and deliberately funny—funnier than any human comedian who ever lived.

refer to eastmans chapter on wit and jokes.

ed wynn was a man who was clumsy, spoke with a lisp, had a bad speaking voice, couldn't sing or dance yet insisted on appearing in public. freedman said he made a brilliant career out of his defects.

in nineteen thirty six max eastman published a book, the enjoyment of laughter. there is an analysis of humor on page __ that appears over the signature of eddie cantor. I wrote it. it follows in its entirety. I have since changed my mind about humor just as the public taste has changed.

get steve allens' book *the funny men*.

THE RITERS

Today's comedians use battalions.
parkinsons law prevails. like drunks in a shooting gallery.

somebody once said that trying to analyze wit was like dissecting a frog. you can see what he's made of but when you get thru the subject has expired.

I bag my first comedian—G. P. Non-com. In captivity they tend to become docile instead of obedient.

APPENDIX 3

Sold Sketches from Philip Rapp's 3x5 Joke File cards

"Mrs. Hamblett Records Her Vote" from *Pierrotechnics*

Mrs. Hamblett is very hard of hearing. She goes to the polls to vote and is asked the usual questions by the men in charge. Half the time she can't hear what they ask, so she answers the questions she thinks they asked her. The men tell her that all she has to do is to take a ballot and put an X next to the name of the man she wishes to vote for. She takes the paper over to a nearby desk. The men tell her to hurry and put it in the ballot box. She does so. The men sigh with relief and tell her she can go home. The woman tells them that they hurried her so much that she didn't have time to put anything on the paper.

"The Mug" from *Pierrotechnics*

A man and a woman are going to work the "Badger Game" on Mr. Percival Purvis, a supposed sucker. Mr. Purvis is given the woman's address by one of her accomplices. He is told that the woman is a Palm Reader. Purvis goes to her apartment and finds her sitting behind a screen through which two holes have been cut. He is told to put his hands through. He does so, and she begins to read his palm. Soon she comes out from behind the screen and they sit down together on the settee. She places his arm about her. Suddenly, the door opens and her "husband" comes in and proceeds to shake down Purvis. Purvis gives him the money. Purvis asks the woman to teach him the palmistry business, he asks her and her "husband" to go behind the screen, put their hands through the holes while he attempts to read them. They do so in order to humor him. As soon as they have their hands through the holes, Purvis takes out a pair of handcuffs and snaps it on their wrists. He turns out to be a cop.

"Noreen" from *Nine to Eleven*

The scene opens in a small country cottage. A man and a woman are sitting around waiting for "Noreen" who is lying in a bed behind a screen hidden from the audience. They are waiting for Father Murphy who had promised to be there to help ease the pain for poor "Noreen." Father Murphy comes and they tell him to step softly lest he wake poor "Noreen." The Father tiptoes over behind the screen. Then Father Murphy's voice is heard. "Pat!" he cries. "The Saints be praised! Noreen has taken the turn! (He appears from behind the screen with a hen in his hands) Glory be—she's laid an egg!"

"John Citizen's Dream" from *Nine to Eleven*

Mr. John Citizen comes to the office of the Inspector of Taxes to see about his income tax. He finds that the Inspector's job is to help people to avoid paying taxes. He tells the Inspector that his income is five hundred pounds *per anum*. The Inspector helps him figure out what he spends in a year, taxis, etc. John Citizen tells him that he uses the subway, except on Sundays. The Inspector then figures that it costs him two-hundred pounds a year for taxis. When he finishes itemizing these imaginary expenses, he finds that he has spent fifty pounds more than John Citizen earns. So he tells him that not only is he exempt from taxes, but the state owes him one-hundred pounds. He gives him the hundred pounds. John Citizen then admits that his income is really a thousand a year—whereupon the Inspector gives him another hundred pounds!

"Comparisons Are Odious" from *Austin Melford's Nonsense*

It is the maid's afternoon off and she is getting ready to go out when her mistress asks her to stay and let her daughter's fiancé, Percy, into the house. The mistress goes away and leaves the maid standing there. The telephone rings. It is the mistress's daughter Phyllis. She hates Percy, and tells the maid to see that he doesn't come again. Percy comes in, and the maid introduces herself as Phyllis's sister. She proceeds to tell Percy about the faults that Phyllis has. She tells Percy that Phyllis has a wooden leg, snores, and has adenoids. And also that Phyllis told her that he, Percy, couldn't make love. Percy, his ire aroused, throws his arms around the maid and starts to kiss her. The mistress enters and berates Percy for making love to her maid. To which the maid replies, "Making love? Say—you ought to see the master."

"A Modern Christmas" from *Vignettes from Vaudeville*

It is Christmas day and little Horace's parents are all set to surprise him with their gifts. Grandpa has electric trains for him. Grandma bought him a bicycle, etc. They all unwrap their presents and go to show little Horace how to work them. Horace stands on the side, bewildered, while the older people play with the toys they had bought for him. He is completely forgotten. Finally, they notice that he is missing and they go to look for him. They find little Horace deep in an armchair—a siphon on a small table at his side—a cigar between his lips—immersed in a copy of *The Sporting Times*.

"The Kiss" from *Vignettes from Vaudeville*

Dennis, who is in love with Cynthia, a married woman, has come to her house to steal her away from her husband. They have planned to go abroad. Cynthia's maid, who has been in her service for many years, hears that her mistress is going away without her. She starts to sob bitterly. Dennis asks her what the matter is. She tells him.

Dennis, feeling sorry for her, gives her a kindhearted kiss. Cynthia enters while Dennis is kissing the maid. She misinterprets the kiss and orders Dennis from her house. Dennis leaves and Cynthia goes to her room. Cynthia's husband enters. He goes over to the maid, and noting her tear-stained face, asks her what she was crying about. She sobs. He tells her to stop crying—takes her in his arms and kisses her.

"WEATHER OR NO" FROM *VIGNETTES FROM VAUDEVILLE*

The two love birds are cuddled in the parlor. They keep kissing each other goodnight. But the boy doesn't go. Finally, he decides that it was time he went home. So he makes to leave. They discover that it is raining very hard, so the girl tells him that he can sleep in her house. He tells her to excuse him for a few minutes. He exits. A few minutes later he comes back soaking wet. She asks him where he went. He tells her that he went home to get his pajamas!

"THE AUTHOR, THE ACTOR AND THE VICTIM" FROM *VIGNETTES FROM VAUDEVILLE*

The author is reading his manuscript to the actor who is to have the major role. One part calls for the actor to sob. The actor refuses the part, saying that it isn't natural, and that no man would do it. The author offers that any man will sob under certain circumstances. They bet. A bell rings and the author tells the actor to get behind the curtain and watch the proceedings. Billy, who is married to the author's sister, enters. The author tells him that his wife has run away with another man. Billy tonelessly asks if he might use the author's phone, saying that he invited some people to play bridge that night and wanted to call it off. He goes into the next room. The actor comes out from behind the curtain and collects his bet. They go into the next room and the author tells Billy that it was all a gag. Billy says, "Do you mean that she hasn't left me?" The author nods affirmatively. Whereupon Billy breaks into heartrending sobs!

"Stalemate" from *The Nine O'clock Revue Book*

The scene opens in a hotel dining room. A girl is seated at a table alone when an old man comes over and sits next to her. He tells her that he is a detective, and that thieves are after the string of pearls she is wearing. He also points out a young man whom he says is carrying five thousand pounds on his person. He says the thieves will get him, too. The old man leaves and the girl begins to cry. The young man gets up from his table and comes over to the girl. He asks her what the matter is. She tells him. Then she unclasps the pearls from around her neck and gives them to the young man. She tells him to guard them for her. He gives her his five thousand pounds as security. The old man comes over and arrests the young man. They leave the hotel together. A waiter comes over to her table; he proves to be the girl's accomplice. She is just boasting to him how she clipped a man for five-thousand pounds with a fake necklace, when her eyes fall on the bank notes—they are counterfeit.

"Arnold" from *Rescued from Revue*

The scene opens in Henry's flat. Henry's wife is discovered in George's arms. Henry suddenly enters. George tells him that he is merely hypnotizing his wife. Henry asks him to do it so that he can ask her questions while she is under the spell. George asks her if she loves him. She, pretending to be under the influence, replies that he is an imbecile. Then George asks her if there is anyone else in her life. She replies that there is—Arnold. George and Henry are both shocked. George asks her when Arnold last visited her. She tells him. Both men see nothing further to live for, so Henry shoots himself, while George takes poison. As George is dying he asks her who Arnold is. She tells him that he is the little plumber who did all the odd jobs in her house. It seems that Henry had a passion for doing odd jobs, so she had to hide him from Henry.

"All the World's a Links" from *Oh—By the Way!*

This sketch has two parts. In the first it shows how the husband feels after a losing day at golf. He walks in the door a half hour too early for dinner and growls when told that it's not ready. Shouts at his wife for making his meat too well done. Asks if there is anything else he can eat. He is told that there is some cheese. He says he hates cheese. Baby starts to cry. He growls. In the second part, it shows how he acts after a winning day at golf. Comes in, kisses the wife. Meat is burnt to a cinder. He says that he likes it that way. Hears baby cry, says it's music to his ears, etc.

"Which Do You Prefer—Silent or Talkie?" from *The W.P.B.*

Manager comes before curtain and makes the following speech: "Ladies and gentlemen, no doubt you are all aware that there is much controversy as to whether the silent or the talkie film is the better. We have, therefore, written a screenplay which will perform as a silent film, and then *a la* talkie."

"Western Love from *The W. P. B.*

This sketch takes place out west. It seems that word has come to the cowpunchers that a lady school teacher is coming to town. Their boss has promised the first of them to get married will have a house to live in for nothing. The cowboys have donned their best clothes and each is secretly confident that he will be the one to be accepted. They go to the train to meet the teacher. She proves to be young and pretty. They all cater to her. One takes her bags, etc. Jeff, the owner of the only hotel, has the best chance. He has persuaded her to stay at this place. Curly and Happy, the two cowpunchers, refuse to leave the hotel. Jeff duels them and kills both of them. He then turns his attentions to the school teacher. He proposes to her and she tells him that she is already married! Jeff shoots himself.

"The Locksmith" from *The W. P. B.*

Sir George, a man about town, is finally getting married. He admits that he has been quite a cad in his day and we find him and his butler disposing of hordes of pictures and letters. A locksmith, who had been called to mend the bureau, shows up. He tells Sir George that his heart is broken. He had bought a cottage for his bride to be, etc. George asks him about the man in the case, and the locksmith gives him a description that fits Sir George perfectly. Sir George is beginning to get very nervous. He tells Sir George how he's determined to track him down. And how at last he's found him. He tells Sir George that he found the man in Portland doing a jail term. The blackout is with Sir George remarking to his butler, "The silly ass! I thought I'd done it!"

"Virtue Has Its Own Reward" from *Straws on the Wind*

The scene takes place in the saloon of a small country village. There had been a contest as to who was the most upright man in the town, and David, Phoebe's boyfriend, had not won. She is terrible upset about it because the winner was to receive twenty pounds. She had promised to marry David if he ever got twenty pounds together. David enters the saloon, where Phoebe is employed as a barmaid, and tells her that he lost, that Jasper Housego had won. She sees Jasper come into the saloon and goes over to him. She asks him why they gave the prize to him. He tells her that he is a bachelor and bachelors are more upright than married men because one can have secret sins without anyone being the wiser. She tells him that he's too old to have secret sins. He says that she ought to see him when he's roused. She puts her arm around his neck and he draws her to him to kiss her, but she tells him that she won't kiss him unless he gives her two of the pounds he has. He gives them to her. She screams, the people come rushing in and see her in his arms, she tells them that he grabbed her. He gives another pound to David, and buys drinks for the house with the rest of the money.

"Tickets, Please" from *Ups and Downs*

Mr. Platt is the humble husband of one domineering woman. She never gives the poor guy a chance to open his mouth. Even his own children step on him. He asks for a new umbrella and his wife tells him that he's only had his for fifteen years, and he shouldn't be so extravagant, etc. One day while looking through the paper, he finds that among the numbers that were published for Sweepstakes winners, was his number, and for a prize of fifty thousand dollars. He tells his family. Immediately everybody caters to him. They go out and buy him an umbrella, get his slippers, etc. But he can't remember where he put his ticket and everybody starts to turn the house upside down in search of it. Finally, he finds it in his other suit. Everybody is happy—but when he looks at the ticket he finds that the number doesn't correspond with the winning number.

"Telephone Tattle" from *Ups and Downs*

The girl is a switchboard operator in a large hotel. She is a busybody and never fails to listen in on any conversation that may provide choice bits of interesting gossip to her. She has a boyfriend, Herbert Brown, whom she suspects of going out with other women. One day a man calls and demands to be connected to a certain movie actress, residing at the hotel, who is known for her way with men. She connects them, knowing that she is about to listen to a choice bit of conversation. She is shocked beyond words when she hears that the man making love to the actress over the phone is none other than Herbert Brown. She immediately breaks into the conversation and starts to call names, etc. The Herbert Brown calling the actress turns out to be none other than the owner of the hotel where she is employed.

"The Very Devil" from *One Damn Thing After Another*

Takes place at a costume ball, everybody in costume. They are all waiting to see Charles, who has been divorced from his beautiful wife. Charles appears dressed as a devil, and tries his best to live up to his costume. He goes around butting into conversations, always making it tough for someone, and he's having some fun. A young man is proposing to a girl whom he is madly in love with. He promises her everything under the sun if she will only marry him. Along comes Charles and tips her off that the man who is proposing to her just went bankrupt the day before. Charles is having troubles of his own; he has to pay his wife alimony, and she is bleeding him until he's nearly penniless. He tells his wife that he came in the wrong costume—he should have come as a woman instead of a devil.

"The Unwritten Law" from *Out of the Box*

The scene opens in a restaurant. A stranger enters, and although there are plenty of empty tables to be had, he sits down at a table already occupied by a man. It seems that he was searching for a clear and unobstructed view of the entrance. He appears to be very nervous, and when he starts to eat the bread belonging to the other man, the other man asks him what the trouble with him is. The stranger asks the man if he believes in the Unwritten Law. Or, in other words, does he believe that a husband has the right to kill his wife's lover. The man says that he does not and that any such man is a murderer and should be high handed. During this talk the stranger has taken out a revolver and is looking furtively at the entrance. Suddenly, when a man enters, he turns to the man at his table and says, "Tell that to him!" The man asks, "Who?" And the stranger replies, "Her husband!"

"The Altogether" from *Out of the Box*

Archie Jeddon is an artist. He specializes in nude paintings for which he uses nude models. He is busy painting a nude girl when it suddenly dawns on him that he has invited his fiancée and her folks to visit him that very day. He frantically pushes his model into another room when he hears a knock at the door. His fiancée and her parents enter. He tells them he is a landscape painter. He has many narrow escapes when they seek to enter the room where his model is hiding, but he succeeds in holding them off. Finally, the door opens and a man comes out . . . it is the model. She has saved the day by disguising herself as a man in the artist's clothing!

"Game to the End" from *The Review of Revues*

Tom is engaged to Joan; she is the pretty but helpless, old-fashioned type. Tom's brother Stephen doesn't approve of her. He is very athletically inclined and believes that Tom should marry a girl who can play tennis, swim, etc. Stephen exits and as he does, Mary enters. She is the exact opposite of Joan. She is the brawny and weather-beaten type, and she wears a man's hat. She, too, is in love with Tom. Tom cannot make up his mind which one to choose for his wife. Joan offers him nothing but her inexperience, her weakness, and her utter dependence on him. Mary offers him her steadiness on the backline, her strength, and a discount on his rackets. Stephen advises Tom to toss for it. So he spins his tennis racket, it stops on the rough side, so he gives his arm to Mary.

"The Rose" from *The Review of Revues*

This sketch has five parts. 1. Wife and husband at breakfast table. They are arguing. Husband takes rose from dresser, puts it in his lapel, and leaves for work in a huff. 2. Goes to office. Hires pretty secretary, flirts with her, then gives her the rose. 3. This scene opens in a restaurant. The newly hired pretty secretary is there with a man. It is not her boss. They have lunch together and she to prove her love gives the rose to him. 4. Scene opens in the home of boss. Wife is waiting for her lover, who is none other than the man seen in the restaurant with the secretary. Lover enters. They make love. He gives rose to her. 5. Husband enters after her love has gone. Both are in good humor. He sees rose she is wearing, asks for it, and when he gets it, he cleans his pipe with it.

"This Marriage Business" from *He Dines Alone*

The actress has been married three times. Her first husband was an author, the second, a critic, and the last, a manager. The scene opens in the actress's bedroom; she is about to retire when in comes her first husband, the author. He tells her what a fool he was to divorce her, and tries to win her back. There is a knock on the door and she tells the author that it's her present hubby; he always comes to her room before he goes to sleep. She hides the author in a closet. Her second husband enters and goes through nearly the same routine that the author went through when, suddenly, there is a knock at the door. She tells the critic that it is her husband, etc. and tells him to get into the closet. He gets in the closet, and her present husband, the manager, enters wearing pajamas and has a rug slung over his arm. He tells her that the roof is leaking in his room, and would she let him sleep on the couch in her room. She goes to the closet and locks the other two ex-husbands in. Then she turns to her present hubby and asks him how long two men could live in a closet. He tells her, for months. She says, "That is all I want to know!" She goes to retire.

"Us Browns" from *Ups and Downs*

Daisy is a young girl who expects to marry Polk, a young man who is employed in a large department store. She invites him to tea one day and Daisy's brother Herbert, who has just finished an eighteen-month stretch for burglary, appears. Daisy is afraid that Polk will be prejudiced against her because of her brother. So she asks her brother to behave while Polk is there. Polk arrives and tells them that six rolls of ribbon were stolen from his store and that the police are after the thief. Daisy looks at her brother. Herbert tells Polk about his jail record. Polk says that he despises thieves. Herbert says that he is going out and if he finds Polk there when he gets back, he will break him in two. Mrs. Brown, Daisy's loving mother, tells Polk that Daisy is the apple of her eye, and that she takes after her very self. Polk calms down and embraces Daisy. A detective comes in and puts Mrs. Brown under arrest for stealing the six rolls of ribbon.

"But Is It Art?" from *Ups and Downs*

The girl is ragged and unkempt. She is an artist. She endeavors to make her living by showing the paintings she made to passersby. All of her paintings are modernistic. A few feet away from her, sits a man. He also has pictures. But his are pictures that he hires at the rate of fifty cents a week. He is not an artist. All the passersby seem to know him and drop money into his hat. To the girl, they give nothing; they don't even glance at her pictures. The man has finally begged enough to buy him a decent lunch and asks the girl artist to watch his pictures while he goes for lunch. As soon as he leaves, she turns her pictures to the wall and goes to sit by his. Soon passersby are dropping money into her hat. Finally, she has quite a few dollars. She looks at her pictures and says, "It isn't art . . . but it is lunch!"

APPENDIX 4

MISC. OUTLINES AND FILM TREATMENTS

SAM GULLIVER'S TRAVELS

According to most authorities on human behavior, people who travel a great deal are divided into two categories: the Irresistible Talker and the Immovable Listener.

As a rule, the listener is not so by choice, but rather is a victim of the designer of trains and commercial planes, undoubtedly an Irresistible Talker. Otherwise, why are seats in these vehicles placed in pairs?

The Talker usually boards at the very last moment, casts a practiced eye down the length of the vehicle, spots his prey and moves in for the kill. The prey, already lured by the diabolical bait of the Talker, the Window Seat, despite his studious appearance, sits in apparent comfort and safety, ostensibly engrossed in a copy of this week's *Time*, actually hoping that his seat partner will be that pretty redhead he saw in the depot. This never comes to pass for the simple reason that the redhead is a waitress in the depot café and had just stopped at the ticket window to return the sixty cents she borrowed on Friday.

In a flash the Talker has deposited himself in the empty seat and immediately transforms the Hoping Traveler into the Immovable Listener. The Talker carries a bulky briefcase which he slides on the floor between himself and his companion, thereby effectively blocking any means of escape. Packages and articles of clothing placed on the empty seat, to be removed at the precise moment the redhead appears alongside, are no deterrent to the seasoned Talker. *You* know that.

Having removed his paraphernalia to his lap, further locking himself in position, the Listener rights his copy of *Time*, which he had been holding upside down, and buries his head in the magazine.

Withdrawing to a book or magazine is no defense against the Talker. Feigning deafness or ignorance of the language is equally ineffectual, and nothing short of calculated insult or a rap on the head with a spiked club will discourage the Talker from talking. Since polite society frowns on these last two methods, escape is impossible.

There is, however, a way of dealing with this scourge of civilization as you shall see when you meet Sam Gulliver.

Sam Gulliver, who resembles the star to be used in this proposed television series, travels for a nationwide shoe concern. He practically lives on trains, planes and busses and is never shown against any other background, unless it is the depot from whence these forms of travel are dispatched.

JOAN OF ARKANSAS
"THE UNDESERTED ISLAND"

At a regular briefing session of Drs. Dolan, Newkirk, and Short, Dolan reviews Joan's progress—or rather, the lack of it. It is a report leading inevitably to Dolan's conclusion—Cerebrac, the computer, goofed!

Dr. Short stoutly defends the protégée of his infallible electric brain, and Newkirk takes the middle position—that Dolan's experiments with Joan have been too drastic, and that this is the cause of the whole project not getting off the launching pad. Dolan retorts that his experiments have been mild as a June breeze, and in any case, his next one is a test that could be passed with flying colors by an infant in arms. As a test of adaptability under adverse conditions he is leaving Joan on a desert island for two weeks, without food or shelter.

Joan—having heard the news—is now seen being comforted by Mrs. Putnam, who is also slipping her a few delicacies to smuggle along on the trip. She is having trouble concealing them as Dolan enters, and Mrs. Putnam accuses him of heartlessness. He stoutly avers that he is the kindest man in the world, but he is also a scientist conducting a vital government project—not the leader of a campfire girl marshmallow roast. Joan's struggles betray the hidden delicacies, and Dolan confiscates them over protest. When Joan demands to know what she can take with her, he produces her tools of survival—a shoemaker's awl and a peavey.

Ready for a take-off by helicopter, Dolan is giving Joan her final briefing. She is to remember the vital secrecy of her mission and training, in the unlikely event of encountering any other humans during the next two weeks. She is also to be given a tape recorder, battery powered, on which she is to record her day-to-day reactions to the experiment. She is also . . . but Joan seems almost anxious to be on her way. Dolan, suspicious, starts a final shake-down inspection for hidden food. Under the pretext of inspecting the rotors of the helicopter, Joan climbs a mechanic's ladder and deposits her treasures on top of the rotor. Dolan inspects, finds nothing, and gives the signal for take-off. Joan frantically climbs up to retrieve her sustenance, just as the rotors start to whirl. After a wind-milling ride, Joan is rescued and led reeling into the helicopter as Dolan shakes his head.

We next pick up Joan on her island, with the helicopter disappearing into the blue. (There is really nothing to worry about, since she has been assured that the copter will appear over the island for reconnaissance in a week . . . weather permitting.) Joan then dictates her first taped entry into the log—that she is starting a search for food, and anticipates no problem, since coconuts are abundant. A montage of her food-gathering attempts follows, punctuated by her remarks in the log. She has misadventures in tree-climbing, in getting hit with falling nuts, and she finally stages a wild brawl in the top of a tree with a monkey who claims prior possession of a coconut. And then, of course, there is the matter of how to open a nut with an awl and peavey, with the pangs of hunger growing all the time.

A day or so later, Joan is confiding to the log that she is beginning to have hunger delusions. Not only does the peavey look like a giant Popsicle, but as she dictates, she has the delusion that a hairy hand is offering her a banana, and finds that the mirage is complete up to the point of the banana having substance and taste. She then sees the face of her benefactor, and records in the log that she is reminded somewhat of Dr. Dolan, although the expression is much kinder. A kiss from the delusion finally convinces Joan that she is dealing with a bespectacled chimp, rather than a hunger-induced delusion. Her strange guest then departs suddenly, with much chattering, leaving Joan wondering what she said to offend him. As she turns around, the cause of the chimp's fright is apparent—an African lion, in close proximity.

Joan takes off up a tree, but has the misfortune of choosing a weak branch, which bends under her weight. It finally breaks, and Joan hits the ground running, only to collide headlong with a fierce-looking savage. This last shock is too much, and she collapses in a faint as we fade out for the end of Act One.

Act Two picks up as a continuation of Act One, with the savage and the lion staring down at the unconscious Joan. A more conventional individual comes on the scene, and we learn through his conversation with the ostensible savage that we are dealing with the members of a movie company on location. Both the second man—who is the director—and the actor are unable to account for the presence of Joan, since they assumed the island to be deserted. The director asserts his intention of calling the producer, one J. B. Dolan, for enlightenment and possible medical assistance. Joan, reviving, catches the name "Dolan" and asks if they have also been sent here by Dolan. She then assumes they are working for a common employer, and asks what role they are to play in shooting her to the moon.

As the two men stare at each other, Joan says that she understands, and knows that they shouldn't talk about the project. Any job they have in mind for her is okay, just so long as there is food on hand. The director excuses himself from this seeming mental case, and goes a short distance to call Producer Dolan on the radiotelephone.

Producer Dolan, in Hollywood, is totally disinterested in the Director's account of the strange woman who is being prepared to fly to the moon, and instead wants to know what is holding up production on the musical re-make of the Robinson Crusoe story. He wants them to finish shooting and get off the island, since for some reason he can't persuade those fatheads in Washington won't give him permission to even be on the island. The Director explains that they are having problems with the female lead, who doesn't want to work with the animals. Dolan shouts at him to double her, and if he hasn't got a double, *get* one. The Director hangs up thoughtfully, and goes looking for Joan.

Back at the laboratory, we find Joan's Dr. Dolan—along with Short and Newkirk—poring over serial photos of the island, taken to check Joan's progress. Dolan is confident that the pictures will show Joan running up the white flag, and begging to be taken off. Short and Newkirk have more confidence in her ability to adapt, but they are more than astonished at what the pictures show.

Joan has apparently built—with her peavey and awl—several large log buildings, pens for animals, has hollowed out a large dugout canoe, and had cleared a large area of land for cultivation. Dolan is completely incredulous, but since the island had none of these improvements when Joan was marooned there, and since it is a government reservation with no visitors allowed, he is unable to offer any explanation, other than the obvious fact that Joan must be very handy with a peavey. He resolves to go see for himself.

On the island, Joan is getting instructions in her new role, without much understanding of its relation to space travel. However, she knows that Dr. Dolan has come up with some weird assignments in the past, and this seems another in that succession. Getting chased into a swamp by a lion and cornered by a crocodile has her on the point of rebellion, however, until she learns that she is to be rescued by the handsome male lead and comforted in his arms. Joan goes through with the chase—with the usual misadventures—but when it comes to the point of being comforted in the strong arms, there is a cut, and the immaculate leading lady takes over for Joan.

There is a montage of Joan's misfortunes as a stand-in, wherein Joan gets the grief and the girl gets the leading man. Joan is finally promised a juicy part in the big dance sequence celebrating Crusoe's betrothal, but her dance turns out to be with the chimp.

We then dissolve to the interior of the helicopter, with Dolan and Newkirk coming to investigate for themselves the progress of their protégée. Cutting to Joan and her Hollywood co-workers, we find that the cannibals have captured both Crusoe and his bride, and are preparing the barbecue. Joan, of course, is braving the flames in place of the bride. The scene is proceeding nicely when the helicopter approaches to hover overhead. The Director and cast try to wave it off, as it is spoiling the shot.

Above, Dolan and Newkirk are shocked by the appearance of the hostile tribe of savages below. Dolan then sees the captive Joan, and resolves to rescue her. A thrilling helicopter rescue follows, with the Director at first screaming imprecations at the intruders, then resolving to shoot the whole thing, and re-write as he goes. The savages surge forward, but Dolan fights them off and assists Joan—thrilled beyond words—up the ladder and into the helicopter.

In the final scene, in the helicopter, Dolan and Joan both learn the truth, but to Joan the important thing is that Dolan came to her rescue in her hour of need . . . even if the need was a Hollywood product.

UNTITLED DANNY KAYE OUTLINE (PARTIAL)

The smash hit musical picture of 1946, *Two on a Straw* was practically the biography of its talented and beautiful star, Iris Moon. In the aforementioned picture, just as in real life, Iris was discovered behind a Hollywood soda fountain dispensing a variety of milkshakes and displaying a blouse full of goodies. An astute talent scout with a fine appreciation for Iris's milkshakes uncovers the rest of her talents and she is soon on her way to film stardom. At the crest of her fame an unfortunate marriage to a lovable but dissolute character, the inevitable divorce, the ensuing battle for custody of the child (a tiny replica of her beautiful mother), and various other vicissitudes bring the career of Iris Moon to a sharp halt. However, through the author's ingenuity and her will to win, Iris whips all her problems, finds her true love and once more reaches the heights never again to be dislodged. That was the story of *Two on a Straw*. Nobody liked it except the public and it grossed eighty-seven million dollars.

A microscopic contributor to this enormous gross was Adam Gorworth, a young man of no small accomplishment himself. Adam could sing, dance, juggle, act, was an expert mimic and pantomime artist, played several instruments, was reasonably attractive both in body and features; in short, Adam had everything including a burning desire to parade these talents before the great motion-picture audience. And so impressed was Adam Gorworth by the story of Iris Moon and *Two on a Straw* that he immediately changed his name to Danny Kaye, gave up his job as a hole-borer in a bowling ball factory and set out to conquer Hollywood. The day he left Glendale he had a spring in his step, apples in his cheeks, and a banana in his pocket.

In June of 1947 Danny Kaye descended on Hollywood, and the town was agog. Producers and directors held their breath, studio executives spoke in hushed tones and the trade papers carried the biggest story of the year. But it wasn't about Danny. Iris Moon had kicked over the traces again—and this latest show of "temperament," as the papers charitably referred to it, meant curtains for the great star. Despite the fact that two million dollars already spent on her current picture would go down the drain her employers decided not to put up with her any longer. And so the career of Iris had come to a sharp halt with no ingenious author to twist the tail of the story and solve her problems. Besides, Iris no longer had the will to win.

All this is by way of a prologue because our story doesn't really start until today. Today Danny, the gifted young man with the urge to conquer pictures, still has his gifts and still has the urge. He is by no means as starry-eyed or naïve as the day he arrived, but he is nonetheless undaunted. Three years of struggling for a break in pictures hasn't embittered Danny but it has made him sharp. It didn't take our boy long to learn a few angles and even invent some that the others didn't know. He soon learned that extras, even those extras with political pull and inside help, rarely earn enough money during any given year to buy the bare necessities. He registered with Central Casting but calls were few and far between. So he filled in the gaps by taking a job outside the entertainment world. Remembering how Iris Moon was discovered behind a soda fountain, Danny is now, by dint of industrious application to the theory that history repeats itself, one of the fastest, most accomplished and personable short-order cooks in the entire chain of Rexall drug stores. His domain is the stove, sandwich and beverage area in the largest Rexall's in Hollywood, and he rules it with a ready wit, a burst of song, a nimble step and a soupcon of juggling. It is in this conspicuous position that he hopes to catch the trained eye of some influential studio mogul but very few moguls are aficionados of Rexall's.

Still, the salary isn't bad, the surroundings are congenial, a great portion of the patronage being confined to picture people either working or hoping, and Danny is relatively happy. If his pay envelope is not consistent in size each week it's because part of his stipend has gone to cover the tab of some less fortunate extra—boy, girl, old man or woman—oh, yes, Danny is what some people might consider a soft touch. But he's well-loved and his enthusiasm knows no bounds.

Pert Cashier, the pert cashier at the far end of the mammoth drug store, is his greatest audience and also conspirator ex post facto in one of Danny's plans to keep busy in pictures. Not satisfied with the sporadic calls for extra parts from Central Casting, Danny Kaye changes his name again. And again, and again, and again. In fact, he has registered with Central Casting under nine different aliases. If a studio issues a call for middle-aged Englishmen, Lancashire dialect, it's more than likely that Central will telephone for Clovis Smith-Paddon. If a Russian aristocrat is needed, Igor Prontovich will fill the bill nicely. Henri Monet is exactly the French apache type, and when Central is searching for a motherly, tender and wise old lady, whom would they call but Katherine Whistler?

It now becomes clear why Danny's small room over the Yucca Steam Baths is loaded with costumes and accoutrements hardly necessary to the calling of a short order cook. Or even an extra, for that matter. But Danny is a special extra! His gift for mimicry serves him and serves him well. Now, you might well ask, what does he do about his phone calls? Wouldn't somebody at Central Casting get wise if he took all his calls at Rexall's? Well, it so happens there are eight public phone booths in the drug store, each with a different number, naturally. Each booth represents an alias to Danny so that when he answers the phone he is immediately prepared to carry out the masquerade. That is, he usually is. Sometimes he gets mixed up when the lunch traffic is heavy and Central Casting is apt to find that Katherine Whistler is answering Henri Monet's phone, or vice versa. *Well, Frenchmen have strange tastes, or maybe there's still life in the old girl*, thinks a puzzled operator. When he's too busy to answer the phone, the little cashier takes his call and summons him to the booth. "It's for you, Danny," she sings out. Danny, busy with his pots and caught with his pans down, rushes frantically for the line of booths.

"Who am I?" he remembers to ask.

"Freckles McGuire."

Grabbing the receiver Danny answers in the adolescent, voice-changing tones of the Huck Finn type. There are long stretches when he doesn't hear from Central Casting at all, then again they might want all nine of him in one day. It remains then only for him to select the day's work that offers the most possibilities to further his career. The fact that he is still a short-order cook is ample proof that he isn't the world's best selector.

When he gets a day's work in pictures he makes up his absence from the store by working on the night shift. And when he's not on the night shift he attends dramatic classes, studies ballet, voice culture, television technique and trap-drumming at one of the duly accredited schools that infest Hollywood and its environs. That cuts another slice out of his meager bankroll and when he's really hard-up he works off the fees by giving instruction in the very courses he's taking. Actually, he's far better equipped to do that than most of the regular instructors at the school.

It is a few minutes before the noon rush when Iris Moon enters Rexall's and seats herself on a stool directly in front of Danny. Iris is as lovely as ever, simply but attractively dressed, and wears dark glasses. Danny has his back to her, and is busily engaged, preparing a huge bowl of tuna-fish salad. The former star glances at the lunch menu and waits diffidently for somebody to serve her. While mixing the tuna salad, Danny is surveying the lunch counter thru the mirror on the back wall, counting the house as it were, and his eyes come to rest of Iris. He recognizes her instantly. Dropping everything, he turns to her and stares. Politely, Iris inquires whether she might have a watercress sandwich on whole wheat toast, no butter, please. And a small Coke. With lemon. No ice, please.

Danny is transfixed. Suddenly he blurts out, "You're Iris Moon!" She doesn't deny it. The noon rush begins but Danny can't tear himself away from his idol. He tells Iris how wonderful he thought she was in pictures. How she was his inspiration—his great desire to work with her. He's always been sure they could have been greater than Astaire and Rogers. Even Lunt and Fontanne. His compliments don't exactly fall on deaf ears. It's been a long time since anybody took any interest in Iris and she's hungry for his flattery. In the meantime the orders start pouring in and Danny, completely engrossed and enthralled, pays scant attention to his job. The dishes and sandwiches he serves, with great rapidity and deftness, are passed along to the hungry diners. One gets a cold slaw milkshake, another a raw egg between two slices of rye bread, others get tuna-fish sundaes, and similar weird combinations. Before the storm breaks Danny has really concentrated on the watercress sandwich for Iris, and he presents it to her with the pride of a Savarin. It's about thirteen deckers, garnished and trimmed, beflowered and goody-encrusted, the most ornate sandwich ever made.

Now the wrath of customers is mounting, and in a series of close shots we see Danny's confused handiwork. A man who ordered a banana split lifts up a ball of pineapple-covered ice-cream to discover two frankfurters in the dish. Between the two halves of a hamburger bun reposes a tea-bag. The startled patron lifts it out by the string and yells for the manager. One by one the angry diners voice their complaints and the harried manager descends on the still-enthralled Danny. While the store manager is heaping contumely upon the smitten young short-order cook Iris, leaving her masterpiece of a sandwich and her sunglasses on the counter, retreats from the scene unobtrusively. Danny is stripped of his apron and spatula and drummed out of Rexall's in disgrace. As he bids all his friends goodbye he spots the glasses left by Iris Moon. He retrieves them and makes up his mind to find her and return the article.

The phonebook doesn't disclose any listed number and all other inquiries about Iris yield nothing. Except a few disparaging remarks to which Danny takes exception. Still, Danny reasons, she must live somewhere in the neighborhood of the drugstore. He knows she left the store on foot. A thorough search of the immediate vicinity of Rexall's leaves Danny terribly discouraged. There are innumerable court apartment houses and he has spent hours scanning the letter-boxes of the individual units for the girl's name. It suddenly dawns on him that she might be living under some other name. Maybe her married name.

APPENDIX 5

NOVEMBER 27, 1984 LETTER FROM MARIAM RAPP TO COLUMNIST JIM MURRAY

Dear Mr. Murray,
The first thing we do when the *L.A. Times* arrives is to turn to your column. No one can equal you and your knowledge, in particular about horse racing. My sons, when they were four and six years of age, wanted to ride and so we bought a ranch in Encino and four horses. We built stables and equipment and rode up into the hills which at that time were hay fields. Today those hay fields are known as the Royal Oaks Estates, but then we could ride for hours and saw only deer and sometimes a snake or two. My eldest dreamed of being a jockey.

My husband was a comedy writer, who was brought out here by Sam Goldwyn to do a motion picture for Eddie Cantor. My husband had been writing Cantor's radio shows. While we loved horses and riding, owning a race horse was something we never dreamed of having. A neighbor of ours in Beverly Hills had a young son whose father owned a race horse, and my son and his playmate told us his father wanted to sell his horse. We decided to buy him for $1,500, but what do we do next? The owner of this horse told us about a jockey who wanted to be a trainer and we were introduced to R. H. Red—as he was called—McDaniel and he got his license and became our trainer.

Well, we had to have silks for our jockey and so another friend of my son's, a girl his own age who lived down the street from us and was a lover of horses too, but whose mother wouldn't buy her a horse, asked if she could design our silks. She was a very talented girl and we said yes, of course she could. This young girl's name was Joan Irvine, whose grandparents left her a ranch which was deeded to them by the Spanish government [in what is now known as Orange County]. Joanie Irvine today is probably the richest young woman in America, but I digress.

Our horse was now ready for the races. He ran about ten races and always finished second. Once he took the lead and another horse rode up beside him, he lost all desire to leave his friend behind. McDaniel said there were horses like that, they just didn't care about winning, they just liked racing for the fun of it. Well, fortunately he was claimed and we bought another horse, who was a big stallion, but had a cracked hoof. McDaniel knew what to do for him and raced him sparingly and only at six furlongs and he won 10 out of 11 starts. He was claimed away from us, and the new owner decided to race him at 1/16th miles and further and the horse never won again and his foot got worse and he was finally auctioned off for $100, but Red McDaniel added owners to his stable. He had owners who included Harry James and Betty Grable and about 10 or 12 other owners. He took a $5,000 claimer and won a $100,000 race with him. He claimed a mare for us for $2,500 who was in foal at the time and she raced against horses and won the Del Mar Handicap and beat the best male horses on the track.

Everyone wanted Red for their trainer, and all the jockeys wanted to ride his horses. He had a language all his own and was a joy to listen to. A quiet little man who soon became the leading trainer in America and held that title for five years in a row. His picture and life's story is well written up in the leading *Horse Manual.* Bill Shoemaker won the second race of his now-long career on one of our horses, and Johnny Longden [American Hall of Fame jockey] won many races with 'Mac's' horses, among them Andy Crevolin's horses that Mac trained.

One day after saddling three winners and about to saddle another horse that the Harry Jameses owned, he suddenly decided he was tired. He may have had one beer too many, but he decided to leave the track (we were racing up at San Francisco) and go home where he was living in Berkeley with his wife and two daughters. After driving halfway across the Golden Gate Bridge in his Cadillac he stopped and got out and jumped off. No one knew why. Maybe he had too many demanding owners, too many horses, too much of racing and decided he couldn't take it anymore. He was a quiet man who had made his life's dream come true, but couldn't handle it any more.

All of the theatrical critics of that era considered my husband, Philip, the finest comedy writer. Jerome Kern told Philip he wished he was 10 years younger so that he could do a musical with him. It was at that time that Philip was called upon to rescue a dying radio show starring Danny Thomas, with a singer by the name of Frances Langford and an emcee by the name of Don Ameche and wrote the Bickersons for two people who had *never* done anything with a comic premise. People who heard this masterpiece started laughing and to this day it is the most popular and most copied and most acclaimed and funniest album ever written. There is a radio station in Washing D.C. that plays only comedy records and the Bickersons is the no. one sought-after record and 90% of his callers for this are young people between the ages of 18 and 24. I guess the many of those who had been listening to this wonderful piece of comedy since 1947 have grown old and died.

Laughter is the greatest medicine in the world and Philip knew it better than anyone else. He has always understood better than most the true meaning of wit and humor, and it will always be loved and enjoyed by generation after generation. He gets depressed and lonely since all the friends and family members he loved best are gone from this world, the only living member of the famous round table at the Hillcrest C.C.

is George Burns, but when Philip feels like Mac did he plays the Bickersons again and he laughs again.

I know you have enjoyed the Bickersons, as much as we enjoy your column and I am therefore enclosing herewith two cassettes. I know you and your family will spend many hours of fun and laughter listening to these cassettes.

I hope and pray that you and your family will have a Happy and very, very Healthy 1985 and live to be 100 years old and keep giving us the pleasure of your writing. You have no peer. Mac was number 1 and Philip Rapp is number 1 and you are number 1. Stay well and keep writing.
Most sincerely yours,
Mariam Rapp. Mrs. Philip Rapp

APPENDIX 6

LETTER FROM PHIL WHILE IN LONDON TO PAUL RAPP

Dear Paisley-baiter,
What a town! I suppose Mom told you about the flight, etc, so there's no need to go into that. It's just wonderful beyond belief here. The people are so fine and the customs so quaint.

This morning we went to Buckingham Palace to see the changing of the guard. It was rather a grey day so I didn't take any movies. We expect to go back there on Thursday so I'll shoot the whole procedure in color.

We've just about walked over half of London, gawking like a couple of peasants. Rich ones, of course. The shops are full of the most amazing things—pretty cheap too, and I'm going to get you some trinkets on our next shopping trip. We've been to all the finest restaurants, done a heap of pub-crawling (boozing to you!) and seen a show or two. Incidentally, when you order a scotch & soda here, that's exactly what you get. The British think ice is something that the fishmonger cools his halibut with. Beer is served at room temperature but most of the rooms are cold enough to freeze the nose off of a well-digger in Idaho, so it isn't too bad.

The hotel is the most luxurious place imaginable. Huge living room, bedroom and bathroom in the suite, with a personal valet for me, and a personal maid for Mom. What a change from hearing the Paisley [Odessa, the Rapps' maid] screaming "Pouull!"

One day this week we're going to the House of Commons and listen to the debate. We'll be the guests of Sir Beverly Baxter M. P., a good friend of Victor Saville [British film producer].

We've changed our schedule a bit. Instead of Saturday, we leave for Paris on Monday. Then to Rome, Xmas in Nice & Monte Carlo, back to Paris & New Year's Eve in jolly old London.

I'll write you from each place and buy a piece of loot for you in every town.

Be a good boy & have a great time in Sun Valley—be careful!
Your Loving,
Poper

APPENDIX 7

BRIAN RAPP'S THOUGHTS ON HIS GRANDFATHER, JUNE 9, 2009

I think my granddaddy's view of reality was entirely based on the romantic notion that truth, beauty and femininity were the most powerful things in the world.

I remember what my mother, Jenny Maxwell, told me when I asked her how she met my dad. Back in 1959 she was Bud's girlfriend in an episode of *Father Knows Best* and Sandra Dee was working on a show in the same studio. My dad-to-be, Paul Rapp, was assistant director that day on another show and he had to choose between Jenny and Sandra for a date. I always say lucky for me he picked Jenny because Mom could handle her "grasshoppers" a lot better than Sandra could her margaritas, but that's a whole other story. Everyone in the Rapp family loved to catch a buzz. Cocktails were the elixir of life that lubricated fun times back then and Mom may have been small at five feet and 100 pounds, but she was mighty. I remember she also loved Bailey's Irish Cream in her hot chocolate and I was always rewarded with my own glass when I finished building the fire in our River Rock fireplace in our cabin up in Idyllwild. She was Norwegian, a real Viking through and through, and Granddaddy instantly pegged her as a fellow fisherman after watching her land a trout at the Sportsman's Lodge in the Valley. Fishing was a way of life in both Hull, England, where he was born and the Village where Mom grew up, and they both passed that *River Runs Through It* vibe to me. Every time I baited my hook as a kid I had this eerie feeling that I would succeed. California's waters in the early '60s were teaming with game fish. My dad had a book in our tackle box to identify all our bounty and I remember I was famous for landing the rarest known species like the Monkeyface Eel and poisonous Skullpin.

Mom's favorite was Mahi Mahi and Dad's was corbena and halibut. Granddaddy was the king of Catalina Island with the record catch of Sand Dabs that he brought in at night by the light of the harvest moon.

When I was a boy nothing was cooler than feasting on our seafood fried up in egg wash and sweet butter. I can still remember the sound of victory in our giant black steel pan. Not a morsel was ever wasted as we dipped our filets in catsup and homemade tartar sauce. Granddaddy always told me a sharp knife was crucial to deboning and he showed me how to push the blade away from my body on his smooth grinding stone. Sometimes I think Granddaddy loved cooking for me even more than catching the fish. The kitchen is where he really entertained me. A boilermaker in one hand and his metal flipping tongs in the other, clad in his Cutty Sark apron, to me, every meal was a grand performance and I was front row at Carnegie Hall.

The stories I heard are the stuff of Hollywood legends, and in all the years of tales, I never heard him curse or speak ill of anyone except Jackie Gleason for stealing The Bickersons from him to produce *The Honeymooners* back when TV started. Gleason was the only person mean spirited enough to stab him in the back, and he never forgave him.

To me, his best stories were how he hung out with bootleggers and gangsters at the 21 Club because they loved drinking with him after *The Ziegfeld Follies of '33*, or how he got Willie Shoemaker and Johnny Longden to ride our horses back in '51, the first year they started racing. Red McDaniel was our trainer until he jumped off the Golden Gate Bridge. Yikes! Granddaddy always told me to treat the stable boy and the parking valet better than the owner of Del Mar. He was beloved by the common man and he always tipped our jockeys with several hundred-dollar To Win tickets in their boots. It gives me chills to think how much we all loved him.

His sheepish grin haunts me, thinking how we walked to our table at the Turf Club, the maitre d' inquiring if Mrs. Rapp would be joining us at the track today?

"No Charlie, I'm with Brian, my grandson, and we've got a hunch in the fourth race on a double book special, Alviro Pirota's aboard and Mare says to bet the farm."

"Good luck, Mr. Rapp. Can I get you your favorite corned beef on rye with mustard?"

"Of course, and the same for my Big B. But make his on egg bread."

We lived for the thrill of victory and survived to fight another day with the agony of defeat.

I was born in July 1960 so I never got to watch a live performance from one of his radio shows but my dad told me he did and that the level of high jinks and fun with The Bickersons cast of Don and Frances, and Fanny Brice with Baby Snooks, made every performance a true classic. The night before the show Phil would stay up all night typing away as a sole creator of all his shows. He said he preferred typing to freehand. He used carbon paper before there were Xerox machines and used the hunt-and-peck method to conserve energy.

We used to love to watch *M*A*S*H* and *All in the Family*. He said on a hit show in the '70s they had a team of writers but when he was king of all writers, we lived like the good life would last forever.

I remember one summer around 1970 I was listening to The Bickersons comedy album, and it really occurred to me that as an artist, Granddaddy was really in touch with the soul of humanity. Phil understood his audience and knew how to make his actors sound real. He knew how people talked; it was his uncanny gift that he was born with. If you listen closely to John and Blanche when they are emotional, you can hear the love they feel deep down coming through no matter how strongly they resisted, just like a typical day in the Rapp residence.

Granddaddy and Grandma were the real-life battling Bickersons with Grandma in her role as didactic know-it-all and Granddaddy as the loveable rebel looking for a safe place in the apartment to hide his afternoon cocktail. And me as referee Mills Lane in the middle of a Mike Tyson fight.

The thing I loved most was when they put their heads together and handicapped the Del Mar racing form the night before a day at the Turf Club. Grandma had a slide rule with times and distances. She spent hours circling horses on the old newsprint to discover any clues to picking a winner. They loved the challenge and looked forward to every post time like a kid going to Disneyland.

CREDITS

PLAYS

Open House (with George Beck, 1939)

Match Please, Darling (with Joel Rapp, 1968)

RADIO

The Chase and Sanborn Hour/The Eddie Cantor Show (1932?–1939?)

Maxwell House Coffee Time/The Baby Snooks Show (1931?–1946?)

Good News (1938–1940)

Drene Time (1946–1947)

The Old Gold Show (1942–1946)

The Bickersons (1951)

FILMS

Strike Me Pink (1936, MGM)

New Faces of 1937 (1937, RKO)

Start Cheering (1938, Columbia)

There's Always a Woman (1938, Columbia)

Up in Arms (1944, MGM)

Wonder Man (1945, MGM)

Ziegfeld Follies (1946, MGM)

The Secret Life of Walter Mitty (1947, MGM)

The Inspector General (1949, Warner Bros.)

Ain't Misbehavin' (1955, Universal)

Wild and Wonderful (1964, Universal)

TELEVISION

Topper (1953-55; writer/director)

Summer Playhouse ("Mimi," 1954; writer/director)

The Adventures of Hiram Holliday (1956–57; writer/director/producer)

> [Adventure of the Romantic Pigeon by Philip Rapp & Doris Gilbert
>
> Adventure of the Swiss Titmouse by Philip Rapp & Robert Riley Crutcher
>
> Adventure of the Christmas Fruchtbrod by Philip Rapp & Robert Riley Crutcher

Adventure of the Sea Cucumber by Philip Rapp & John Kohn and Bernard Drew

*Adventure of the Hawaiian Hamzah

Adventure of the Wrong Rembrandt

Adventure of the Attaché Case

Adventure of the Monaco Hermit Crab

*Adventure of the Dancing Mouse

*Adventure of the Lapidary Wheel

Adventure of the Surplus General by Rapp & Richard Powell

The Tab Hunter Show (1960; director)

My Favorite Martian (1965; "I'd Rather Fight Than Switch")

Songs

Ballad to an Amber Lady (by Philip Rapp and Crissingers)

Morning Song

Translucent Carriages (by Fonnie Lee Harley, Philip Rapp and Herodotus)

---

* Published in *The Hiram Holliday Scripts* by Philip Rapp.

That's a Rapp!

INDEX

Adventures of Hiram Holliday, The **195**, 204-212, 248, 357, 391-392
Allen, Gracie 14, 128
Alley Oop 268-269
Ameche, Don 2, 3, 113-117, 119, 120, 155, 157-158, 159, 160, 161-171, 173, 174, 175, 230-237, 238, 259, 313, 343, 344, 355, 383
Arlen, Harold 13, 53

Baby Snooks 2, 3, 14, 61-74, **95, 105, 106,** 117, 151, 250, 280, 294-306, 343, 354, 389, 390
Bennett, Constance 183, 184
Benny, Jack 2, 47, 157, 211, 355
Bergen, Edgar 158-159, 357
Berle, Milton 9, 127, 134, 135, 137-140
Bickersons, The 2, 3, 85, 113-118, 125, 126, 153, 156-181, 182, 185, 187, 189, 190, 191, **201**, 202, 212, 230-237, 238, 245, 250-252, 259, 264-266, 268, 270, 273-274, 275-279, 280, **288**, 342, 345, 346-352, 355, 383, 384, 388, 289, 390
Bishop's Wife, The 136, 142-144, 343
Blue, Ben 3, 202, 203, 355
Bolger, Ray 136, 189, 356
Brady, John 205-207
Breen, Bobby 47, 55-58, 343
Brice, Fanny 2, 14, 47, 61-74, 79, **105**, 151, 250, 306, 342, 343, 353, 354, 356, 389
Burns, George 11-12, 14, 306, 353, 384

Cantor, Eddie 2, 11, 12, 13, 34-51, **52**, 53-60, 61, 62, 68, 72, 84, **90, 91**, 204, 342, 343, 353, 354, 358, 381, 390
Carroll, Leo G. 183, 184
Cavalcade of Stars 175-176, 349
Cohn, Harry 123-124
Como, Perry 236, 237, 250
Conte, John 68, 72, 128, 172, 173, 343
Corman, Roger 85, 188-189, 241, 242, 254, 255, **282**
Corwin, Norman 153, 159
Cox, Wally **195**, 205-212, 355
Crandall, Jack 45-46, 47, 48, 50

Davis, Eddie 47, 48, 204
Davis, Joan 3, 73, 189-190, 214-218, 355
Dee, Sandra 187, 387
Denove, Jack 179, 182, 184, 190, 191

Deputy Seraph **196, 197**, 219-228, 275
Disneyland 205, 209, 210, 211
Donna Reed Show, The 187, 189
Durante, Jimmy 42, 138, 299
Durbin, Deanna 47, 343

Ed Sullivan Show, The 175, 191, 230, 248, 345
Erickson, Rod 206, 208-209, 212

Father Knows Best 187, 387
Fibber McGee & Molly 2, 156
Fine, Sylvia 144, 146, 150
Freedman, David 12-14, 34, 43, 47, 49, 51, 59, 61-63, 67, 68, 72, 182, 342, 353, 354, 358

Gardner, Reginald 82, 83
Gleason, Jackie 3, 175-178, 179, 181, 229, 342, 347, 348, 349, 355, 388
Godfrey, Arthur 205, 209, 211
Goldwyn, Samuel 48, 53, 84-85, 142, 146, 149, 151, 202, 244, 343, 345, 357, 381
Good News Show, The 63, 68, 343, 354, 390
Grant. Cary 142, 143, 183, 184
Gregg, Virginia 156, 191
Grey, Virginia 182, 191
Gruskin, George 205-206, 212, 225-227, 346, 355

Hartman, Don 85, 257
Highway Patrol 256-257
Hines, Mimi 249-250
Holiner, Mann 68, 256
Holtz, Lou 11, 61, 62, 68, 342, 353, 354
Honeymooners, The 3, 175-181, 346-352, 388

Hope, Bob 5, 44-45, 117, 356
Hunter, Tab 245-248
Hunt, Marsha 159-171, 344

I Married a Dog 237-238, 249
I Married Joan 190, 214
Inspector General 149-150, 151, 244, 273, 345, 391
It's the Bickersons 179, 182-183, 190, 191, 202

Jeffreys, Anne 183, 184
Jessel, George 11, 47, 50, 353, 354
Joan of Arkansas 214, 215-218, 242, 372-376
Jocks Talk, The 120-122, 313-341

Kaye, Danny 2, 77, 84, 136, 144-151, 244, 345, 353, 357, 376-380
Kean, Betty 189, 230
Kupferman, Theodore R. 177, 178-179, 229, 342, 346
Kurnitz, Harry 150, 244

Lahr, Bert 82, 83, 353
Langford, Frances 2, 3, 113-117, 157-158, 159, 172, 173-174, 175, **193**, 230, 236, 237, 238, 250, 259, 270, **285**, 344, 345, 351, 355, 383, 389
Lesser, Sol 55, 57, 224
Levoy, Gordon 176, 178-179, 273-274
Lewis, Jerry 140-141, 356
Life Begins at 8:40 13, 342, 354
Lillie, Beatrice 14-33, 48, 353
Lombard, Carole 69-70, 72, 343, 356
Loveton, John W. 183, 185

Making of Robert, The 269-270
Man of the House **198**, 237

March, Hal 237, 247
Martin, Dean 140-141, 356
Marx Brothers, The 2, 3, 53, 83, 113, 218-228, 242, 275, 299, 356
Match Please, Darling **200**, 259-266, 390
Maxwell, Jenny 187-188, 387
Mayo, Virginia, 144-145, 149
McCarthy, Charlie 158-160, 344
McConnell, Lulu 61, 342
Meadows, Audrey 175, 177
Merman, Ethel 48, 53, 54
Mexican Jumping Bean 229-230
Mimi 249-250
Miranda, Carmen 133, 134, 135, 137
Mr. Peepers 206, 207, 211
Moore, Sam 12, 73, 353
Moore, Victor 14, 146
Morgan, Frank 68, 69, 72, **109**, 119, 155-156, 294-312, 343, 344, 356
Morris, Bobby 7, 43-44, **88**
My Friend Irma 183, 351

Newson, Ted 205, 218, 224

Oakie, Jack 14, 354
Odd Couple, The 245, 264
Open House 14, 343, 390
Oppenheimer, George 183, 184, 186

Parker, Lew 171, 172, 173, 174, 175, 182, 189, 191, 230, 342, 345, 348, 349
Parkyakarkus 37, 47, 50, 54, 57
Powell, Richard M. 189, 202, 203, 207, 210, 217, 219, 249, 392
Price, Georgie 9, 10-12, 353
Pryor, Ainslie 206, 212

Rapp, Brian 188, **289**, 387-389
Rapp, Joel 3, 6, 8, 13, 51, 79, 84, **100**, 123-124, 140, 149, 184, 187, 188, **194, 199, 200,** 206-207, 218, 242, 245, 254, 255, 258, 259, 260-264, 271, 279-280, 390
Rapp, Paul 2, 3, 6-8, 51, 75-79, 83-85, 94, **101, 103,** 110, 117-118, 122-123, 124, 125, 126, 127, 144, 171-172, 184, 186-189, 191-192, **194, 198,** 212, 223, 229, 239-242, 245, 254-255, 263, 267, 272, 273, 274-275, 276, 277-278, 279, **281, 282, 283,** 286, **287, 290, 291, 292,** 387
Rapp, Mariam 7, 10, 12, 51, 60, 77-79, 85, **92, 93, 96, 97, 101, 110,** 117, 120, 122-124, 126, 187, **199,** 239-242, 262, 267- 268, 274-275, 279, **285, 289,** 353, 381-384, 385, 387-388
Raber, John U. 12, 47, 60, 353
Reed, Alan 72, **95,** 354
Regal Reproduction 11-12
Riggs, Tommy 14, 354
Rooney, Mickey 119, 237
Rose, Billy 67, 72, 73, 74, 356
Rose Marie 137, 138, 140
Rubin, Benny 50, 66, 79, 172, 174

Saturday Night Revue 176, 177
Schubert, Bernard L. 182-183
Scorsese, Martin 83, 189, 254
Secret Life of Mitty, The **112**, 146, 147-149, 223, 391
Sellers, Peter 238-239, 269
Shaw, Mel 118, 124-125, 126, 176
Simon, Neil 257, 264
Smith, Thorne 183, 184
Spring in Brazil 127-141, 172, 230, 343, 355
Star Time 171-172, 173, 342, 345, 349

Stafford, Hanley 63-66, 68, 69, 70-71, 72, 73
Sterling, Robert 183, 184
Steve Allen Show, The 175, 189, 191
Stop! You're Killing Me 150-151
Streisand, Barbra 73, 249
Strike Me Pink 48, 51, 53-55, 390

Tab Hunter Show, The 245-248
Thomas, Danny 49, 151-152, 244, 344, 383
Three Worlds of John Bickerson, The 250-252
Topper 183-187, 214, 223, 245, 355, 391

Watkin, Lawrence E. 142, 343
Winchell, Walter 11, 34
Wonder Man 144-145, 357, 391
Wynn, Ed 182, 202, 345, 355, 358

You Bet Your Life 221, 223, 227
Young, Robert 67, 69, 343
Young, Roland 183, 184

Zanuck, Darryl 119, 135
Ziegfeld Follies of the Air, The 61, 63
Ziegfeld Follies of 1933 68, 72, 342, 354, 356, 388

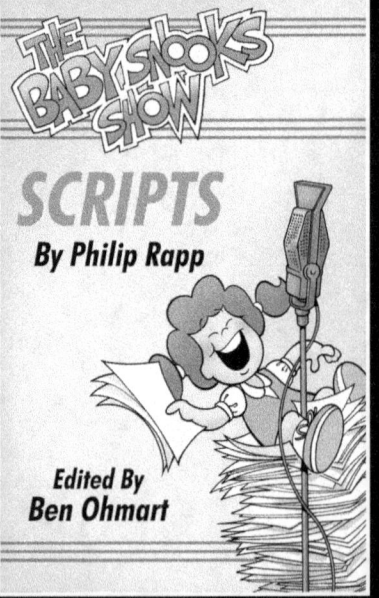

www.ingramcontent.com/pod-product-compliance
Lightning Source LLC
Chambersburg PA
CBHW051624230426
43669CB00013B/2172